JOY OF
FINANCIAL
PLANNING

www.amplifypublishing.com

Joy of Financial Planning
7 Strategies for Transforming Your Finances and Reclaiming Your American Dream

JASON HOWELL COMPANY
Visit our website at http://www.JasonHowellCompany.com

Photography by Astri Wee
AstriWee.com

For more information, please contact:
Mascot Books
620 Herndon Parkway #320
Herndon, VA 20170
info@mascotbooks.com

Library of Congress Control Number: 2019908903

CPSIA Code: PRV0919A
ISBN-13: 978-1-64543-059-9

Printed in the United States

*To my girls, Audrey and
Eden, and my lady, Jenn.*

Thank you.

JOY

of

Financial Planning

7 Strategies for Transforming
Your Finances and Reclaiming
Your American Dream

JASON J. HOWELL, CFP®

amplify

CONTENTS

Strategy V: Joy of Legacy: Estate Planning

Strategy VI: Joy of Opportunity: Investing

Strategy VII: Joy of Time: Retiring

ACKNOWLEDGMENTS

To all of the people whom I absentmindedly leave off of this list, I thank you most wholeheartedly. You quietly, subtly, and gracefully breathed friendship and support that silently transformed me into believing I was born this way. Thank you.

Next, and perhaps most importantly, I would like to thank **David Green** for his support of this book. (Mostly because we joked that I should thank him first, so I'm just following through.) All kidding aside, you are one of the people who unexpectedly kept asking about the book, and that was great motivation to get it done. While I am talking about people from my church, I will also thank my pastor, **Bryan Mickle**. Bryan, I hope you find something valuable to preach upon in here, as per your request. Thank you to the members of our church's children and youth ministry team, including **Sarah Dianne Jones**. I happen to be writing this on your last Sunday. Yes, I hope you feel guilty for taking your awesomeness to another church (but like a good Christian, I forgive you). **To my fellow Elders** (former and present), thank you for making me take a pause from work, family, and book writing to think of the bigger picture. **Peter Lipsett** especially: your faith in me as a friend and in support of my business (and my book), has meant a lot over many years. You will always be "Christian of the Week" for that. **Rob Tobiassen,** thank you for teaching me to keep a skeptical eye on institutions of all kinds and to make time for friends when they need one. **Claire, Jeff,** and **Alma Nobel,** thank you for your confidence in me. **Halsey Rogers, Aromie Noe,** **Tayae** and **Tajin Rogers,** thank you for being friendly examples of dedicated volunteers, even when you're really, really busy. **Cooper Bosland,** thanks for reminding me that just saying "hello" can start a long-term friendship. **Jim Gallagher** and **Blair Moorhead,** thank you for teaching me that, no matter what I do, I should look good doing it. **Pete Hause,** thank you for teaching me the same fashion lesson. Also, thanks for reminding me that we're dead a lot longer than we are alive, so we better "*carpe diem.*" **Madeline Jarvis,** thank you for lunch and Sunday hugs. **Rick Schadelbauer,** thanks for saying, in not so many words, that I am a good writer. It means a lot coming from, you know, a writer. **Dana Edwards,** thanks for your example of grace, **Kathy Kobe,** thank you for making my service to the church easier. And **Lynnette Yount,** thank you for teaching me that, no matter what, just smile.

Thank you to all of my beta readers who suffered through the first public draft of this book, including: **Pam James, David Green, Gina Weatherup, Dave Merrill, Barbara Kay, Sarah Machacek, Jennifer Weisberg, Christine Landoll, Pam Horack, Brian Kelly, Deb Merriner, Max Prilutsky, Amy Scanlon, Jeanette Franzel,** and **John Gustavo Blair.** John and Jeanette, you two particularly went above and beyond on your feedback, and with everyone else, helped to make me think. Also, a big thank you to the people who served as experts in the book, including: **Patrick Holland, Kevin Rockman, Franziska Moeckel, Michael Feinberg, Gabriel Cruz, Kelly Blanks, Nikki Jerome Ouellette,** and **Ryan Brown.** Ryan, thank you especially for letting me quote you more than a few times. Ryan and Patrick, thank you both additionally for serving as perennial guest speakers for my personal finance class at American University. You inspired me with your expertise. Nikki, **Katie Parkes,** and **Nicole Kelly,** thank you for always being in my corner. **Becky Anderson, Sumeet Shrivastava, Michael Gallagher, Curt "Sunshine" White, Chaimaa Fekkak, Chuck "Call Rhonda" LaRock III, Kristin Discher, Michael Ly, Dave Roe,** and **David Atkins**, thanks for your ongoing mentorship on the George Mason School of Business alumni board. Special thanks to the Hine family, led by the incomparable **Scott Hine**. Scott, your friendship, not only with me but with the entire Mason family, matters a lot.

To my publisher, Mascot Books, and especially **Ben Simpson** and **Andy Symonds,** thank you for reaching out to work with me on this project. Special thanks to **Kiley Garrett** for your project management, and **Ricky Frame**, for your skill and patience with the cover design. **Naren Aryal,** as the owner of the firm, thank you for saying hello during my first visit. It was a nice touch. Special thanks to **Lauren Kanne,** my lead editor, tasked with the formidable job of clarifying my run-on sentences, grammatical errors, and hanging phrases. You helped to transform thousands of words into something that resembles a book.

A big thank you to **Astri Wee** for taking a couple hundred pictures so we could find one good enough for the cover of this book. Astri, your energy, love for opera, and talent made taking pictures fun. Everyone should write a book, if for no other reason than to hire you for a photo shoot. It would be worth it. Thank you also to **Lars Kroner,** Virginia's favorite personal trainer, for teaching me that nothing matters more than shoulders. And to all of my fellow BNI members at the Reston Referral Network, thank you for believing in me.

To the family of clients who support Jason Howell Company (JHCo.) by allowing our firm to serve your families, thank you. I hope you have learned as much from me as I have from all of you. And to my business partner **Doug Tees,** thank you for having faith enough in the plan for JHCo. to buy in (literally). And thank you for supporting the development of the brand by supporting my efforts to write this book. Your mix of operational expertise, sense of humor, and genuine respect for people are rare qualities to find in one person. Our clients are lucky to have you, and so am I. And **Deb Tees**, I know our clients and I are lucky you let us have him.

Of course, no list of acknowledgements would be complete without sharing my appreciation for **Michael Kitces** and **Alan Moore**. Thank you for founding the groundbreaking XY Planning Network and for making **Maddy Roche** your first hire. Each of you have inspired me and unquestionably supported my success in this profession. Thank you also to **Paul Franklin**, who, after my political campaign loss years ago, bought me breakfast and reeled me into the personal finance profession. This was all before I had time to start crying in my beer. Thanks. Additional thanks to **Brian Arezzo, Anne-Day McCabe Triana, Cady North, Jon Yankee, Justin Castelli, Liz Clough, Jennifer Davis, Greg Smolen, Jason Smolen, Rebecca Geller, Jeff Schatz, Jennifer Myers, Patrick Ortman, Chuck Donalies, Breanna Reish,** and **Brad Hawkins.**

Finally, to my wife, **Jennifer Taylor Howell.** The biggest compliment I have ever received and will ever receive came along after four and a half years of dating you: I finally started believing you wanted me to propose! So, I did, and you, remarkably, said yes! It's been years of adventures since then, and through them all, you have steadfastly believed in me and that our journey would take us to a good place. Thank you for your partnership, your faith, and your personal sacrifices. Thank you for always believing we would win. There would be no book, no company, and no run for office if you hadn't said yes in 2010. Thank you for all of the courageous years of "yes" since then. In a life filled with many ups and downs, in an imperfect world in need of a heroine, you give me hope, courage and peace. Jenn, *you* are my joy.

PREFACE

American Dreams

Would you ever run for United States Congress?

In 2012, I ran for Congress against a twenty-year incumbent in Northern Virginia as an independent. I wanted to solve the country's economic challenges, working through the political system I had followed closely for years. I wanted to be part of creating the American Dream for anyone who dared to believe. But I lost.

I have always believed in a certain kind of "American Dream." My personal version of the dream was the kind that started with an idea, solved a simple but important problem (maybe ending a disease, like they did with polio), and ended with giving most of my wealth away to my alma mater.

Though attending college was supposedly a "no-brainer," I had always set my sights on entrepreneurship. In fact, on one quiet Sunday afternoon in 1993, after "great thought," I told my dad that I intended to drop out of college. My dad had just innocently walked down to the basement (where I usually was) to say hello when I coldly announced that I would no longer transfer to George Mason University after completing an associate's degree at Northern Virginia Community College. No, that plan was old news. Too pedestrian. I would instead focus on becoming a successful *entrepreneur!*

THE STUDY AND PRACTICE OF FINANCIAL PLANNING HAVE GIVEN ME A ROADMAP TO THE AMERICAN DREAM.

My dad looked at me thoughtfully and kindly. Rather than sharing his internalized shock, he merely said, "Son, why don't you keep going to college, for me."

I looked into his eyes, noticing an odd mix of disappointment flecked with hope, and instead of defending my half-baked plans, I quietly conceded: "Okay, Dad."

Thankfully, my dad's wisdom saved me from missing out on a great formal education and the overall university experience. I did indeed eventually transfer to what is now the largest research university in the Commonwealth of Virginia, George Mason University. And I graduated with a bachelor's degree in accounting. (How dreamy.) I had a straightforward career path as a corporate accountant ahead of me, but I couldn't help continuing to dream.

For over twenty years, my full-time career has involved the subject of money. From my college job as bank teller to my positions as an accountant, headhunter, and United States Congressional candidate, and now as a CERTIFIED FINANCIAL PLANNER™ practitioner, I have made the business of money my profession. Making money work for families—rather than just the other way around—has become my personal mission. The study and practice of financial planning have given me a roadmap to the American Dream.

Why Write a Book?

There is no doubt that writing a book has a cachet all of its own, and for good reason. Many of us raised in the Western, Christian religions are familiar with the phrases "the Good Book," "the Holy Book," and "the Book of Truth" in reference to the Holy Bible. Other religions and cultures have their holy books (or collection of books) too, like the Tanakh, the Quran, the Book of Mormon, the Vedas, the Tripitaka, and others. We learn to study with books as children and continue into adulthood. As an adjunct college professor, I can attest that even now, "the book" is where the test questions come from (and, by default, the answers). We are born and raised to revere books more than any other medium. Search "Why do we love books?" online and you will find over 2 billion results.

When I first began my study of personal finance, I had many options from which to learn, and in 2019, I have many options with which to teach: seminars, webinars, gamification tools, videos, podcasts, and on and on. I will utilize these tools to spread the messages I have for the public, but for me, and perhaps for my generation, education begins with a book. So, I just *had* to write one!

I graduated college in 1997, during the heyday of national booksellers. Barnes & Noble, a decade off of acquiring bookstore chain B. Dalton, launched its consumer website that year and became a publicly traded company in 1999. Borders Books was still expanding; it opened its first international superstore that year in Singapore. The country's third largest bookstore was based in my metropolitan area of Washington, D.C., and it peaked in size during the 1990s. After graduating, I had the opportunity to read any books I wanted, and there was no shortage of bookstores. On many Friday nights, I would take the short drive to Borders to avoid rush hour traffic and flip through a book while listening to an open-mic performance. On weekends, I would walk into another bookstore and just stare at the business books, wondering which one to buy, *knowing* that "the truth" of entrepreneurial success was staring back at me among the catchy titles and striking covers.

I never went to the bookstore to meet new people (to my chagrin), but rather to learn and sometimes decompress. It was, in many ways, a sanctuary where I could do some great thinking about what I wanted to do and who I wanted to become. So, I love books and I love the bookstore. Though the mega-bookstore chains have diminished since the boom-boom of the 1990s, the independent bookstores are making a comeback. Hopefully, you will do some of your greatest thinking in one of them and find a book like this one (and others) to inspire your truth.

A friend asked, "If I read this book, why would I need you as a financial planner?" I told her she wouldn't. This is a book of curated information that anyone can take and "run with," if they choose. It is a book of options, but those options are ever-changing; as a professional, it's my job to keep up with them. I believe your success in life is determined by constant financial planning, which can be a full-time job. It just happens to be my full-time job.

The Biggest and the Smallest

What has, anecdotally, made the United States of America unique in the world is a muddy version of capitalism that allows for something more than "haves" and "have-nots." Our country has no official caste system, so economic mobility or stagnation have almost always been choices. Even though the starting line hasn't been the same for every race, creed, and gender, America hasn't always required that where you started was where you needed to finish.

If our grandparents or parents didn't pay too much attention to national economics or "the markets," that was okay. Economics kind of worked out for most of them, with the post-World War II boom and the rise of a nation that was unparalleled in the 20th century. But in the complex, competitive economic world of the 21st century, we are either haves or have-nots. We are either rich or broke. The world is moving faster and the country is moving further apart, socially and economically. Gaining a personal financial footing has become more elusive. Achieving the American Dream seems to be just that—a dream.

I believe our generation still has so much to offer the world. I believe we are the ones the rest of the world has been waiting for.

When I say "our generation," I am actually referring to two generations of adults: Millennials and Xers. I am a member of the latter, the smaller of the two. Xers, members of Generation X, were born between 1965 and 1980. We are typecast as cynical and skeptical, and we used to be known as the slacker generation (before we inevitably grew up). We have seen and experienced so much. We are old enough to remember a time before the internet, yet young enough to know how to use it. We grew up at a time when parents got divorced (a lot), and we came of age in the 1990s, when music still had categories. Many of us were in our twenties on 9/11 in 2001, and we still sense that life has never been quite the same.

Now, most of us are married, have a couple of kids, and are left wondering what we did with our cassette tape collections. (We still have our compact disc collections, even though we don't own CD players.) As we were promised, we have had multiple jobs and, some of us, multiple careers. We might have two or three 401(k)s from different employers hanging around, and we think we've seen statements recently (but we're not sure).

We did not turn out exactly as we had hoped, but then again, we didn't hope for much. (After all, the skeptical part was true.) We have been called the "middle" or "forgotten" generation. We are no longer consistently on the cover of popular magazines (except for maybe *AARP Magazine*). We're just not a big enough marketing target, I guess. Regardless, somewhere between the Boomers and the Millennials, we still exist.

The larger generation, Millennials, were born sometime between 1980 and 1997, so the oldest are approaching the big "4-0." They are nearly digital natives; they have grand ideas and they are culturally open-minded; they are also (predictably) the current "punching bag" generation. (Everyone likes to make fun of Millennials except the Millennials I know.)

They have also seen their share of crises. They were even younger during 9/11, and for the majority of their adult lives, our country has been at war in the Middle East and with "terrorism." They experienced the Great Recession of 2008 just about the time they were old enough to start investing, and they haven't seen the securities markets the same ever since. Millennials are the ones with crushing student loan debt, who graduated into a changing economy that promises them "gigs," but not much else. Like Xers, Millennials have had multiple jobs and careers, and they recognize that nothing is promised; they have seen that no institution is sacred. They will most certainly be on the business end of the economic, environmental, and (if the most alarmed among us are correct) social uprisings we will face.

Our generation's American Dream is not lost, but we face different financial challenges than prior generations. The cost of housing and college have grown faster than inflation, and the trajectory of pay and interest rates have slowed. The safety nets of Social Security and Medicare are both on unfunded trajectories. Our macroeconomic outlook is dubious, with over $22 trillion in debt in 2019, and a federal income tax rate that has been trending lower. There is no telling how far out-of-balance our federal budget will grow, and what that will mean for your employer, your pay, and your family.

Problems

Joy of Financial Planning was written to solve a big problem. It was written for adults who woke up one day and realized how complex financial life had become. No one told us that life insurance was something we would have to worry about. No one told us estate planning was something for people under ninety. Seemingly all of a sudden, there are 101 things necessary to "handle" just to keep the promises we made to our growing families and ourselves.

You are working so hard and have become so busy. You really don't have time to go through all of this financial stuff (but you know you are supposed to). You have parents and children to worry about (the term "sandwich generation" applies to you). You think your kids may have to work even harder just to keep up with the pace of change. You really just want to reduce your anxiety around money, enjoy your family life, achieve the American Dream, and change the world. Is that so much to ask?

Great Words

Two speeches in U.S. presidential history seem to sum up the best of what American Dream idealism conjures up. One of those speeches was President Ronald Reagan's farewell address on January 11, 1989. Our 40th U.S. president gave us an illustration that served as the perfect epitaph to one of America's most remarkable presidencies.

> *I've spoken of the shining city all my political life, but I don't know if I ever quite communicated what I saw when I said it. But in my mind, it was a tall, proud city built on rocks stronger than oceans, windswept, God-blessed,*

and teeming with people of all kinds living in harmony
and peace; a city with free ports that hummed with com-
merce and creativity. And if there had to be city walls,
the walls had doors and the doors were open to anyone
with the will and the heart to get here. That's how I saw
it, and see it still.

I was old enough to have watched that farewell address live, but I can't really remember if I did. In the years since, I've watched it online and I have imagined our country at that time. The freedoms expressed may not have been *felt* by everyone in the 1980s—or even now, for that matter—but they still serve as an ideal of what America could strive to become as a nation of opportunity. Opportunities we hope to all enjoy as individuals and families.

Our 35th president's life was cut short, and though I wasn't alive when John F. Kennedy died, I am overwhelmed with emotion whenever I listen to his inaugural speech. He too sums American Dreams and ideals. Known more for two sentences, I hope that I can encourage you to watch the entire speech online or at least read the text in the Appendix of this book. A snippet, in his words:

In the long history of the world, only a few generations
have been granted the role of defending freedom in its
hour of maximum danger. I do not shrink from this
responsibility—I welcome it. I do not believe that any
of us would exchange places with any other people or
any other generation. The energy, the faith, the devotion
which we bring to this endeavor will light our country
and all who serve it—and the glow from that fire can
truly light the world.

And so, my fellow Americans: ask not what your country can do for you—ask what you can do for your country.

Gets me every time.

Our generation of adults does indeed have a role in defending freedom—our own economic freedom. The bipolar nature of not just our politics, but our economics, is dimming the light of our "shining city." It is up to our generation to dust it off, or replace the bulb if necessary! We have to take a much more intentional role in the planning of our financial lives than our predecessors if we want to accomplish great things. It is not only important that our generation becomes financially successful, it is necessary. Our efforts on a personal scale will determine the success of our generation collectively.

Your Real American Dream

What is the *real* American Dream? For many, it is a very personalized belief about the greatness of the United States of America. For others, it is an aspirational ideal enshrined in our founding documents in 1776 that propels us forward, despite our human imperfections. For others, it reflects upon a dream of "good ole days" that have long since passed, leaving us with whatever and whoever we are right now.

Since 1993, my American Dream has included starting a successful business, which has now finally been realized. I want to continue the success of my firm while being present for my family and creating success for the families of all of my clients and their children. And as I approach the sunset of my life, I want to contribute to solving one of the world's biggest problems. Of course, those are big dreams—but those are the best kind.

What's yours? Do you dream of outsized financial success, like Bill Gates or Mark Zuckerberg? They created enough wealth to sign up for the billionaires-only Giving Pledge (a pledge to give away half of your wealth during your lifetime). Do you dream of feeding the hungry, curing disease, fighting for social justice, cooling the earth, or setting a positive example of drive and ambition for your kids? Or, at some point, did you give up on dreams altogether? Do you feel like you're just getting by, that faced with a manic economy, getting by is the best you can do for you and your family right now?

No matter what your dream, money will play a role. Mother Teresa didn't need a financial advisor or an estate planner to effect change, but we need to have our finances in order to achieve our versions of greatness for ourselves, our families, the United States of America, and the world at large. Just getting by is no longer good enough; in fact, it's no longer possible. Many of us have been using an old financial playbook. It worked well for some in our grandparents' generation, just barely for our parents', and it is not working for ours. You either have or you have not in our new economy. No matter what your American Dream is, achieving it takes a different set of skills. It is up to us to learn those skills; teaching what I consider the basics of financial skills is the purpose of this book.

The *real* joy of the American Dream was never about buying a house, going to college, having one job (or career) for thirty years, and then retiring until death do you part. It has always been about transformation: becoming a better version of yourself, providing for your family, and leaving a positive legacy for the benefit of your community. This transformation includes self-realization, exceeding natural limitations, and executing on good ideas. *Joy of Financial Planning* is about the joy of the American Dream, transforming your high potential into measurable success for yourself, your family, and your community. If we were all empowered with that mission, imagine what a dreamy place this world would be.

A Word About Prejudice & Finances

My father preached that America was not prejudiced by "black or white," but rather by green—as in money. I grew up believing that financial status could overcome prejudice around nationality, race, gender, religion, politics, sexual orientation, physical appearance, physical stature, or whatever other ways our fellow humans find to segregate the "in" from the "out" group.

Though I didn't internalize the injustice of the insider-outsider divide when I was younger, I noticed it in the movies. In *First Blood*, John Rambo was a Vietnam veteran who wandered into a small town after being discharged. Rather than reward him with the deference a U.S. soldier deserves, Rambo was antagonized, his undiagnosed post-traumatic stress disorder (PTSD) was triggered, and he, unfortunately, went to war with the local police and National Guard. Despite the repeated injustice of his experiences, (spoiler alert) the movie ends with him being taken into custody. *Rambo: First Blood Part II* begins with John Rambo in jail.

It isn't lost on me that I am a black man thriving in a traditionally Caucasian man's profession. Less than 5% of CERTIFIED FINANCIAL PLANNER™ professionals are people of color, and fewer still own and manage a wealth management firm (as I have and I do).

My last name, with its British and Welsh roots, has never betrayed the confidence of my race or culture. In fact, I once had a client ask me if it was my "real" name. He was about my age, and admitted to the memory of the television show *Gilligan's Island*

and the wealthy character named Thurston Howell III. Indeed, mine is my given name, and I suppose it has helped me somehow along the way of life.

Though I have never worn my race on my sleeves, I have consistently and undoubtedly worn it on my skin and in the tight curls of my hair. People in my generation and younger have had the good fortune to have been born into this country after slavery, Reconstruction, and the Civil Rights eras. We have been lucky; still, the inequality that past generations of color have faced have adversely affected the progress of their descendants. Financial inequality due to race, has a source that can be easily traced to historical inequality.

My life experiences with race have been mitigated by how I was raised, where I have lived, and where I live today. I live in Virginia, and regardless of the racial challenges that this quasi-Southern state still faces, we are a long way away from the Jamestown of 1619, when the first slaves arrived. Any challenges I face living in Virginia seem silly in comparison to those of the generations before me. So, this is not a book about experiences with microaggressions (everyday insults communicated intentionally or unintentionally), though I have and will likely continue to experience them.

Some of you reading this book may live in neighborhoods or family situations that outsiders are curious about. They may ask, "Why don't you just leave?" With my gilded name and mostly fortunate experiences, I have, at times, found myself asking that same unenlightened question of those I see on the news who are economically disadvantaged. With maturity earned through experience, I have learned that one answer is that it is easier to stay "together" in a place where you know your place, than move to an unknown location where you are decidedly alone.

Moving from being an insider to becoming a suspected

outsider comes with very clear and imminent danger. Better to be poor and accepted than take a chance on wealth in another town and get arrested. I understand that for an insider, hanging out at the same bar or coffee shop is akin to real-life versions of *Cheers* and *Seinfeld* (two of my favorite cancelled shows). As an outsider, your presence at a local pub or bookstore or other establishment might be watched with suspicion.

Having spent my twenties working with local unsigned musicians in the Washington, D.C. metropolitan area, I am aware that bias is not limited to race. The musicians I served as band manager, business manager, and music rag writer were mostly Caucasian men and women. I was drawn to their musical talent. Though some of them and their fans were part-time hobbyists who have successfully moved on, others did not leave the ever-shrinking, low-pay music community. Fans supported musicians and vice versa, but the number of bars that support original music has decreased over the years.

TT Reynolds was a music venue where outsiders turned into insiders. For a time, whether you had a lower-back tattoo, one on your ankle, or one on your neck, you were welcome. Even a guy who tucked his shirt in with no tattoos and an aversion to alcohol was welcome. It was frequented by people who, at the time, were on the lower end of the financial spectrum. Eventually, it was closed down for irreconcilable differences with the City of Fairfax (or the gravitational pull of gentrification). And where did all of those unwanted, loud-music-loving, mostly tattooed young people (outsiders) go? Somewhere else.

Prejudice is not limited to skin color or anything else. My dad seems mostly right that, in effect, the rich get richer (no matter where they come from). But the spirit of this book is that it is possible to change your station despite outside forces that would prefer you succumb to the inertia of your current path.

I argue that the rich get richer because the rich get help. I hope this book can help you become a better version of your financial self, no matter where you come from, who you love, who you are, or what you are. The strategies laid out here are a good foundation for meeting the challenges of our economy and changing the direction of your financial life. You will not always get help from the people around you; that's part of life. But this book will put you ahead of where you are today, no matter what is in your way.

INTRODUCTION

This generation of adults needs updated financial planning skills more than any other generation in American history. This book is about the economic challenges we face as a generation, losing the joy of your American Dream, and finding that joy again through the magic of financial planning. We need to get better at money; our families and our country are depending on us. We also need to step back for minute to understand where we are today.

Our generation—whether you are an Xer or a Millennial—faces very different economic challenges than our parents did. The meteoric rise in housing, college, and medical costs, without equal rise in wages and social safety nets, put our economic futures in precarious positions. One or two financial mistakes and we can easily slip into the proverbial "have-nots" category. If you ask most adults what's holding them back from achieving their dreams, they will eventually whittle their excuses down to one word: money. In the 21st century, your ability to navigate the complexity of finances determines your level of personal protection, the height of your hopes and dreams, the preservation of your values, and whether your potential will be realized or wasted.

In a world of hyper-partisan politics and bipolar wealth distribution, the politicians can't save our environment, fight for social justice, ethically end disease, slow the rise of poverty, or accomplish anything that's hard to do. We can't either—not as long as we're worried about paying the mortgage, saving for college, and working again this weekend.

My oldest daughter loves butterflies and rainbows. When she was four-years-old, I could ask her any day of the week what she'd dreamed about the previous night, and the answer would be the same: "Butterflies and rainbows." I have no idea if that was true, but I know it doesn't matter. She "dreamed" of what brought her joy. We're not kids anymore, but let's start over, let's step back and dream again (like we used to). If you are holding this book (or reading this on your phone), there are things that used to bring you pleasure, passions you care about deeply that would bring you joy—if you had time to follow them. But you don't, because you choose to be responsible (read: a grown up).

Well, I'm here to tell you that you can live responsibly *and* with passion, if you dare to live with intention. *Joy of Financial Planning* is a discipline around finances that will transform your life by freeing you from the economic challenges we face as a generation. The concepts in this book are your opportunity to dream again.

You are the one you have been waiting for. It is your turn. It is your time.

Get Hit and Move Forward

Financial planning is life planning. The *process* of planning is what prepares us to "Get hit and keep moving forward," as Sylvester Stallone says to his son in *Rocky V*. (Yes, I saw it in the theatre.)

If you are like me, you have already made plenty of "mistakes" in your life that have affected where you are financially today. For example, I have never picked the correct six numbers in the Powerball, despite having played the lottery *numerous* times! I wish I could have predicted how Amazon or Facebook or Netflix or Cintas stock would have performed after the Great Recession of 2008, but I could not (at least, I did not). More practically, I stopped saving in my twenties to start a business that didn't quite make it. (Okay, three businesses.) I also ran up credit card debt in my twenties that took me years to pay off.

In retrospect, they weren't all bad decisions. I did make *some* good choices. I decided to live with and support my dad until he died at the young age of sixty-five. I bought life insurance soon after getting married. I said "No!" to drugs (thank you, Nancy Reagan). I committed to a profession—yes, financial planning—that brings me joy. And I said yes to starting a family, despite the financial fears that go along with raising kids.

Life is full of challenges to your thinking and options for your choosing. Sometimes things will work out as you expected, and sometimes they will seem to work against you. If and when you implement a financial planning strategy, don't be surprised, for example, when the amount of money you intended to save for a home down payment gets spent on an emergency. Our 34th president, General Dwight D. Eisenhower, once said, "Plans are nothing; planning is everything." General George S. Patton, a member of Tom Brokaw's "Greatest Generation," once said, "A good plan, violently executed now, is better than a perfect plan next week." One of the many things these two generals had in common was a rock-solid belief in the benefits of *planning*. It is a belief I share, and I have developed a strategic approach to financial planning in order to share this belief with you.

How to Read this Book

Unlike other books on finances, this book acknowledges that millionaires and "thousandaires" alike have complex webs of financial tools that need to be put in place. (Your financial life is not easy!) It also acknowledges that adults in this century will need to be more than "accumulators" of wealth; we must *create* and *curate* value on an ongoing basis. I'm here to teach you how to do that.

The book is divided into seven strategies (or "joys"), which, taken as a whole, represent a comprehensive view of financial life planning. These are the same personal wealth strategies I share with my clients. Each wealth strategy is also subdivided into multiple parts, which form the basis of each of the chapters. These "joys" do not cover every single topic in your personal financial life, but can serve as a primer to continue your financial education. All of the strategies are important, if for no other reason than they are interrelated.

It is difficult to order the strategies according to priority, because your priorities will depend on what's missing in your current financial life. Your current financial state is based uniquely on the goals, concerns, and challenges you are facing right now. Chances are that you don't really want to read this entire book. Having written it, though, I believe all of it is useful information, and taken together, will lead to the transformation of how you view the role of money tools in your life. You can, however, read this book out of chronological order and gain even more value than had you first read through portions that, for you, were less relevant. This book can also be read episodically, which is to say, if you want to read about life insurance because you are about to meet with a life insurance agent, you can skip to the Joy of Safety section and the chapter on life insurance. Afterwards, you can put the book down until your next financial adventure.

The world didn't necessarily need another book on finances, but it *did* need a book that spoke to our current economic concerns by an author who was willing to get personal. Rather than just write a generic book of financial terms, I decided to share personal as well as professional experiences that will give you a window into my life's run-ins with these financial concepts and help you identify your own. You will also discover financial history you haven't read before (like where the name "Blue Cross/Blue Shield" comes from) and concepts that you've heard a dozen times or more. This book isn't meant to be a dissertation, but rather an explanation of the concepts you need to succeed.

Your personal transformation through application of these strategies is *Joy of Financial Planning*'s greatest value. Of course, to properly apply any of the concepts in this book fully, I suggest working with a CERTIFIED FINANCIAL PLANNER™ practitioner and other financial professionals. What you can become by walking through and implementing these wealth strategies will change your approach to goal-setting and the milestones you achieve in life. *Joy of Financial Planning* is about helping the families you and I are building today by recognizing who we were yesterday and developing the legacies we want to leave tomorrow.

Section I: Joy of Harmony (Family Governance)

"Harmony" is a pleasing combination of sounds, sights, or in this case, financial strategies. What makes this section harmonious is how it helps you match your financial strategies to your family's values. In this section, we will focus on the laws that matter most: the laws (or rules) you set for yourself and your loved ones. I outline what the wealthiest families have done historically to pass not only family wealth but family values to the next generation. You will also be introduced to a new juxtaposition of phrases: "Kitchen Table-Family Governance."

Section II: Joy of Enough (Earning, Spending, & Taxes)

"A penny saved is a penny earned" is one of the simplest money maxims, but often ignored. To accumulate any sum of money, you need a few things to go well; most importantly, you need more income coming in than the expenses you're paying out. We are taught early that we need to get jobs for income, but not enough time is spent in school on how we can *create* our own jobs. In this section, we focus on income, side-income (or the "gig economy"), spending, and entrepreneurship. Look out for my four steps to creating income.

We'll delve into explanations for emotional responses to spending on things you need, things you want, and even things you don't want. Finally, we'll talk through federal income tax planning and how to make sure you are paying just enough.

Section III: Joy of Balance (Cash, Credit & Debt)

Once you have income beating your expenses, it's time to get the interest you earn to beat the interest you pay to banks. The balance between the interest you pay and the interest you earn is an important metric, which life often teaches us in costly lessons. I put special attention on how home mortgages and student loans work, since they are two of the biggest culprits keeping people upside down.

There's focused attention on net worth in this chapter. I also talk about debt payoff strategies, the benefits of using cash as a barometer, and how to positively impact your credit score for future leverage opportunities. Debt is leverage, and when used correctly, can be a powerful wealth-generating strategy.

Section IV: Joy of Safety (Risk Management)

"Safety" references risk management tools, like insurance. Emergencies funds are important, but the risks you've decided you *can't* afford (i.e., self-insure) can be shared with insurance companies (and the friendly pools of premium payers they call clients).

Risk management is recognition that you have something at risk, something to lose. It is a form of appreciation, something that all of the happiness gurus recommend you take time for daily. You appreciate your life, your health, your good name, your shelter, perhaps your independent mode of transportation (car), and your net worth. These are things for which insurance was invented.

I'll talk about the origins of insurance and explore why most people only buy insurance that is legally required, while wealthy people pay for insurance as an affordable trade-off of risk.

Section V: Joy of Legacy (Estate Planning)

These are plans you put in place not for yourself, but for your legacy, commonly known as estate planning. Like other topics in this book, estate planning is mostly used by the wealthy, but is valuable for all of us.

Planning for your "estate" is a polite way to talk about making it easy for other people to deal with your health and financial affairs when you are not able to. These situations include when you're out of town, incapacitated, or if you are dead (I know, how pleasant). Our financial and medical lives are complicated, and sorting it all out in legally enforceable documents lifts a heavy burden off of your survivors.

Inherent in legacy planning is identifying the contributions you want to make to family members and society at large. This section will help you walk through those decisions.

Section VI: Joy of Opportunity (Investing)

Investing is all about the opportunity to take advantage of viable trading markets. The power of participants in the securities markets is leveraged by entrepreneurs to raise capital, and the participants are leveraging the power of entrepreneurs to grow their money faster than inflation.

The business of investing and the ability for consumers to invest on their own has changed over the years. Understanding this history will help you gain deeper insight into the benefits, dangers, and our insatiable attraction to the securities markets.

In this section, I talk about the power of compounding effects on money invested (again, mostly in the traditional securities markets). We discuss some basic investment philosophy, why, when, where, and how to invest, bringing some method to the madness of irrational markets. The goal here is to highlight the important difference between an investor and a trader—a difference that could mean a million dollars or more to you over the course of a lifetime.

Section VII: Joy of Time (Retirement)

With apologies to my peers in the financial industry who advertise during professional sports events, retirement is not a goal. Retirement is a made-up word to get older people out from behind their desks and into rocking chairs. Science is going to keep us alive too long for any of us to choose that lifestyle. I will use *that word* in this section only for reference purposes. We will focus on the latter stages of your life, which will hopefully be a time of renewal, reflection, and time. What would it be like to live like a philanthropist, an activist, a wisdom worker, or just someone who has the best working body on the tour bus to Alaska? Yes, we will review the benefits of good health and attention to income, rather than simply accumulated wealth and sick care. With good income and good health, you should never run out of money! I will show you how to create some options.

Finally

You are the kings and queens of your money. In my professional life, I am just an adviser; for the purposes of this book, I am just an author. Nothing in this book can be taken as gospel without first consulting many and various professional experts about your personal situation. For example, you may want to meet with a mortgage loan officer, a student loan specialist, a professional philanthropist, an estate planner, insurance agent, or even an independent financial planner (hey, I'm right here). Throughout the book, I've used a few quotes from these specialists to give you an idea of what they would say (from the proverbial "horse's mouth"). Use this book as a curated information source. It can prepare you for meetings with almost anyone in the personal financial field. After reading this book, you should have little fear of going in "naked" to a meeting/conversation with people who wear cuff links and/or power suits for a living. Use what you read here as a guide for asking these kinds of professionals questions about your financial life. I know many that would give you a free consultation, especially just over the phone.

As you march through the challenging world of adulthood, my hope is that I can brighten, even if just a little, the dark mysteries of finances and wealth building. We shouldn't be surprised that managing a household and a life is a little harder than it seemed as a kid; alas, it is. We are not wrong for feeling stressed about paying down debt, saving an emergency fund, saving for college, and preparing for retirement. It's hard. I chose this profession on purpose: to have one less thing to figure out during my "free time." Most people consider managing finances a full-time job; it just happens to *be* my full-time job. Becoming known for teaching these concepts is part of my American Dream and the reason I wrote this book. I hope this book helps you develop your American Dreams and eventually, the legacy for which you can take pride.

JOY OF HARMONY

Family Governance

"Let all your things have their places; let each part of your business have its time."
~ Benjamin Franklin

CHAPTER I

BACKGROUND & HISTORY

Family Governance in Family Offices

Wealth has a history of its own. Over time, it has been concentrated among the few, usually handed down successfully over at least two or three generations before being unintentionally squandered or lost. Part of the wealth preservation phenomenon is due to the skill and dexterity of the little-known organizations called "family offices." The cornerstone of these traditional single-family or multi-family offices is a governance structure that ensures all family members are on the same page and that tax obligations are properly managed.

The Roman Empire, beginning in 27 BC and headed by Gaius Julius Caesar Octavianus (aka Julius Caesar), was a heady time for concentrated wealth. Nearly 25% of the world's goods and services were produced by Rome, and most of the assets were owned by Caesar. Major wealth accumulators like Caesar (or the Emperor of China and the King of Timbuktu hundreds of years later), all worked with small teams, akin to what we now call a family office, that managed their resources.

A more recognizable family with a governance structure is the House of Windsor, the current royal family of the United Kingdom. That family's wealth is managed by a Sovereign Grant from the "Crown Estate," or property held within the United Kingdom. Though it has varied over the years, 15% of Crown Estate's profits are paid to Queen Elizabeth II annually.[1] This arrangement goes back to 1760, part of a compromise between King George III and the UK Parliament to have a fixed amount of income to the monarchy be managed by the House of Commons.

A modern-world example of family offices is provided by the Rockefellers, who became the American pioneers of the single-family office in 1882. Jan Van Buren, co-founder of Foss Family Office Services in Switzerland, wrote in *Tharawat* (a magazine for family businesses) that John D. Rockefeller Sr. was worth the equivalent of $255 billion when he died in 1937. Co-founder of Standard Oil Company (which controlled up to 90% of the world's oil), Rockefeller was unique in setting up an office, complete with employees, specifically to manage his family's wealth and trusts. Some of those trusts still exist today. Undoubtedly, those office employees and his family worked through a governance structure that separated the family business from the wealth and the emotional hurdles of dealing with family and money.

Initially, single-family offices were each designed by a wealthy family to serve them alone; think the Rockefellers, the Morgans (of wealth giant J.P. Morgan Chase), or the (Bill and Melinda) Gates. Consulting firm Ernst & Young, in collaboration with investment bank Credit Suisse, published a guide stating that

---

1   You can actually find the "Royal Household Framework Agreement Relating to the Sovereign Grant" on the Royal.UK website.

there are approximately 3,000 single-family offices set up around the world, and *half* were set up in the past fifteen years. As wealth has continued to grow and centralize, some families open their offices to others (with a minimum wealth buy-in between $100 and $500 million), creating multi-family offices.

The allure of pooling investments, administering assets, and coordinating endowments, trusts, and other philanthropy makes the hassle of setting up a family office well worth the significant expense—at least, for the very wealthy. But couldn't others use a hand shaping the history and true value of their families?

Firms that specialize in family business, family trust, and family foundation management offer something that families of every wealth level can use today: an intentional structure. This structure preserves not only the financial wellbeing of the family, but the culture and relationships up and down the family tree. Beyond wealth, family governance is a long-acknowledged cornerstone for family safety and longevity. It is something I imagine that the Waltons, the Kennedys, the Bushs, the Mars family, and many others have known about all of these years. I am building that cornerstone for my family, the Howells. Now, it's your family's turn.

CHAPTER 2

FAMILY GOVERNANCE

A British bank is run with precision
A British home requires nothing less!
Tradition, discipline, and rules must be the tools
Without them—disorder! Chaos! Moral disintegration!
In short, you have a ghastly mess!
~Mary Poppins

The idea of family order being the mother of prosperity is high-lighted in two classic movies starring Julie Andrews: *The Sound of Music* (1965) and *Mary Poppins* (1964). In both movies, Julie Andrews plays antagonist to a male figure who is too rigid with his children. In *The Sound of Music*, Captain Georg von Trapp is a retired naval officer raising seven children, sometimes by use of a whistle. Julie Andrews plays the role of the family's new governess (a common position in wealthy European families). *Mary Poppins* is set in turn-of-the-century England (1910), and Julie Andrews plays nanny to the two young children of the prudish banker Mr.

Banks. In both movies, her character impresses upon the men and their families (and by default, the viewers) the value of creativity, the lessons of play, and the many contours of love. Combined with the solemn structure provided by an early 20th century patriarch, it was a recipe for inevitable family success.

AND WHAT I WANT, MORE THAN ANYTHING, IS THE ABILITY TO GIVE THE GIFT OF PERSONAL ACHIEVEMENT TO MY CLIENTS

The history of family governance outside of the ultra-high net worth family office structure is not well documented. How does one create a system of family governance, with or without the assistance of a governess or a nanny (or just Julie Andrews and a Hollywood ending)? That's what I wanted to find out and bring to my clients.

Believing that financial planning is life planning leads me to seek out the harmony it's possible to create by coordinating our financial world with our day-to-day lives. I believe that the discipline afforded by good financial planning is a predictor personal achievement. And what I want, more than anything, is the ability to give the gift of personal achievement to my clients (who are already on that journey). Behind all of the talk about insurance and investing and taxes, I know that's what they want as well—for themselves and their families.

PERSONAL EXPERIENCE

As a relatively new father myself, I have been on the lookout for best parenting practices, along with tips for co-equal management of the family household with my wife. There are bits of guidance provided by our religion; social norms exhibited by fellow parents at our kids' daycare and school; and the pristine model of the 1950s-1960s "traditional" nuclear family. A classic Gen X story, I am a product of a "broken home" (divorce) who also became a member of a "blended family," all the while remaining the son of an immigrant family. My family history is as muddled as my (permanent) tan. My wife's immediate family tree provides a more simplified family history. Just two generations back, we share a foundation of farming in our family lines, even though our grandparents were farming in different countries. The roots of our families are similar, but we were raised by parents with very different experiences. These are the experiences that are reconciled by family governance.

Learning to become a good parent, spouse, son, and sibling while actively performing in the roles is a little like flying an airplane while refilling it with gas. Along the journey, I started writing up what could be considered a list of family values centered around the concepts of order, overall fitness, and relationships. As an entrepreneur, I committed to sharing the progress of my company with my wife, so she understands what's going on with the future of our largest asset. We have targeted one day a week when we can talk about family finances, chores, aspirations, and life. (Like most, though, we hit these topics randomly throughout evenings and during naptime on weekends—but we hit the topics.) Working with clients, I wanted to create something more, and so my research dive into family governance began.

PROFESSIONAL EXPERIENCE

Admittedly, when I first rolled out family governance for my clients, I didn't quite have the wording down. Here's what I knew:

1. High net worth (HNW) families have a long history of structuring their financial life.
2. Financial planning is life planning.

I began deeper, sometimes-awkward conversations with my clients about how they spent their time, from running their households (chores) to scheduling leisure activities (hobbies), what their family values were (knowing they likely weren't written down anywhere), and when the principals made time to talk about money. What I was really looking for was a way to harmonize the financial life they had asked me to help them build with the regular world they had to manage as the kings and queens of their households. I wanted to uncover a kind of "kitchen-table family governance." I knew I was asking some of the right questions, even though I still seemed to be only grazing the surface of what a successful financial life looked like beyond the numbers. This was a challenge worth battling until I could find the proper research around the defining topics of family success.

I found that there were people who had a grasp on the communication, the life skills, and the financial world we live in. And they had that luxury because they were getting instruction from a myriad of people who specialized in family business consulting for the wealthy families among us. I wondered why this couldn't be translated to families with smaller businesses, or no business besides the business of family. I decided there was no reason it could not be done. These best practices and their harmonizing effect should be and need to be articulated for all of our families.

In the following section, you will find the results of my research. I challenge you to take additional steps in identifying how to spell success for your family and your family's legacy.

A Family Governance Process

There are many definitions of **family governance**. Here's mine:

> *The system for creating family harmony, preserving family history, and nurturing family values and wealth though the purposeful structure and stewardship of the founding family members.*

An even easier definition is, "The wealthy family's system for nurturing values, traditions, and wealth that is passed on to the next generation." Or, you could just say that family governance equals family decisions. That the history of family governance is tied to the business of money is beside the point. Money is a tool that can be used to reinforce the mission of the family (once they articulate one). Families have purposes that stretch further than the dollar. Each family is in the business of life. Families have a natural purpose, providing for the physical and emotional needs of the individual members. We do our best, but as flawed humans, we come up short more often than we'd like. Even families that start businesses must first work on communication between family members before they can expect any continuity or future success of their business. It might take a team of psychologists to diagnose and remedy the challenges we endure as family members. But to create family governance, a roadmap for current and future generations to navigate an unpredictable future, well, that just takes some time.

Forming a family governance system begins with identifying what matters most to the principals. Who gets to be the principals? Well, the first ones to get this started! I looked around my own family and I didn't see anyone handing out iron-on family seals or crests (not that those are required), so I rightfully reasoned no one had quite gotten started on identifying our family motto or mission either. It was up to me! And yours may be up to you.

This is exciting once you get going, but nerve-wracking at the start. Who are you to create a system typically designed for the wealthiest families? You are a member of the most important generation of Americans: the current adults. You don't need a literal "family business" or $100 million to see the benefits of this process. The following five steps outline how I have translated family governance for (W-2 income) families.

Step 1: Tell Your Story

When I think of what I would like people to remember me by when I'm gone, it surely isn't my money; it's my story. Your children and your children's children will not understand a thing you are doing with their inheritance if they don't understand your story. If you are in your mid-forties or younger while reading this, you may think you have plenty of time to tell the story of your last name to your children. You might; you might not. And you might think your significant other of many years understands the nuances of your story—they might or might not. The act of writing down the highlights of your **financial story** brings a specificity and a structure that will be revealing, even to yourself.

Your story can begin wherever you'd like. You can start with your parents or grandparents and walk down memory lane to the best of your ability (this is another reason to write it while you are young). You can write about how they met, what they might have endured, and how that shaped your upbringing. You can then start talking about your relationship with your spouse or significant other. Invite them to write in their family story too, and share these family stories with each other. You will learn something more about each other just by completing this exercise.

Of course, you will want to talk about your experiences with money. Write about the messaging you heard growing up and how it affected you. Here are some of the questions you should ask of yourselves and each other:

- What phrases did you hear about money when you were growing up?
- What did your parents/grandparents teach you about money?
- How did you earn your first dollar/paycheck?
- How hard has it been to save money over the years?
- What was your most successful financial moment or year?
- If you could go back, what one financial change would you make from your past?
- What do you believe about money in relation to the overall economy?

Depending on how old your children are, some or all of your discussion should be shared with them. This doesn't need to happen all at once; most parents I know drop little stories about themselves over time. (Usually, it follows, "When I was your age…") I am not qualified to judge how well those piecemeal revelations work, but as a fellow parent, I know I want to be more intentional.

Begin with the end in mind when it comes to building your family governance system: tell your family story. If your children are old enough, have them start writing theirs.

Step 2: Identify Your Current Lifestyle

You already have family norms when it comes to life and money management. You make money, you save, you spend, and you probably invest. You work a lot and your probably think you don't work enough (you do). Maybe you talk about money frequently, maybe you do not talk about money unless it's an emergency. Identify what you are doing now. Stepping back, without judgement, to talk about what you actually *do* when it comes to money is the next step in determining what you *ought* to be doing. Start with the following questions:

- Who earns money in your household, and is this by choice?
- Who makes the spending decisions and pays the bills for the household?
- Who makes the savings and long-term investing decisions in the household?
- How do you handle financial disagreements? Are there "ground rules?"
- If someone is earning an allowance, what does it represent?
- How has charity or posterity influenced your financial decisions?
- Considering how you spend your time, what do you actively value the most?
- What does money mean to you and your partner/ spouse and/or kids?

Step 3: Reveal Your Aspirations

In the late 1990s, I was lucky to have that special friend that perhaps only a few of us ever have (though I hope you did too). She took to me all of the best (read: craziest) parties, and quiet get-togethers were spent watching quirky movies (on videotape) that I was too nerdy to have otherwise seen. One of those movies was the 1994 film *Swimming with Sharks*, starring Kevin Spacey as Buddy Ackerman, a Hollywood boss from hell, and Frank Whaley as Guy, his assistant, who turns out to be not-so-nice a guy either. Guy kidnaps Buddy, and Buddy asks his captor, over and over, "What do you want?"

I have forgotten most of the movie, but that question lingered with me the night I watched it, and has popped in and out of my life ever since. It is one of the most important questions you can answer if you aspire to reap the benefits of family governance.

After you share some of your family story, write about your life aspirations—the ones you have achieved and the ones you still have to accomplish. You are writing this while you are very much alive, so feel free to write down aspirational goals that seem improbable. (Napoleon Hill, author of one of the most famous personal development books, *Think and Grow Rich*, recommends writing your goals down and reading them every day—try it out, it's a great exercise.) Below are some examples of questions that can help you get your answers:

- What do you want money to do for you and your family relationships today?
- What do you hope money will do for you and your family relationships in ten years?
- What, specifically, do you wish to teach the rest of your family about money?

- What do you wish your partner/spouse and/or kids understood about you and money?

Step 4: Draft the Family Mission Statement

After writing your stories, what you have done, and where you intend to go as a family leader, forming your **mission statement** and **family motto** will come a lot easier. These are how you hope each member of the family treats each other and what you want your last name to mean in the community. What do you want your family reputation to mean in society? How will you motivate your family (while you are alive *and* after you have passed away) to nurture that reputation?

You can get as detailed as you like here, but brief missions are more easily remembered. For example, if "Respect boundaries and give each other space, but be generous when a need arises," is part of your mission, it will work. Sometimes, though, one word can mean so much. It's why mottos stick, while mission statements just stick on a wall.

Mission statements assume the people reading them are old enough to "get it." The way you position a mission statement for a family with adult children may be different than how you would for a younger family just desperate for Junior to make his bed in the morning. If you don't have adult children, chances are the same aspirations you have for yourself will work well for your kids. Examples include:

- We will always be honest.
- We will confront challenges, even though they are hard.
- We will treat others with kindness. Even our siblings!
- We will take responsibility for our actions.

- We will clean up after ourselves and help each other.
- We will save up for things outside of our normal budgets.
- We will believe in a higher power and follow x or y or no religion.

Note: If you have family members with special needs, then specificity is required and can be detailed in a mission statement and in your last will and testament. The services of an estate attorney licensed in your state (along with a tax attorney) will suit you well.

Step 5: Create Space for Family Meetings

After walking through your story with your spouse and writing out your preliminary mission statement, it's time to meet with the family (your family, that is—my apologies if you were thinking of someone else's). Rolling out these concepts should probably start with your nuclear family.

The first **family meeting** is an opportunity to create excitement around the potential of *your* family! It is announcing your intention *to live* with intention. It is an invitation for the other members of the family to join you on a journey that coordinates the financial and perhaps social life of the family.

This meeting is the first of what should be many. If you are the kind of family that regularly (or at least once in a while) shares a meal together, you can host "meetings" at the dinner table; first casually, then formally. It can be a safe space to come together on relevant issues of the day. If it's just you and a partner, then reviewing values and aspirations while sharing a meal is something you may already do. If your meals include other family members, then you can go around the table asking questions.

Step 6: Draft a Family Constitution

There are many boutique firms that specialize in drafting formal documents for how family businesses will be run. For families, though, there aren't many. Completing the first five steps prepares you to draft a friendly **constitution** for your family. You are now in a place to outline roles, responsibilities, decision-making structures, goals, discipline, and process for review. This family constitution can be as formal or informal as you like. Here are some elements to include:

- Outline the financial roles and responsibilities of each family member
- Specify how often the family will meet to make decisions, review goals, etc.
- Describe how financial decisions will be made and by whom
- Outline how to resolve arguments and what to do when "laws" are broken
- Decide when third-party professional financial expertise will be used (i.e., advisers)
- Create a reporting mechanism (style, frequency, distribution, etc.)

Having a document that summarizes these elements is clarifying for the entire family, especially the future patriarchs and matriarchs who choose to lead (that's you).

CHAPTER 2 TAKEAWAYS

Family governance is not just for family businesses and the ultra-rich. It's an organizing principle for people who want to lead their families in directions that matter. Family governance is a system that has more to do with values than money (though we may express our values through our decisions with money). We come to the proverbial table with stories that affect our finances and, consequently, the direction of our lives and the lives of the people who are around us. You can take specific actions to guide yourselves and your family members. That is the promise of family governance.

Actionable Strategies:

- Take the opportunity to explore family governance examples in business and religion
- Write and share your money-life stories
- Identify what's working and not working your current lifestyle
- Reveal what you *really* want out of life for your family when it comes to money
- Draft a family mission statement that the whole family can commit to
- Create space for family meetings to review and share what's working
- Draft a family constitution that outlines how you will execute your plans

CHAPTER 3

FAMILY BUSINESSES & GOVERNANCE

Family business is not only big business; it is also big *businesses*! During my research, I learned that many public companies are family businesses. According to a *Harvard Business Review* article by a senior adviser with Boston Consulting Group, family businesses account for 30% of businesses with over $1 billion in sales. (Their definition of family business included public firms where a large percentage of stock was owned by family members and family members had positions on the board of directors.)[1]

Not every family business is huge, but they can all benefit from governance. Because the "family business" is usually the largest asset within a family, the importance of a formal structure can't be overstated.

---

1   Kachaner, Nicolas, "What You Can Learn from Family Business," Harvard Business Review, November 2012, https://hbr.org/2012/11/what-you-can-learn-from-family-business, 2019.

Shirtsleeves to Shirtsleeves

There is a famous Japanese saying that has been adopted in many cultures around the world: "Rice paddies to rice paddies in the three generations." It's the not-too-hopeful phenomena when the first generation of your family achieves success and creates wealth through visible hard work; the second generation, out of respect, continues that success by preserving the wealth through conservative living; and the third generation blithely squanders it all.

It has become a cottage industry for astute advisers to service families in the category of "family business consulting." Try an internet search for the term; you can scroll and scroll for days (or at least pages). There are plenty of books and conferences helping multigenerational businesses solve the "shirtsleeves to shirtsleeves" problem.

One of the most important categories of governance within the family business "industry" is **succession and/or ownership**. Worldwide consulting firm McKinsey & Company, in their 2010 article, *The Five Attributes of Enduring Family Businesses*, wrote, "Large family businesses that survive for many generations make sure to permeate their ethos of ownership with a strong sense of purpose." McKinsey also noted that attention to family governance is an attribute of long-lasting succession.

We have already covered the basics of family governance in the previous chapter. In the following sections, I will mention just some of the additional formality necessary when your family includes a successful business.

Family Business Council

The **family council** is often comprised of the founders and other family members with whom business, property, and/or other assets are shared. This is the group meant to handle family governance or, more specifically, the decisions that need to be made by owners of the family business.

This might include:

- Defining the values and mission of the family and the business
- Managing the interaction of the board directors with the family
- Reviewing financial statements and business management reports
- Discussing succession planning for the family business and the council itself
- Updating estate plans of the founders and others who share assets
- Outlining the financial education of other family members
- Evaluating options for philanthropy and posterity
- Determining if other professionals/advisers are needed

There is also an inherent responsibility to address the social aspects and communication needs of the family:

- How goes the relationships east and west, north and south of the generations (e.g., siblings, spouses, and parents)?
- How financially aligned are spouses to the family members of the founders?

- What conflicts need to be resolved?
- How are financial transitions affecting family members?

A family council is hard work. It is like any board of directors, except in this case, the work couldn't be any more personal. Members must have a fiduciary duty to the mission of the family, which might evolve and change as the family grows.

Family Business Constitution

You will want a blueprint for how your family governance is run. For example, if you're going to have a "board of directors" (like the family council), then it is a best practice to outline how long the members will serve. Do you really want to hold the reins of the family governance into your late eighties and early nineties? Does your spouse? How will you handle shareholders of the family business? What happens with divorced spouses? What happens if a family member gets arrested or jailed? How much financial support do family members receive, and under what circumstances? All of these should be documented in the **family business constitution**.

The United States Constitution was a labor of love, punishable by death if the colonists were caught drafting it. This is why the signatures on the bottom meant so much (especially the big and bold "John Hancock"). Writing your constitution for your family with your family business (wealth) in the mix may feel more than a little awkward. It may seem like a chore, but the impact of the legacy you leave for future family members is infinite. It's a weighty and important task, and thankfully, there are many experts who help guide families through this process.

Because you can hire consultants to help you draft this

document or run your council meetings, it may seem that all of your decisions are set in stone once made. They are not. This is your family, and you can change as you learn. Family constitutions are living documents, with elements that will change over time. All of the family council discussions will become building blocks for a constitution likely oft amended for the first few years.

General Family Business Meetings

Family business meetings are different from family council meetings; while the work of council meetings is serious (like working on a board of directors), family business meetings should be more informative and partially social (though the formality of the event is up to you). This is not a meeting where major decisions are made, but rather where major feelings are shared after members are informed of decisions. (Hopefully those feelings are mostly supportive and loving.)

One of the largest family businesses in history is Walmart Inc. Before going public in 1970, the Walton Family owned twenty-four Wal-Mart stores.[2] In 2015, the Waltons recommitted to owning 50% of the company's stock.[3] As you can imagine, the living family members are some of the richest people in the world. Can you imagine what it would be like if their entire family was included in a business meeting? It would be chaos. In Walmart's case, they have layers of management for the day-to-day, a board of directors for corporate governance, and likely family directors for family governance. I imagine the family reunions are

---

2   "Our History," Walmart, Inc., 2019, https://corporate.walmart.com/our-story/our-history.

3   Reuters, "Wal-Mart says Walton family to sell shares to keep lid on stake," April 10, 2015, https://finance.yahoo.com/news/wal-mart-says-walton-family-221221853.html.

informative but most social in nature.

An annual meeting makes sense, since anything more frequent might be too much to coordinate; once every couple of
years (like a family reunion) is also a possibility. Obviously, family
members who share business ownership, real estate, trust responsibilities, and other assets should be invited, but you will also
want to invite future heirs and spouses. Family members who
would like a stronger voice in leadership could be invited to the
more formal and frequent family council meetings. Usually the
founder of the business would "lead" these meetings, at least to
start. Eventually the founder will relinquish that role and hopefully the next most responsible person will take his or her place.

CHAPTER 3 TAKEAWAYS

The stakes are high when a family business is the employer and sustainer of a family's wealth. The formality of family governance for family business are often supported by consulting firms and so-called experts, but the family dynamics will have to be managed by the patriarchs and matriarchs of the family, whomever they are. If that person is you, then the development of a family council and a formal family constitution is critical to the long-term success of the family wealth. The goal is to prepare ahead to avoid conflict, and to ease communication when conflict inevitably arrives.

Actionable Strategies:

- Outline how the long-term goals of the family business match those of the family
- Recruit and evaluate experts in the field of family governance for family businesses
- Nominate formal family council members to manage the business and the family
- Conduct (annual) family business meetings for select family members
- Ensure constant communication between family members who share ownership

CHAPTER 4

A WORD ON
FAMILY VALUES

Historically, when I've read or heard the phrase "family values," I've cringed a little. It has been more of a political phrase than denoted by the words. But my research on family governance took me through interesting arguments regarding the family and family values; I'll share some insights (and history) that were new to me.

I enjoyed learning about award winning author Stephanie Coontz and her "provocative" (according to a *New York Times* review) book, *The Way We Never Were: American Families and the Nostalgia Trap.* Her thesis is best summarized by the first line on the back cover: "*Leave It to Beaver* was not a documentary." That nostalgic family picture of the mom and dad and a couple of kids easily managing day-to-day life did not represent every family of the post-World War II period, and it didn't represent much of the pre-war period either. But even today, it stands out as an ideal.

The politics of the phrase "family values" has stripped away our opportunity to even talk about a topic that is more valuable than money to many of us. For some of us, successful development of our families and the community impact of our values are the entire purpose of wealth. Herein lies the largest problem: our guilt tying our level of financial success to our ability to reinforce our family values. Have you ever thought, *If only I could afford to spend more time with my kids/spouse/parents, I would, right?* Net worth does not equal self-worth, but it *feels* that way sometimes. Why?

Perhaps that can be explained in part by historian and award-winning author Elaine Tyler May. In her article, "Family Values: The Uses and Abuses of American History," she writes revealingly about the connection between "traditional" values and national history:

> To understand this concern with "family values," we need to examine the relationship between the family and the state. The United States is not the only society that places huge ideological and social meanings upon the family. But in the United States, a young country founded as a rather risky democratic experiment, most of the institutions that provided social order and a sense of identity were initially absent: the aristocracy with its implicit ideal of noblesse oblige, royalty grounded in kinship ties of the rulers, or even the deeply-rooted historical markers of identity grounded in a national soil, common traditions or customs.

> Lacking those characteristics, the United States invented its own traditions, and placed the family in the center of the polity, as the institution where citizens are bred and nurtured. Believing in the rights of the individual, but fearful of tyranny from above as well as anarchy from below, the nation's founders invested in the institution of the family the responsibility for maintaining social order in the democracy. Perhaps that is why the framers

of the Constitution dismantled virtually all vestiges of old-world hierarchies with the single exception of coverture, the common-law practice that rendered a married woman politically and legally "covered" by her husband. As a femme couverte, a married woman exercised her obligations to the state through her role as wife and mother in the family. In that capacity, she was expected to civilize the society and render the republic safe from the potentially dangerous excesses of democracy...

I have been motivated to read (and re-read) even more of May's work; I find her writings fascinating, having seen them for the first time while researching for this book. One more excerpt is necessary to close this line of thinking:

From the beginning, however, the reality of family life defied those definitions and strained against the normative ideal. The vast majority of Americans lived on farms, or in households that required the productive labor of all adult members of the family. The prevailing middle-class norm in the 19th century that defined "separate spheres" for men and women never pertained to these families, nor did it reflect the experiences of African-Americans, either during or after slavery. Only the most privileged white Protestant women in the towns and cities had the resources that allowed them to devote themselves full-time to nurturing their families and rearing future citizens.

If the ideal of family values is immediately shattered by the existence of blended families and working mothers, then very few of the families I know or work with can be considered "ideal" (including mine). Good. We can get on with the business of creating our own ideals and standards, and by that token, our own family governance structures that we believe work for the success of our families, the communities we serve, and yes, the country we love.

JOY OF
HARMONY

Summary

Harmonizing your life begins with expressing and sharing your personal story. It requires taking a factual look at what you are doing now with your time, energy, attention, and money.

We are part of a generation that must run faster and jump higher just to reach where our parents were at this time in their lives. And many of us have taken on that challenge with courage. Family governance asks you to slow down, reset, and refine what you really want for yourself and your family, then create a system for achieving those goals. It allows you to draft your values, write your mission, and pass those on to the next generation.

Creating a system of family governance will create rules for steady progress towards the goals of your family (and perhaps your family business). These are unlike the rules you just had to follow as a kid; these are the rules that, as an adult, you negotiate and put in place. You decide your family values. You decide the impact you want your family to have on the community and the country. More importantly, you get to be intentional about how your family members treat each other when facing conflict, financial decisions, and life experiences. You are likely the first to take this formal step in your family's history. You have the opportunity to become the patriarchs and matriarchs of your family, heavy responsibilities that will make an impact for generations to come.

A Final Word on Harmony

"Decisions are the ultimate power," says Anthony Robbins, world-famous life coach and creator of the wildly successful *Personal Power* series. At its heart, family governance is about making decisions. Imagine a world where more of us made intentional decisions to improve the harmony of our families, our ways to make a living, and the ways we support our communities. Imagine the difference it would make if we monitored our time, energy, and attentions to ensure they were consistent with our intentions. I see a future world in harmony with the earthly needs of the environment, the spiritual needs of humanity, and the business needs of trade and commerce. We begin by improving how we communicate with each other (namely our spouses or significant others); recognizing that we can be the patriarchs and matriarchs of our families and communities going forward; seeking first to understand then to be understood; and taking what we know of each other and aspiring together and passing it on to the next generation. We extend those dreams wherever we interact: our places of worship, our non-profit boards, our co-workers and our friends.

We the people can set the example for the institutions that have long been craving our leadership.

JOY OF ENOUGH

Income, Expenses, & Taxes

"A penny saved is a penny earned."
~Benjamin Franklin

CHAPTER 5

BACKGROUND & HISTORY

Earning

Before getting a handle on the concept of earning an income, it helps to understand how your paycheck got to where it is and why that matters, then discover what you can do about it.

Most people are at least anecdotally familiar with the wealth gap in the United States. In 2013, Pew[1] reported that the wealth gap between upper and middle-income households is the largest since the Federal Reserve began collecting data: upper-income median net worth is nearly 700% greater.[2] But that's not the only story. A study of middle-income households showed that the

---

1   The Pew Research Center is a non-profit, non-governmental, nonpartisan "fact tank" based in Washington, D.C. It does not take policy positions, but it does provide a lot of information on social, economic, and demographic trends.

2   Fry, Richard and Rakesh Kochhar, "America's wealth gap between middle-income and upper-income families is widest on record," December 17, 2014, https://www. pewresearch.org/fact-tank/2014/12/17/wealth-gap-upper-middle-income/.

median income levels in 2016 were equal, after adjustments, to the median middle-income level in 2000.[3] How is that possible and when did this start?

One has to look all the way back to the Industrial Revolution beginning in the 18th century to fully appreciate how we got here. As America (and Europe) started growing up, labor was in high demand. Many moved into the cities and worked hard—seven days a week for 100 hours or more. After many years of organized labor walkouts, strikes, and rallies, the pendulum swung to allow the signing of 1938's **Fair Labor Standards Act** standardizing a five-day, forty-hour work week. By the end of **World War II** in 1945, nearly 12 million workers were a part of a union, and the concept of **collective bargaining** (negotiating between employers and groups of employees) became a thing. Unions became a lobbying force in American politics, eventually siding with the successfully progressive Democrat Party. Despite their initial lack of support for minorities and women in skilled jobs, unions did a lot to bolster the post-war boom of America, including America's middle class. From 1945 through 1970, wages grew as much as 300%.

Now, despite nominal wage growth, real average wages (accounting for inflation) haven't really grown in forty years—in part because corporate leaders are rewarded almost exclusively for high stock prices, no matter the cost to employees, consumers, or the environment. In the bestselling book *Who Stole the American Dream?*, Pulitzer Prize-winning journalist Hedrick Smith outlined the shift of political and economic advantage back to big business that began in 1971. He noted that, "From 1998 to through 2010, business interests and trade groups spent $28.6 billion on

---

3   Kochhar, Rakesh, "The American middle class is stable in size, but losing ground financially to upper-income families," September 6, 2018, https://www.pewresearch.org/fact-tank/2018/09/06/the-american-middle-class-is-stable-in-size-but-losing-ground-financially-to-upper-income-families/.

lobbying compared with $492 million [by] labor, nearly a 60 to 1 business advantage." What that means, in regard to your paycheck, is that companies took back the political and (with that) the economic advantage. Collective bargaining hasn't been effective since before the Ronald Reagan era of the 1980s. Despite nominal wage growth, real average wage growth (accounting for inflation) hasn't really grown in forty years.[4] One of the reasons wages are not growing (as Hedrick Smith writes about) is that corporate leaders are rewarded almost exclusively for high stock prices, no matter the cost to employees, consumers, or the environment. For employees, a significant cost has been wage stagnation for decades. In the brave new world of earning an income, a whole new way of thinking is necessary.

Spending

To understand our own spending habits, we have to understand what we're up against. Consumer spending has always been an important metric for the US economy. From 1950 through 2010, as a share of Gross Domestic Product (GDP), our consumer spending has grown, on average, from 62% to 70% of the overall economy.[5] That's a big deal! You will hear the phrase "consumer sentiment" thrown around by financial analysts and economists who are trying to predict how you and I feel about buying. Collectively, we spend about two-thirds of our personal income on services,

---

4 Desilver, Drew, "For most U.S. workers, real wages have barely budged in decades," August 7, 2018, https://www.pewresearch.org/fact-tank/2018/08/07/for-most-us-workers-real-wages-have-barely-budged-for-decades/.

5 "Personal Consumption Expenditures/Gross Domestic Product," Economic Research at the Federal Reserve Bank of St. Louis, 2019, https://fred.stlouisfed.org/graph/?g=hh3.

mostly housing and healthcare. The other third of course is spent on goods, mostly food, followed by cars, recreation and energy.

The Personal Consumption Expenditures report (PCE) is released monthly by the Bureau of Economic Analysis (BEA), a division of the U.S. Department of Commerce.[6] PCE helps economists and stock analysts predict how much we will spend now versus save for the future. High PCE levels (spending) predicts good things in the short term for the economy, while low PCE levels (saving) predicts good things for the long-term growth of the economy. That data is translated to corporate boardrooms across the country by the executives whose compensation is tied to their company's stock price. The minute stock analysts get a whiff of low PCE in a certain sector, the companies in that sector feel it in their stock prices. You can bet that once the stock price is affected, the chatter in those corporate boardrooms is centered around how to get you and me to spend more than we save.

Consumer Behavior & Public Relations

"We must shift America, he wrote, from a needs to a desires culture. People must be trained to desire, to want new things even before the old had been entirely consumed." That line is from the 2002 British television documentary series *The Century of Self*, which traces consumerism back to the end of **World War I**. As the story goes, Edward Bernays, the nephew of Sigmund Freud, was invited to join President Woodrow Wilson at the **Paris Peace Conference** in 1919. Bernays had been employed as a press agent to promote America's benevolent involvement in the war effort;

6   "Consumer Spending," Bureau of Economic Analysis, https://www.bea.gov/data/consumer-spending/main, 2019.

now, he was being asked to use that skill to promote democracy in Europe alongside President Wilson. Bernays noted how popular President Wilson was in Paris, and figured that if you could "use propaganda for war, you could certainly use it for peace."

Since propaganda was a loaded term, he coined a new term: "public relations." Bernays' niche was using his uncle's ground-breaking psychoanalytic research to influence buying behavior—selling people on products and ideas alike through emotion rather than information. With the American Tobacco Corporation as a client, he convinced women—who didn't smoke at the time—that cigarettes were connected to empowerment and independence. According to the documentary, Bernays invented movie product placement, the sex symbolism of cars, and emotional expression through fashion. Not coincidentally, he was also responsible for the U.S. popularity of Sigmund Freud, a then-struggling neurologist in economically-compromised Vienna, Austria, dedicating invaluable "public relations" work in the late 1920s. (Sigmund Freud is the only neurologist I have ever heard of.) Watch the documentary to learn how we began being sold based on our "unconscious desires."

In *The Hidden Persuaders*, a 1957 book by Vance Packard about the motivational techniques markets use to sell, the public was introduced to the controversial new "subliminal advertising" technique, a term coined by market researcher James Vicary. Vicary alleged that millisecond-long ads in movie theatres contributed to a 18% increase in sales of Coca-Cola and a 58% increase in popcorn. (Vicary would later admit his study was falsified.)[7]

7   Kessler, Benjamin and Steven Sweldens, "Think You're Immune to
     Advertising? Think Again," INSEAD Knowledge, January 30, 2018, https://
     knowledge.insead.edu/marketing/think-youre-immune-to-advertising-
     think-again-8286?p=Philippe%20Evrard&c=3232&by=title&p=Philippe%20
     Evrard&c=3232&by=title#ijyKyWixG8YbAomj.99, 2019.

The ability to encourage behavior at the subconscious level has been a subject of study ever since. Because subliminal advertising in hard to prove, there is no particular U.S. law that bans the practice, though the Federal Communications Commission (FCC) does have rules against marketing deception and will revoke a company's broadcast license if outright public deception is proven.

Claims of subliminal marketing have continued over the years. Controversial author Wilson Bryan Key wrote a handful of books on corporate advertising, including the widely circulated *Subliminal Seduction* in 1974. He spoke of the media's use of sex and violence to affect behavior, presumably at a subconscious level. Professional studies on a concept called "neuromarketing" have been documented since 1984. Neuromarketing studies began by using brain imaging to understand the neurological process of decision-making and grew to include eye tracking, heartbeat, body temperature, and even skin response. (We won't even mention what metrics can be collected and measured about your buying habits online.) British-American author and motivational speaker Simon Sinek has made a career out of his 2009 TED talk, "How Great Leaders Inspire Action" and bestselling book, *Start with Why*. In his original talk (which now has over 42 million views), Sinek speaks to his "discovery" of the "Golden Circle." He says inspired leaders and organizations speak (sell) from "why" to "how" to "what." Sinek argues that our neocortex responds to facts and figures, but it is our limbic brain that makes decisions and controls our behavior. In other words, how we feel (or how we are led to feel) is how we buy.

We have a long history of spending, and our habits weren't just passed down from our parents. They were curated by the smartest marketing scientists hired by executives with the greatest incentives in the world.

Federal Taxation

According to the December 2015 *New York Times* article, "For the Wealthiest, a Private Tax System That Saves Them Billions," tax planning is a core function of family offices. Unlike family governance however, tax avoidance—both legal and illegal—has always been a part of American culture.

In fact, the United States' aversion to taxes (at least, taxation without representation) began years before the country's formal founding. The **Stamp Act of 1765** was a kind of sales tax on printed materials imposed by the British Parliament upon the colonists and the British citizenry (and rebuffed by both groups). It was a precursor to the more infamous **Tea Act of 1773** that precipitated the **Boston Tea Party** and eventually, the **American Revolutionary War** (1775-1783).

Tax and War

Known for his heroics leading the Union through the **American Civil War**, President Abraham Lincoln was also quite the politician. Faced with a budget deficit, a volunteer army, and the fate of the Union, Lincoln opened a special session of Congress to raise funds through the first federal income tax. The **Revenue Act of 1861** launched (among other taxes and tariffs) a 3% flat income tax. It wasn't enough. The **Revenue Act of 1862** levied an additional excise tax and introduced the first progressive tax system. A means for collecting these taxes was also created, introducing what we now all know as the Internal Revenue Service (IRS). Over the next few decades, Congress repealed and reassessed the way it would tax. The **16th Amendment to the United States Constitution**, proposed by President William Taft in 1909 and ratified in 1913, authorized Congress to levy income tax without basing it on the population of individual states, and the IRS tax form 1040 was introduced to the public.

The **Revenue Act of 1918** simplified the income tax structure and added a top tax rate of 77% on income above $1 million. **World War I** was funded by the increased taxes assessed by the **War Revenue Acts of 1917 and 1918**, which included an excess profits tax on corporations with marginal rates as high as 60%. In reality, the Federal Reserve Banks of the day lent money to the government by purchasing "war bonds," but the progressive tax system was now set in place for the future.

The advent of **World War II** coincided with another milestone in tax history, the **Revenue Act of 1942**. This act increased individual and corporate income tax rates while reducing personal and dependent exemptions. A 5% "Victory Tax" was also part of the new law, with the promise it would be credited after the war. At the beginning of the war, about 4 million Americans paid income tax; by the end of the war in 1945, that had jumped to over 42 million.

Federal Income Tax Evolution

By 1969, the federal income tax had entered a new phase: identifying ways to tax even those who might purposely avoid being taxed. The **Revenue Act of 1969** created the Alternative Minimum Tax (AMT), meant to catch wealthy filers who avoided paying even a modicum of their tax liability. President Reagan's famous **Tax Reform Act of 1986** was sponsored by Democrats to eliminate loopholes of the so-called "rich" and simplify the tax code so that it was considered fairer. It created an AMT for corporations, bolstered the AMT for individuals, required Social Security numbers for dependents, and greatly reduced tax shelters.

The cost to Democrats? A drastically reduced top tax marginal tax rate, from 50% to 28%. It also raised the bottom rate from 11% to 15%, a seemingly regressive tax rate change that was a first for U.S. policy. This dramatically changed the ratio direction of the highest marginal tax rate to lowest marginal tax rate towards where we are today. The high/low rates have gone from 7:1 ratio (7% rate to 1% rate) in 1913 to 3.7: 1 (37% to 10%) today.

Lost in these details is the reality highlighted by the Tax Policy Center, a non-partisan think tank in Washington, D.C.: from 1979 to 2015, the average income tax rate for all income quintiles has barely changed.

Payroll Taxes

The Current Tax Payment Act of 1943 was signed into law to make it easier to collect taxes of all kinds: federal, state, and local. It introduced payroll withholding (and quarterly tax payments) at a time when the United States was at war and had no desire to run after people for tax collection. (Incidentally, this provision was in the original Revenue Act of 1913, but it had been repealed three years later.) Federal tax withholding began to include Federal Insurance Contributions Act (FICA) payments. FICA was created to financially support the Social Security Act of 1935. For Social Security, we each pay 6.2% of our salaries up to $132,000 (2019).

Tax laws are written through legislation that comes out of the U.S. Congress, particularly the House of Representatives. Like all laws that begin in the House, they are next sent to the U.S. Senate for reconciliation, then the president for signature. In many instances, the president submits a plan to Congress, then it goes through the legislative process before returning to the

White House for signature. When President Roosevelt submitted the **Social Security Act of 1935**, he didn't initially cap the wages that the 6.2% would be collected on. He just assumed people at a certain level of wealth wouldn't need Social Security, so in his original plan, they were left out. But before the bill got out of Congress (and back for his signature), there was a cap and all income earners were included in future Social Security benefits (obviously much lower in 1935). Since a lot of people make less than $128,000, there is a political argument that the cap is unfair, because higher income workers are escaping a tax burden that everyone else pays dollar for dollar. The other side of the argument is that higher income earners benefit less from Social Security, because the future payments are a smaller part of their net worth. Again, taxes are political.

Non-citizens are subject to withholding rates of 30%, while investment revenue (including interest) is subject to backup withholding of 28%. You have heard all of these phrases; you were born into a world that had already accepted that there would be a difference between your gross paycheck and your net paycheck. That was not always the case.

Revenue Act of 1978

Before 1978, beside taxes and maybe health insurance, nothing else was "taken out" of your paycheck. The **Revenue Act of 1978** was written by Congress, sent to the White House, and signed into law by President Jimmy Carter (much more quietly than the Social Security Act). This law kicked off the opportunity for companies to make another withholding from an employee's paycheck (something we had now grown used to with taxes), setting aside compensation that would not be taxed until the employee reached the age of 59 ½ via Internal Revenue Code, section 401(k).

Did you know that we didn't have 401(k) plans until the early 1980s? That's the power of tax law. Within just a few years, half of all large firms either had a plan in place or were working to replace their pensions with 401(k) plans. Another sign of the "tail wagging the dog" was the invention of Thrift Savings Plans (TSPs) that began for federal workers in 1986. By 1990, there were over 19 million participants in 401(k) plans across the country.

Is it any wonder that with portable 401(k) plans instead of pensions, we were told that we would have multiple jobs over the course of our careers? Prior generations were *encouraged* to stay in their jobs for life with a pension "carrot" dangling at the end. We can take our 401(k)s anywhere—wiping out a whole culture of employee loyalty.

Tax law has consequences.

CHAPTER 6

EARNING

Imagine you had a machine in the basement that printed money—cold, hard American currency. Imagine that it was legal to print this money. Imagine it's been working for twenty years, and it's likely to work for twenty more.

Now, imagine that machine is you.

Some people get their "machines" to work in perpetuity (e.g., musicians with their royalties) and some people have multiple "machines" (e.g., athletes with music, team, and shoe contracts). But you don't have to be a successful musician or athlete to have multiple, perpetual streams of income. And thankfully, you don't have to have a machine that prints money (that's illegal). **Joy of Earning** is about designing a strategy so that money is always coming in (preferably from different sources), and bringing this money in without the "mission creep" of increased expenses.

Most people fail to accomplish their personal life missions because they fail to solve the riddle of their basic financial survival. (Which is understandable—financial survival has become an overwhelming riddle of dos, don'ts, and don't-forget-the-latest-financial-products.) But generating higher income with less effort over less time while managing expenses is not just the riddle of survival—it's the riddle of wealth. Even millionaires need to ensure they are generating income that outpaces expenses; the world is expensive, and even fortunes have limits. Understanding the power of income, the cost of spending, and the deception of credit is the subject of this section.

PERSONAL EXPERIENCE

I wanted to earn money when I was thirteen, but I was too young to get an authorized work permit from my junior high school. So, I did what any soon-to-be entrepreneur does: started knocking on doors and offering home services. I would rake leaves and clear out backyards, but my best business was mowing lawns. I didn't own a lawnmower, but my neighbors did, so I would just use theirs—a true service business.

After I graduated college, I enjoyed the peace of a paycheck that came every two weeks as long as I showed up to this place called "work" and worked. I also learned to value vacations and the perk of receiving that same paycheck even when I was *not* working.

"FIRST YOU WORK FOR EDUCATION, THEN YOU
WORK FOR MONEY, THEN PEOPLE WORK FOR
YOU, THEN MONEY WORKS FOR YOU."

I spent my first career in private and corporate accounting, which allowed me to have a side-business. That business was leveraging my knowledge of accounting and my passion for music by starting an accounting firm for unsigned musicians. In Northern Virginia, I had the entire market of unsigned musicians to myself.

Because I started this business in 1999, I decided to purchase my name URL: JasonHowell.com (which I still own today). Unfortunately, I soon found out why I was the only accountant for unsigned musicians—there was no money in it! It was standard in the 1990s to charge 5% of a band/musician's gross income as compensation. But since the bands I worked with mostly topped out in the low four-figures per month, I didn't always charge them. Maybe it was the technology or maybe it was just bad choices, but I wasn't too good at building side income in my early years.

Flash forward many years later, and that nearly no-income accounting firm for unsigned musicians has turned into a quickly-growing financial planning firm for my generation—an educated, skeptical group with high expectations. I've had many interests over the years, and looking back, I realize that I started a few firms; it was not until I decided to not be a "jack of all trades" but to master one instead that my business started to make a difference. The biggest difference was I was finally adding value, through the accumulation of expertise that can only be honed through effort, education, and experience. That's what the Jason Howell Company will always be: an accumulation of expertise honed through effort, education, and experience. The firm is profitable and growing, and our niche in growing, dual-income families is solid. We are bringing back the joy of the American Dream to families by sharing how the *Joy of Financial Planning* can transform their finances and their lives.

The 4 Step Process

First you work for education, then you work for money, then people work for you, then money works for you.

In college, I was told that most CEOs began as accountants,

so I felt great about being an accounting major. After eight years in accounting, I became a recruiter for an accounting and finance staffing firm (okay, a "headhunter"), which was a sales job. There, I learned that "nothing happens until a sale is made." I also learned that in college, marketing and sales people were told that most CEOs began in sales. I wonder if those who major in basketweaving hear, "Most CEOs began as basketweavers."

The truth is that my college professors and headhunting coworkers had all reached partially correct conclusions. A leader needs to have an eye on what's happening (accounting and finance) and what they're going to make happen (sales and marketing). And what's true for the corporate world, in this case, is true for people. You are the CEO of your money, and to ensure its overall health, you must create a consistent flow of income.

Financially successful people seem like they are just "printing money." Creating multiple streams of income is a strategy that many successful people, from (all of) the Kardashians to LeBron James to Gary Vaynerchuk, employ—but before you focus on multiple, let's focus on one.

The majority of people reading this have one stream of income, and that's their salary. Contrary to popular belief, a regular paycheck is actually a good thing. Something about your education, attitude, and presence convinced an employer that hiring you was more profitable to their organization than hiring someone else or no one at all. A job that pays regularly is valuable; unfortunately, it's just not dependable. Relying on someone else—your boss—to determine your income is a viable strategy in the short term, but in the long term, you will need to depend on yourself.

How do you do that? First, recognize that even if you work for an organization, the people who truly pay your salary are the clients, customers, members, or taxpayers. Your indirect or direct value to them is the long-term play for generating income for a lifetime. Second, refresh that value over time by repeating the four-part strategy you began as a teen in college.

Step 1: You Work for Education

Most people don't get wealthy without having an income. And most people trade time for money to earn their income. Your first goal is to get an education that will put you in the position to demand premium payment for your time. Now, it doesn't matter much what kind of education you get, as a long as it's applicable to the work you're going to do. Said another way, it doesn't matter what expertise you develop, as long as that knowledge and experience can eventually be used to deliver value to clients, customers, members, or taxpayers.

It also doesn't matter much at this point whether you get another college degree or learn everything there is to know about a subject in a more diffused method (for example, learning through what's available on the internet). I teach personal finance at American University in Washington, D.C. One day, I had a student come to me during office hours to discuss how mortgages work. We'd had a loan officer as a guest speaker in the prior class, but since this student was managing English as a second language, he didn't catch everything. After about twenty minutes with him, I could tell that not everything I explained was sinking in. I went to YouTube and showed him the many videos on the topic of calculating a mortgage, and his eyes lit up. He recognized what I knew: there were plenty of instructors online who were available to say things in a different, perhaps slower way. I suggest that all students review the chapters before class; for him, I also suggested that he watch YouTube videos on the upcoming topics, so he'd have a subject matter baseline.

Does online education put the traditional professor's job in jeopardy? Maybe, but probably not. The benefit of higher education has long been the process of attaining the knowledge, more than the knowledge itself; the responsibility it takes to attain a four-year degree, rather than the degree itself. Institutions of higher learning have more to offer than just the learning. They also offer the practice of life management during the learning process. This is a practice we are forced to continue post-graduation if we want to remain valuable to our future customers: our co-workers, our bosses, and/or our ultimate clients.

Step 2: You Work for Money

Traditionally, working for money means getting a job and earning hourly or salary compensation. That model works for millions of people, and it can work for you too. Working for money under an employer provides that beauty of a consistent paycheck. The apparent stability of this model at a time in your life when you are raising kids, supporting or preparing to support parents, and building your retirement accounts is understandably attractive. Most employers reward formal education, so the expertise you earned/paid for in college will get your foot in the door for interviews, salary increases, and promotions. An employer also provides benefits to support you and your family.

Another way to work for money is through entrepreneurship. Entrepreneurship rewards creativity, tenacity, and *all* kinds of education. I believe entrepreneurs are born *and* made, but that some of us are attracted to the idea of creating wealth out of ideas early on. I was one of those people who knew from a young age that I wanted to start a business from scratch. I started a few businesses, all in the financial field: an accounting firm for musicians, accounting software for business managers, and finally, a registered investment advisory firm for our generation. Along the way, the formal education and the education I earned through experience prepared me to earn an income in financial services. The toughest part of these businesses was not coming up with the ideas, but executing them. In business, execution is offering services at prices consumers are willing to pay that also cover your costs and then some. The "and then some" part is what you pay yourself. To become at least viable (which could take a few years), what you pay yourself should at least cover your personal cost of living. If your business can earn enough to cover its costs, reinvest in growing the business, cover your costs, and a little for you to save some money, then you're a champ. The next level is to earn enough income to pay for someone else.

Step 3: People Work for You

Leverage is the concept of using one thing to assist with affecting another thing. (At least, that's how I describe it.) If you're part of my generation, then you remember your parents using you to change the channel on the TV (before remote controls).

One of the great opportunities to use leverage at work is when you are part of a team and/or asked to supervise. When you are seen as an expert and have proven your worth as an employee, an opportunity to supervise will usually arise. Along with all of that responsibility will come a promotion and hopefully a raise.

My dad always used to say that the job of a leader is the easiest job. And leadership can be easy, assuming you know to delegate and motivate the people you are in charge of (and navigate the management above you). People can also "work for you" as team-mates and equal co-workers. Some of the best leaders say, "My employees work *with* me, not for me." Even if you typically work alone, your work is part of a larger team, and everyone's input is part of the leverage that works *for* your success.

When you run your own company and consider a new vendor or employee, your job is to first evaluate whether you can "profit" (essentially, create additional leverage) by adding that new relationship. If the answer is "yes," then you hire; otherwise, you do not. If you make the decision to hire, then that new employee or vendor should provide more money for you and/or your company.

That leverage you create beyond yourself is what provides the "extra" money in your life. The money you made just managing yourself (step 2) at work or in business for yourself covered your personal spending needs. When people work for you (step 3), you are "making money" beyond your level of needs; then, you have some discretion over what you want to do with that money. Or, said another way, you can choose what you want that money to do for you.

Step 4: Money Works for You

At this stage, you can start putting your money to work in banks, in the housing markets, in the stock markets, or in your own business!

Most people want to jump straight to this stage. I get questions all of the time about what to do with an "extra" $1,000 or $10,000. My answer is always, "It depends on your financial plan." That's not what they want to hear. What they really want to know is what stock they should buy or how else can I get their money to work for them. But you'll never successfully get to this stage if you haven't learned an expertise and earned an education, received a job or started a business, and don't have people working for you to create leverage. Only then can you successfully give your money enough time to stay invested—in savings accounts, stocks, businesses, or houses—so that it can grow.

If you have completed steps one through three and you are ready to make your money make money, congratulations! So, how exactly does that work? Through the nearly magical power of compounding.

Side Income

Depending on your full-time job, you have varying levels of flexibility to add a part-time job. For example, if you are a part of a regulated industry, like finance, you may not be able to do some things "on the side" without getting authorization from your compliance department. In the Washington, D.C. area, jobs in politics and government frequently put restrictions on side jobs. If you don't have restrictions and/or can work around them, consider a side-business or a side job. When I worked in accounting, I had a side job once in a mall store taking baby photos. It was very little money per hour compared to what I made as an accountant, but after two weeks of very part-time work, those hours added up to a nice little check.

The internet has provided a world of side income platforms that weren't available fifteen years ago, when I was taking photos of babies. George Mason University Professor Kevin Rockman completed research featured in the *Journal of Applied Psychology* that was one of the first published studies of the "gig economy." Rockman was quoted as saying "Maybe in 20 years, it won't be working for one firm, but having a portfolio of firms that workers can choose from..."

If you are reading this book, you are likely curious what skills people will pay for. The website Fiverr.com (current tag line: "Don't Just Dream, Do") was created for freelancers to offer services on demand. Buyers and sellers go to exchange value and money for service. Their basic listings are merely ideas (because there are likely hundreds of options), but to give you an idea, I'll include a few here:

- Graphics & Design - logo design services, business cards, etc.
- Digital Marketing - social media services, content marketing, etc.
- Writing & Translation - proofreading services, resumes, etc.
- Video & Animation - brand videos, animation, etc.
- Music & Audio - voice-over services, composing, etc.
- Programming & Tech - WordPress services, programming, etc.
- Business Services - market research, business plans, etc.
- Fun & Lifestyle - relationship advice, crafts, etc.

Fiverr.com is just one of many website platforms offering access to thousands of buyers and sellers of services. To create my company logo, I used the site Upwork.com to turn my PowerPoint version into something I could send to Vistaprint to create my business cards. There is also FlexJobs.com, VirtualAssistants.com, and probably five more that have popped up since this book was published.

You have probably used one of the more popular "gig economy" services, a ride sharing application like Uber or Lyft. I only recently started using their applications for rides, and as a consumer, I understand the appeal! If you are willing to keep your car clean and like meeting people, providing driver services is another option for side income. For more hands-on work, you can look to sites like TaskRabbit.com or Handy.com.

If you merely want to provide your knowledge to others, it

used to be you needed to write a book (look who's talking, right?). Today, you can provide content through online courses created and made available through a myriad of online platforms, including Udemy.com, Click4Course.com, Ruzuku.com, OpenSesame. com, and Teachable.com.

Finally, I'll mention pet services. Many people I meet love animals, and they could use this love to make money on the side. Check out sites like Wag.com and Rover.com to provide dog walking services, enjoy part-time pets, get fresh air, and make some side income all at the same time.

Unlike taking a side job at a department store, in a side-business, you won't net a profit for the first few hours of your investment—but your hourly rate will snowball once you build a reputation and start seeing clients on a regular basis. It's that regular, consistent work that will provide income that will make a difference in your financial life.

Businessman and motivational speaker Gary Vaynerchuk is known for a lot of blunt talk about the opportunities available to our generation in the world of income generation based on the ability to "day trade attention." I've watched more than a few of his YouTube videos describing the modern-day simplicity of going to a free page of Craigslist, collecting a bunch of items, and reselling them on eBay or Facebook Marketplace. Picking up free stuff to resell used to involve running around the neighborhood for garage sales, then hosting a bunch of your own. Now, reselling one person's junk as another person's treasure is a lot easier (and if time is factored in, a lot more profitable).

Compounding

Compounding is what happens when you reinvest earnings. For example, you have $10,000 invested in an account that pays 5% interest per year. After the first year, your money earns $500 ($10,000 x .05). Assuming you leave that extra $500 in that account, what does your money earn the second year? $525 ($10,500 x .05). Your original deposit of $10,000, which came from your work (working for people), was slated to earn $500 per year in the 5% savings account. But that $500 of last year's interest was left in the bank account, so now the $500 you did not earn from working is going to work for you, generating another $25 per year. That extra $25 is the result of compounding; it is your money making money upon itself, and it is the key to exponential growth of your wealth.

"Compound interest is the eighth wonder of the world. He who understands it, earns it, he who doesn't, pays it." Allegedly, this is a quote by famous scientist Albert Einstein. Funny thing about quotes is they are often attributed to someone famous (and dead) to make them seem more powerful. My dad told me long ago that it's not always the message but often times the messenger that makes a difference. Whether or not Einstein articulated that quote exactly (there are variations also attributed to him, like, "Compound interest is the greatest invention in history") doesn't matter; regardless, we want compounding to be on our side when it comes to money. When our money's earnings is making earnings, it saves us time, because our earnings from work don't have to be as much to take care of our needs. So, the more we can save, the more our money can earn money, or "work" on our behalf. If we can't save, then we are destined to work for every dollar we receive for the rest of our lives.

Leveraging the power of compounding is a big step towards creating the kind of wealth that will give you access to your

American Dreams. Money working for you is similar to the leverage of people working for you, except money is bound to provide value, based on the hard and fast laws of arithmetic, and it will never call in sick.

You can start putting your extra money into a savings account. You will be able to find bank accounts online willing to pay almost 2% per year, but not too much more than that. If the bank is insured by the Federal Deposit Insurance Corporation (FDIC), then start your empire by opening an account. Whether you are twenty-five, forty-five, fifty-five, or seventy-five, if you have never been a saver, today is always a good day to start.

Later, as you accumulate $5,000, $10,000, or more, you can start looking at other choices. You might take on more risk (no guarantees of FDIC insurance), but you'll potentially have more opportunities for your money to work harder (i.e., grow faster). Risk and reward usually go together. The more risk you take with your money, the more you should expect to receive in return. For example, if you put your money to work in an FDIC insured bank account, you can safely assume that your return (the interest rate) will be fairly low. In that example, your money isn't "working" that hard for you, but you're not at all likely to lose your money, even if the bank goes bankrupt. Alternatively, you could buy lots of houses, like many people did in the run up to the 2008 housing crisis. If 2008 didn't happen, those people would have continued to receive a large return because of the leverage that buying a house with a mortgage loan gives you. Their money would have worked "hard" for them. Unfortunately, the Great Recession of 2008 did happen, and many home investors lost all of the money they'd put to work. That's the double-edged sword of risk: you could double your money or cut it in half in the same amount of time.

CHAPTER 6 TAKEAWAYS

Earning money is not a haphazard endeavor. The market value of your time is based on your education, your experience, and your ability to lead others. Many people trade time for money, but soon find out that trading a limited resource (time) for a nearly unlimited resource (money) is shortchanging their future goals. Some people see this disconnect and choose to work a side job to hone other skills that they can leverage more efficiently in the future. Unlike any other time in history, there are online platforms today that can sustain any "side-hustler" in the gig economy.

Wealthy people eventually use the leverage of working with others to create excess capacity in the form of money. That money can then be used to compound over time. Money that compounds over time is like have a silent employee that never takes a day off and can work forever.

Actionable Strategies:

- Increase the market value of your time by working for more education
- Increase your income by working more (time)
- Leverage your expertise by managing others to create capacity
- Use that excess capacity (money) to become a silent worker through compounding

CHAPTER 7

SPENDING

PERSONAL EXPERIENCE

I began earning (and spending) money from a young age. When I had the money, I did what I think most Americans do: spent it aggressively! Once I had money, the cost of things only mattered to determine whether I had enough money or not. There was no nuance about how much it *should* cost or what intentions I had for money beyond spending. There are studies that say people take joy in spending (duh!), especially spending on experiences that build memories.

In May of 2001, I visited France all by myself for eleven days, splitting the time equally between Paris and Lyon. I knew one person in each city, and figured I should visit while I still had those connections. Looking back, I had a few mini-adventures, like meeting a Swedish student on my first day and getting lost in Paris every day. I got locked out of my friend's flat the last night and would have slept in the stairwell, had it not been for another friend who arrived from the United States to share the space. All of this was before Airbnb!

It was an adventure, but one of the more lasting memories was my first day back to work. I thought about the money I had spent on the trip versus what I would usually spend on weekends and eating lunch out at work. There wasn't a big difference. For a fleeting moment, I realized there were some things worth the delayed gratification of spending. I committed to saving all my discretionary income for travel!

Now, I'd like to tell you I economized, budgeted, and maintained a monk-like discipline until my next international vacation. I'd like to tell you that, but it wasn't true. Despite the extraordinary experience of my first solo international adventure, I was the same person who didn't pay much attention to what I spent. So, not long after my next paycheck, I ate out for lunch, I probably bought new music, and over the course of the year, I spent money on things that were not a high priority for me. And the only things that hemmed in my spending were the non-discretionary expenses, like rent and my car payment. Sound familiar?

PROFESSIONAL EXPERIENCE

Discretionary spending is something that can be hard to see, especially when there are smaller, variable expenses. In my initial meetings with new clients, I begin the work of helping them really *see* what they spend: how often, when, and on what. My first step is to invite them into a professional-grade, secure site, built for financial planners to work with clients. There, clients have the option of breaking out each of their expenses. By the time they've entered the data, they are half-way towards seeing some of my monthly spending advice already.

Some financial planners practice a "goals-based" approach to giving advice, which more or less ignores the current budget a person has. Those financial planners estimate a target date for retirement, an "appropriate" amount to live on, and give advice that amounts to not much more than, "You should save more." I prefer when clients give me the detail of their expenses, because it allows me to serve them better with what's called "cash flow-based" approach. This takes the details of their real-life dollars, cents, and time, and helps to show them what they can do (versus what they "should do"). In my third meeting with clients, I present them the same numbers they presented to me, but I might highlight discretionary expenses (i.e., optional expenses, like entertainment, dining out, lawn services, etc.) alongside non-discretionary expenses (like rent, loan payments, and transportation).

There is never a judgement on what "should or shouldn't" be spent. I always tell clients they are the kings and queens of their money; my job is to highlight what they may not see. I suggest they take the highlighters themselves, and color what is discretionary in yellow and non-discretionary in blue, then take note of how much yellow there is on the page. My clients are well-educated, savvy, and aspire to greater things in life. Once they see *their* numbers, the advice given by me to reach *their* goals is well-received.

Neuromarketing

In 1992, the National Livestock and Meat Board launched a campaign that I still obviously think about: "*Beef. It's what for dinner.*" I would like to launch a similar campaign that sticks in your head: *Spending. It's not your fault.*

Well, it's not *all* your fault. As Daniel Pink will tell you in his bestselling book, *To Sell is Human*, we've been selling (and therefore been sold) to each other for a long, long time. With neuroscientists, psychologists, economists, and behavioral scientists all working with companies to better market (sell) to us, it's a wonder we don't spend all of our money all of the time! Have you ever heard of "ethnographic study?" I hadn't either until I started researching for this book. Apparently, ethnography has a lot to do with the study of people in their own cultural and social situations. It's what marketing firms are doing now, instead of just A/B testing us on our website activity. Our interactions with products and services are being observed like some random Discovery Channel rerun of lions chasing gazelles.

"Neuromarketing" is now a mature enough field of study to have its own global trade association with members in over 100 countries: the Neuromarketing Science and Business Association (NMBSA). In an internet world with fewer areas of asymmetric information, we no longer feel helpless walking into a car dealership or buying a plane ticket. So, in place of outright lies about the costs of things, business has deftly moved into the area of brain science, brain activity, and your innate reaction to marketing stimuli. In other words, they're just skipping past your logical assessment of value for your less consciously-regulated emotional response. According to reporting by Nat Ives of *The Wall Street Journal*, a neuroscience research study conducted by Neurons, Inc. for the Mobile Marketing Association identified how long it took consumers to react emotionally to advertisements *in milliseconds*. (It took only 400 milliseconds to react to mobile ads and just a few seconds to react emotionally to desktop ads.) The vice president of marketing and consumer acquisition for Choice Hotels International Inc. was quoted in the article as suggesting that marketers need to shift from sixty and thirty second ads to "Focus in on that zero-second branding." There are people out there who know that our brains are actually wired to reward our impulses rather than our logic. Buyer must still beware.

Whenever you go online, turn on the TV, or go outside, understand that you are in a financial war with professionals (scientists) who are doing everything they can to encourage your spending. Practice pausing before spending by asking yourself questions before making a purchase: "Do I need this or just want this?" "Will this add to my long-term goals or detract from them?" "Will this purchase still make me happy a day, a week, or a month from now?" These pauses and questions are critical to ensuring you are giving your logical brain time to kick in before making a decision that you may later regret.

Conscious Spending

If and when you do buy something, set up a system to track your spending. When it comes to managing (or reducing) expenses, nothing works as simply as just paying attention to your spending. When I worked as a bank teller in the early 1990s, the people who kept up with their spending were those who came into the bank branch asking for a "printout," a partial statement (rather than waiting for the one that arrived in the mail at the end of the month). Back in those days, there was no internet for the public, so of course, you couldn't just "go online" to figure out what you'd spent money on. When I left the banking world for accounting in 1995, I was pretty happy to still have access to my printout, since by then, online banking had been invented. Thankfully, there is a lot of technology available now to help you monitor your spending. One of the oldest software programs for tracking your expenses is Microsoft's Excel, and one of the most popular phone applications comes from Intuit, Mint.com. What you use is not as important as consistently reviewing what you spend money on.

Because we often use plastic to buy everything, it is pretty important to go online and see where money is going. We often know about the origins and the amounts of the big, regular purchases. For example, when I work with clients, they always know how much their rent/mortgage costs, but how much they spend on food or entertainment per month is usually a mystery.

There are all kinds of things that we could pay less for if we first gave them our attention. For example, consider the cable bill. Tech website CNET.com had a great post called "5 Ways to Lower Your Cable Bill." In it, they list Billcutterz, BillFixers, and BillShark as companies that will help lower your cable bill on your behalf.[1] Of course, if you have a little time, one of the oldest ways to lower your bill is to call and threaten to cancel. Cable and internet are good examples of rather large expenses that, oddly, fluctuate. Without attention, that bill can easily creep to the $200 level before any action is taken. That's what happened to me: I waited two or three months to cancel my subscription, despite $10 upticks along the way. Left unchecked, this kind of compound growth to your payments will steal every extra bit of money you thought you had. The sad thing is, because **inflation** is a thing (the costs of goods keep going up), your money is always susceptible to being spent a little more this month than it was last month. This requires us to be aware of when it's happening, where it's happening, and making changes to protect the growth of our money.

1   Broida, Rick, "5 ways to lower your cable bill," CNET, August 29, 2018, https://www.cnet.com/how-to/ways-to-lower-your-cable-bill/, 2019.

Viewer Discretion is Advised

Dividing your expenses into discretionary and non-discretionary categories will make them easier to truly "see." This is because just making a long list of expenses (even I was surprised at how long my family's list was when I did this exercise) will paralyze us, rather than activate our feelings of control.

Once you have your expenses divided into things you want to spend on (**discretionary**) and things you feel you have to spend on (**non-discretionary**), take a new look at how much you're paying for each item. Remember, cost is what you pay, and value is what you get. Do you want to pay almost $200 for cable and internet service? Do you really need to pay over $100 per month for cell phone service? Are you really using your gym membership? Do you like eating out, or is it just a default way to meet up with friends?

I once had a client who wanted to pay off her debt and save $1,000 per month for a house down payment, but couldn't find the money. All we had to do was list her expenses; we found her second largest expense was working out. When you added the cost of the gym membership, the parking, the personal trainer, and the protein shakes, the total came to—you guessed it—just under $1,000 per month.

Now, even as a fiduciary financial planner licensed to give advice, I can't just *tell* people how to spend their money. The "workout expenses" fell under the discretionary category, but no one beside my client could decide whether they were worth it. My most important job when it comes to expenses is to ask my clients if they *intend* to spend the way they do. It turns out, she didn't. The next month, she signed up to workout at the county recreation center for just under $300 per *year*, and she paid off her debts in short order. As for the house, well, she took a long-awaited international trip instead. And this is why I tell my clients—and remind myself—that they are the kings and queens of their money; how they allocate resources is ultimately their decision.

It's important to note that expense management is a process. No two months will be exactly the same, because some expenses are positioned differently around the calendar (e.g., birthdays, back-to-school days, holidays, property tax day, etc.). And some expenses just come up, like a flat tire, a new water heater, or date night. The continued review of these expenses is more about living intentionally than it is about "sticking to a budget." Remember, you are in charge! You don't have to feel bad about your spending unless *you* didn't want to spend the money. Unless those neuro-marketers tricked you into doing it. That's why you monitor and review what's happening on a monthly basis. Maybe you just won't walk by a certain store in the mall, or maybe you'll mute the commercials while watching TV. They can't control you!

Saving vs. Spending

We often think of ourselves as "savers" or "spenders," yet those are not opposites. Both believe in cash flow; one just believes that cash flowing outward is much more fun than cash flowing inward. Like most partisan fights, however, the truth is somewhere in the middle. In reality, clients of mine who build up a habit of saving, after just a few months, are just as excited to describe the "wins" of flowing money into their savings account as they used to be when describing spending on restaurants or online stores. This happens most often when you decide to "pay yourself first." Upon receiving income (paychecks or a check from a client) determine how much you would like to save; set that aside, then pay your bills. Whatever is left over is your "budget" until the next paycheck.

As mentioned above, one important habit to develop is giving your logical brain time to kick in by taking a pause before succumbing to the impulse of buying and its associated dopamine boost. What if there's a real, tangible dopamine boost for saving, but it just takes a few more months to see? Wouldn't it be worth it? The clients I talk to say it is.

CHAPTER 7 TAKEAWAYS

Excessive spending is not entirely our fault; we are taught it, encouraged to do it, and manipulated into it. There are scientists whose sole purpose is to get us to buy, either consciously or subconsciously. Whether this is a legal practice depends on the laws of the country you live in; whether it is ethical is another question entirely. The greatest defense against unintentional spending is awareness.

Spending and saving are not opposite activities; they are at cross-purposes, but there are similar "highs" to be had with both. There is a "high" associated with spending that we can easily blame the neuromarketers for stimulating. There is also a "high" associated with the discipline of saving, once the results begin to accumulate. Give yourself time for the latter, and (as we cover in another section) you will give yourself the **Joy of Opportunity**.

Actionable Strategies:

- When shopping online or offline, take note of the ways you are being "sold"
- Divide your prior three months of expenses between discretionary and non-discretionary
- Make a decision to "pay yourself first" before spending on the discretionary
- Review your spending monthly by category (using online banking or a phone app)
- Engage online services to go through your regular cell phone and cable bills for savings you are missing
- Ask yourself (monthly) if you are spending on your most desired priorities
- Take note of online neuromarketing tactics that trigger your impulse to click/buy

TAX PLANNING

Tax law sets the rules of the financial road, and since financial planning is life planning, it affects the rules of life as well.

There are of course many types of federal, state, and local municipality taxes (just ask any lottery winner how many taxes they pay before claiming their check), but federal taxes demand the highest level of attention because of their complexity. Federal income taxation and other income withholdings are the subject of this chapter. Though not a comprehensive survey of tax law (you're welcome), these are the areas that are common to most people reading this book.

Federal taxes play a role in risk management, estate planning, investment planning, debt management, and retirement. Because they are a part of nearly every financial decision, taxes intersect with nearly every part of our lives. You can make a profit in your investments, for example, but tax law will tell you how much you get to keep. You can pass money and property and life insurance benefits to anyone you want, but tax law will determine how much. The tax system provides the largest revenue line on the federal government's income statement, and paying taxes is part of our shared responsibility to each other. Most services provided by the federal government are funded by the very taxes we and our employers pay. Striking the right balance between paying what is asked of us by our country, paying too much, and illegal tax avoidance is largely an effort of understanding. There are over 70,000 pages of tax code, and deciphering what could and should apply to our personal situation is nearly impossible without the assistance of some good tax software or a professional tax preparer (CPA or tax attorney). In this section, you will read about some of the largest deductions in the U.S. tax code (that relate to income and savings), why they are there, and how they relate to your American Dreams.

PERSONAL EXPERIENCE

My interest in taxes goes back to college. Choosing an accounting major was based mostly on my interest in money, the easy class I took in high school, and the pages of job openings I saw in the Sunday newspaper (yes, the printed newspaper). Why I was looking at job listings in high school is a good question, but I didn't have to look hard to find all of the accountant positions (since the jobs were listed alphabetically).

Of all of the accounting courses I took in college, the one I looked forward to was federal tax. It was the only subject in the wide array that accountants have to study that other people actually care about. Learning what was "deductible" seemed to me like a superpower, because only a few people knew the answers. And those people were accountants!

Well, I eventually became an accountant, and over the course of many years, had a simple tax return that included mostly wage earner's income. I paid taxes without giving it much thought. Paying taxes only got interesting after my first year of business as a financial planner. Starting a business is tough, and my Individual Retirement Account (IRA), if it still existed, would back me up on this. I drained it to fund the lean months in this business. As anyone with a basic of understanding of tax-deferred retirement accounts knows, you are supposed to "defer" taking any of that money out until you are 59.5 years-old. The consequence, otherwise, is paying the taxes that were previously deferred—and a 10% penalty on any of the money you take out. I did that. Well, I should say that I eventually did that, because when my tax bill came, I couldn't pay it.

So, what do you do when you can't pay your tax bill by the date that it's due (typically April 15)? You file your taxes anyway. Why file at all if you can't pay? Because eventually, the IRS will find out how much you owe them, and there are additional penalties for not filing.

Note: The penalty for late tax payments is .5% per month it's late. The penalty for late filing is 5% per month (1,000% more)! This is why you file; that, and you want to be a good citizen, right? Of course.

So, I filed my taxes, and I waited for what felt like months for the IRS's response to my apparent insolence. They dutifully sent me a letter that annotated what I already knew about the taxes I owed, but had not paid on time. (The funny thing is when you prepare and file your taxes, you're the one telling the IRS how much you owe; you know that number before they do.)

What I was given the opportunity to learn (that's how I like to put it) was what happens when you owe taxes and haven't paid. Drumroll please: The IRS sends you a bill. And on that bill is a toll-free number to call to organize a payment plan. You can also go online and create your own payment plan, as long as you owe less than $50,000. This is exactly what I did, and I paid down my tax bill over the course of a year until I was free and clear. And boy, was that a great feeling!

Your federal tax bill is one of the few bills that can land you in jail (typically only if you refuse to pay, but still. Whenever I've had the opportunity to council someone on federal tax debt, we talk about how to prioritize it over all others. And then it just gets paid. How do you avoid a situation where you owe taxes or debt or anything else that might hold you back from your American Dreams? Keep reading.

PROFESSIONAL EXPERIENCE

Since tax plays a role in all areas of financial planning, it is a topic that I indirectly address throughout the planning process. Most people are familiar with tax preparation. Like car insurance, it's legally required. Where most families fall short is in the area of tax planning ahead of the tax filing deadline. Some might argue that their taxes are "simple," which may be true. If you are just filing for yourself as a W-2 wage earner, then tax preparation is easy. Both the IRS and software companies have free solutions waiting for you.

Tax planning, however, is still a must. The Tax Cut and Jobs Act of 2017 proved that even the simplest of returns can create surprises, come tax time. Many people at the beginning of 2019 made anecdotal news after having their tax returns prepared and being surprised by the lack of refund or worse, owing taxes. What they didn't take into account was that their withholding adjustment formula had been recalculated for them throughout 2018. If they got $20 or $30 more per paycheck, they may not have even noticed until it was time for tax preparation.

Now, imagine you file your taxes jointly, you have two or three children, one of you owns a business formed as a corporation, and the other is just a plain ole W-2 wage earner. This is a common example of clients I see, and the advice I give all of them touches on the changes they should consider from year to year. And then I refer them to a tax preparer (CPA or tax attorney) before the end of the year. That professional can help project what their tax liability might be, and it will give them time to make changes or just plan ahead for what's coming. That's tax planning, and it always works in your favor.

W-4 vs. W-2

Most people are familiar with the **W-2** (Wage and Tax Statement) tax form. You remember it because you have to wait for it to file your taxes every year. You know that your W-2s have your total income made and total tax paid, along with other details that tax preparers salivate over to prepare your federal and state tax returns. What you many have overlooked is how your W-2 form is affected by your **W-4** form (Employee's Withholding Allowance Certificate).

When you were hired at your company, you had a whole bunch of forms to fill out. One of those forms was the W-4. This form helps your employer determine how much federal and state tax to retain from your paycheck on your behalf. During tax season (January through April 15), you are effectively reconciling your tax payments on your tax return. You get those numbers from the W-2 your employer sends. So, here's a tip: if you don't like owing a lot in taxes or having the IRS owe you a big refund, you should adjust your W-4 form. Though most people don't touch that form after they first get hired, you have the ability to change it at any time. When should you? Whenever you go through certain life events or see a pattern you don't like year to year come tax-time.

Here are the life events that should trigger reviewing and perhaps adjusting your W-4:

- Getting married
- Your spouse changing jobs (for different pay)
- Having a kid (or kids)
- Getting divorced
- Starting a business

Any one of the above will cause your income (and, by default, your tax burden) to change. If none of the above happens but you haven't liked the tax refund/tax bill you've received over the past couple of years, you may also look to your W-4 withholdings as a place to make a change.

Some people "game" this system by making their withholdings as high as possible during the year, so when they go to reconcile their tax burden (which is what I call filing your taxes in April), they can expect a large refund. This turns the IRS and the U.S. Treasury into places to save money. Most people don't recommend this strategy, known as "giving the IRS a 0% interest loan." Not having the money to spend (because your employer is taking it out and "lending it" to the IRS) is a tough way to learn good savings habits, but some people do it.

Another way to save is to have your employer direct deposit any amount that would typically go to the IRS into a savings account you try not to touch. This is a way to start teaching the discipline of saving without keeping the money away from you and your family for a year.

Tax Politics

You can't do comprehensive financial planning without paying attention to federal taxes. Taxes and tax law drive nearly every part of the planning process. *Fun fact: your income, arguably the most important facet of your wealth, is taxed at higher rates than your wealth.* The thinking behind this is that your wealth was created by your already-taxed income, so why should the federal government "penalize" those who have saved some of it? Others believe that wealth, particularly wealthy estates, should be taxed more heavily; otherwise, you have the same people and families passing down accumulated wealth versus spreading some of that wealth, through taxes, to others in the community. As you can imagine, tax law can quickly become political. And it has always been political. What this unfortunately means is that to pay your respects to taxes and tax law, you must also pay attention to politics. To some of you, I wish to express my condolences; for others, yeah! You now have an excuse for watching all future presidential debates!

Tax Deferred is Not Tax Denied

Our 401(k) and traditional IRA account contributions are generally pre-tax, which means that the money that funds them was subtracted from your paycheck before you had the *joy* of paying taxes. Those taxes, however, are only deferred (delayed). You or your beneficiaries will pay taxes on that money at some point in the future. This was the inspiration behind Internal Revenue Code (IRC) Sec. 401(k): to defer paying taxes, since the top tax rate at the time was 70%. The hope was that when money started being withdrawn, it would be taxed at a lower rate. For those retiring in 2018, the new top tax rate is 37%—so they won! At

37%, the tax rate is about half of the 1970 top tax rate, so the tax deferring gamble paid off.

During that same amount of time, however, the United States national debt has risen from approximately $772 billion to nearly $22 trillion. In other words, the debt has grown by 2,800%! What does that mean for the rest of us? Is it likely that tax rates will be lower later? Should we still be deferring our tax liability in these pre-tax retirement vehicles? That's a big fiscal policy question, and unfortunately, a financial planning conundrum. As we have seen over the years, regardless of the U.S. debt burden, it's unpopular for politicians to campaign on tax hikes, so they usually don't. Is that sound fiscal policy? Probably not, but it's a political reality. Many of my clients with access to a (tax-me-later) 401(k) and eligibility to contribute to a (tax-me-now) Roth IRA consider splitting their retirement contributions. When it comes to your future tax burden, you too may want to hedge your bets if possible. Oh, and vote.

Gaining on Capital

In addition to income taxes, capital gains taxes are an important consideration when it comes to building wealth. The great thing about capital, or wealth, is that you've already earned it. Look at your savings account. Go ahead, log into your bank account and look at the money that is there. Unless you found it, stole it, won it, or inherited it, you earned it. That's why the old maxim, "A penny saved is a penny earned" rings so true: if you don't spend it, you can actually see what you've earned! Any of your money that you spend is truly energy, time, and attention spent. It is gone. Any money that you keep is energy, time, and attention retained. And you can add any wealth (or capital) that your money made for you through investment to that potential energy.

Money working for you is a pretty efficient way of growing wealth. It's so efficient that you're not going to get away with enjoying all of it without it being taxed. Wealth that is taxed is called "**capital gains tax.**"

Capital gains tax is interesting because, like most taxes, there are incentives built in for what the federal government would prefer you do. There are two sets of rates: short-term capital gains tax and long-term capital gains tax. With short-term, if you sell an asset, like a stock or a bond, within a year, any profit (or gain) on that sale will be taxed at your regular income tax rate (equal to what you are taxed for work). If you hold your assets or investments for over a year and then sell them, you will be taxed at the likely lower rates of 0%, 15%, or 20%, depending on your other income.

So, what's going on here? The federal government's policy is to encourage investment for the long-term versus the short-term. You are penalized, for example, for buying a stock today, watching it shoot up 15%, and selling it tomorrow. In truth, this is a case where the federal government sides with good financial planners (like me), who encourage clients to invest in the market only with a long-term investment horizon. In this case, I will give the government a virtual high-five for its policy and its attempt at controlling behavior.

Capital gains tax highlights another incentive for using a retirement account. Retirement or "**qualified**" accounts not only save you initially on income taxes, they also save on the annual cost of capital gains on the growth or profit made on your investments. Regular brokerage accounts or "**non-qualified**" accounts will incur taxes on your gains or profits whenever you buy or sell securities. You will also be taxed when you receive any profit sharing through dividends, either at your income tax rates or capital gains tax rates. In contrast, qualified retirement accounts allow you to earn dividends and capital gains tax-free until you take the money out (usually at retirement age). The positive compounding effect of untaxed capital gains and untaxed income is the "sell" for qualified accounts. Understand, however, that you are taxed on all of that beautiful growth as you take the money out of your account at retirement. So, if the top tax rate is 35% when you retire and the amount of money you take out of your account is above that the top tax rate, you will pay 35% on those dollars.

I don't think most people realize that you are taxed on the amount of money you take out of your retirement account. So, if you are seventy-five-years-old and you take out $150,000 that year, you will be taxed on $150,000. Many people assume they will be taxed at a lower rate because they assume they will be spending less in retirement. This doesn't make sense! Yes, you might have Social Security, but ten, twenty, or thirty years from now, you are likely to be spending more merely due to inflation. Other assumptions that are not reality based are that your house will be paid off, your kids won't need any money, and you won't want to travel as much—all false in my experience. Adjusted for inflation, it's better to assume you will spend at the same level in your future life as you do present-day. This is especially the case for the first ten to fifteen years of "retirement," when you will still be young, interested in travel, and willing to spoil grandchildren. Later, you may change your mind about all three, but for tax planning purposes, assume you will pay taxes on a similar income; the income just may be coming from your savings.

Roth

Established by the **Taxpayer Relief Act of 1997**, the **Roth IRA** is a hybrid of a regular brokerage account (where you can be taxed every year on after-tax gains) and the traditional IRA. The Roth IRA was named after Senator William Roth, the chief sponsor of the legislation, which allowed for a retirement account that did not defer taxes, allowing you instead to compound your investment earnings without being taxed ever again. Many financial planners suggest that most twenty- and thirty-year-olds should choose the Roth option while they are still on the lower side of their career salaries. This is because paying taxes on a $50,000 or even $100,000 salary today and sending a portion to a Roth IRA could be cheaper than the taxes you might have to pay on a $200,000 or $300,000 withdrawal when you start spending the money.

Special Interests

If you watch politicians compete against each other, the phrase "special interests" usually comes up as a negative. A familiar title around the Washington, D.C. area is "lobbyist," a person who advocates on behalf of a cause or interest professionally. Thanks to lobbyists, we have exceptions in our tax code that allow for some people to have advantages over others; that's just the way our system of taxation works. Who gets these exceptions depends in large part on how influential the lobbyists are and how well a politician can spin their support as "for the good of the country." Take, as an example, the National Association of REALTORS®, a trade association that represents the interests of about 1.3 million REALTORS® and 75 million property owners, according to their website. On behalf of these real estate professionals, the association pays attention to the national flood insurance program, fair housing, and of course, tax reform. They have a federal taxation committee specifically focused on tax reform to preserve the benefits of investing in real estate and buying homes in general. This not-so-indirectly supports their member REAL-TORS® and their interests in selling properties, but coupled with their $50 million (plus) annual spend on lobbying, the rest of us never have to worry too much about losing our mortgage interest deductions. Though the home mortgage interest deduction was not initially designed to spur homeownership (when it began in 1913, most people paid up front for their homes), this is the way that NAR currently spins the reasoning behind their support.[1]

According to data collected from the IRS by the non-partisan Tax Foundation in Washington, D.C., home mortgage interest was the third highest deduction for those with incomes over $200,000. The Peter G. Peterson Foundation pegged the deduction of home interest as the sixth largest deduction ($61 billion) for taxpayers overall in 2016. The annual cost of supporting the home interest rate deduction is high, but not as high as the preferential treatment of dividends and capital gains ($196 billion), or employer contributions for medical insurance ($341 billion). It is often said around the Washington, D.C. area that "budgets are moral documents." If that's the case, then our nation's morals heavily support medical insurance (contrary to popular rhetoric), capital investment, and home ownership. With today's tax code, buying a home, investing in capital markets, and receiving health insurance benefits through an employer is the highest value for your consumer dollar.

---

1   Prante, Gerald, "The History of the Mortgage Interest Deduction," Tax Foundation, March 6, 2006, https://taxfoundation.org/history-mortgage-interest-deduction/, 2019.

Business Ownership

No list of deductions or lobbyists would be complete without mentioning the large amount of money spent annually by the business lobby. The Center for Responsive Politics, a non-profit, non-partisan research group based in Washington, D.C., reported that in 2017, "big business" spent over $450 million in lobbying our federal government, including members of the U.S. House of Representatives and U.S. Senate. The top three players were the Business Roundtable ($27,380,000), the National Association of REALTORS® ($54,530,861), and the U.S. Chamber of Commerce ($82,260,000). This is all in one year.

With lobbying comes rewards. Our country has long supported capitalism, and nearly $500 million per year of lobbying surely isn't going to waste. Pro-business policies abound in the United States, but for the purpose of this section, the tax deductions that allow you to start, manage, and grow your business are the most important. Thomas Stanley, PhD, co-author of *The Millionaire Next Door*, believes that more than 80% of millionaires are self-made. So when it comes to creating wealth, it appears that starting and properly executing a business idea is the surest path. Our tax code supports business through deductions for depreciation, mileage, utilities, meals, interest on business indebtedness, insurance, advertising, and a lot more. In this sense, our budget heavily supports the morality of entrepreneurship and one of the original ideas behind the American Dream: that you can follow your passions, grow with your neighbors, and eventually give back to your community.

CHAPTER 8 TAKEAWAYS

The American tax system is large and complex, but much of that complexity is designed to promote causes that our federal government supports. Some of the largest causes are home ownership, capital investment, health insurance through an employer, and support for your own entrepreneurial endeavor. As your financial plan allows, taking advantage of these tool for wealth creation can benefit your family and the causes you wish to support.

Your greatest wealth creation tool is income, and withholdings from your paycheck make a difference. Your position on Social Security deductions, health insurance tax exemptions, and federal tax rates are not just opinions: they are political stances. If you want to change tax law, you are required to get involved in politics. Some people say they are "not political." Those are people who have the luxury of feeling like they are not being affected by what the rest of us see. If you pay taxes—and especially, I suppose, if you don't—you are affected by tax law and tax policy. Call your congressman and senator; contribute and vote for the causes you believe in.

Actionable Strategies:

- Review and adjust your W-4 withholdings if you have a life change
- Adjust your W-4 withholdings if you don't like your annual tax return/liability
- Revise your W-4 withholding form if you receive large federal tax refunds or bills
- Enroll for the health insurance offered through your employer
- Compare your standard deduction to itemizing with a home purchase or mortgage refinance

- If you invest in capital markets, compare the benefits of cashing out annually versus the tax savings associated with long-term investing
- Review your employer's Roth retirement options to compare their long-term benefits against traditional options
- Estimate the value of your expertise on the open market as a future business owner to compare the tax advantages with remaining a W-2 wage earner

JOY OF
ENOUGH

Summary

How much money you make is not determined by how you start out. If that were the case, we would all be "making" $0 per year. There's a natural four-step process to earning money that never has to end: first, you work for an education; then, you work for money; then, people work for you; then, money works for you. You have the capacity to create a platform that allows you to earn the income you want, consistently over time, forever. And if you're not creative enough to create a platform, then there's the "gig economy" waiting for you to share your skills in exchange for money. Once you're earning money, the goal is for the money to earn money for you. When money makes money, the magic of compounding begins. If you put your money to work, it will work and earn you more.

When it comes to your expenses, the difference between discretionary and non-discretionary is a matter of perspective. Get very clear about your expenses so you can get very clear about your spending. The ability to choose how you spend your money is usually a matter of awareness. If you know what you want, then the mini mental rewards triggered by scientists infiltrating marketing departments will affect you less. Neuroscientists are working every day to help you make subconscious decisions about spending you otherwise would not have. Your spending is not derived exclusively from your conscious thinking; in fact, some would argue that your spending decisions come not from thinking, but from emotional impulses triggered subversively by corporate scientists. Having enough is as much about earning as is about spending. Working on increasing the former and minimizing the latter is the bottom line to getting control of your financial life.

"POVERTY EXISTS, NOT BECAUSE WE CANNOT FEED THE POOR BUT BECAUSE WE CANNOT SATISFY THE RICH."

Federal income and payroll taxes are generally expenses that we are required to pay (we are at least required to file a tax return). Understand the differences between capital gains taxes and income taxes, Roth, and traditional retirement accounts, and apply them to your situation. Manage your tax burden. It begins with the W-4 Employee's Withholding Allowance Certificate and the selections you make. If you don't like how your W-2 translates into your annual tax return filing, it's probably because of your W-4. Starting a business is not only a great way to create long-term wealth, it's also subsidized through the federal tax system, which can mean savings for you.

Taxes provide an organized way for individuals to contribute to the greater good of the community. Politicians don't always get the balance right, but paying enough (not too much, not too little) will ensure you are on the right side of the law. And the discipline of doing what's right will create opportunities to make even greater contributions to your community and your country in the future.

A Final Word on Enough

In *7 Habits for Highly Effective People*, bestselling author Steven Covey admonishes us to, "Begin with the end in mind." He dramatically portrays a funeral scene with the reader playing the starring role and asks what you would like eulogist to say about you. In a similar sense, when all of the earning and spending is done, how will you know you've had enough? That's the question I ask my clients, and now I'm asking you as well.

In a country where we throw away enough food to feed the world,[1] we know well the famous, anonymous quote that "Poverty exists, not because we cannot feed the poor but because we cannot satisfy the rich." When we learn to have "enough," I see a future where everyone has enough to eat, workers earn a living wage, scientists spend more of their time curing diseases, and taxation is equitable, uncomplicated, and fair. I believe that when we think of the "end" in our own lives and consciously live toward what we know is meaningful, our governing institutions will follow our lead.

---

1   "Fighting Food Waste With Food Rescue," Feeding America, 2019, https://www. feedingamerica.org/our-work/our-approach/reduce-food-waste.

JOY OF BALANCE

Cash, Credit, & Debt

*"Make no expense, but to do good to others
or yourself; i.e., waste nothing."*
~Benjamin Franklin

CHAPTER 9

BACKGROUND & HISTORY

CASH

For bills that are decidedly uncolorful, U.S. currency has had a fascinating life so far. Going from notes to greenbacks to representing gold to representing "trust," our money history parallels the miraculous rise of the United States of America.

The American Revolution brought on the first separation from Spanish, French, and English currencies. The union of former colonies, known as the Continental Congress, issued the first recognized paper currency in 1775. It was meant to help finance the military, but when that financing fell through, states turned to their own currencies. The first bank was established a few years later; soon after, the Continental Congress presented a nationalized currency in the unit of dollars.

Along with more banks, the 19th century brought us to the Civil War, which needed to be financed. Initially, it was funded through the most widely used currency at the time, demand notes, before turning to greenbacks. They were easily distinguishable from state-issued currencies, which were blank on the back. Gold certificates were issued by the U.S. Department of the Treasury in 1865. They were backed by gold, and the national bank notes that followed created the first currency stability.

The Federal Reserve Act of 1913 was intended to bring more stability, and in fact has, up through present day. This act created the Federal Reserve Board, which governs twelve regional Federal Reserve Banks. This act essentially required all nationally chartered banks (the big banks) to become members of the new Federal Reserve System. And the money changed too. From then on, the Federal Reserve Note has been the currency of the United States of America.[1]

Three decades later, the United States was an important party to an international monetary agreement called the **Bretton Woods System**. Bretton Woods, New Hampshire played host to the **United Nations Monetary and Financial Conference**. Adopting monetary policy to stabilize international exchange rates was a global goal in the midst of ongoing **World War II**. When it came time to decide how currency would be stabilized, the gold standard made the most sense, and the United States was well positioned (holding most of the world's known gold supply). The International Monetary Fund (IMF) and the World Bank were born from this twenty-day conference in the summer of 1944. It was the formal beginning of the gold standard and the hope of kinder, gentler international exchange rate policies. It also established the United States as the major player in global finance, with countries reconciling their currencies in U.S. dollars.[2]

---

1 "The History of American Currency," U.S. Currency Education Program, https://www.uscurrency.gov/history, 2019.

2 Ghizoni, Sandra Kollen, "Creation of the Bretton Woods System," Federal Reserve History, https://www.federalreservehistory.org/essays/bretton_woods_created, 2019.

The economic success of the United States may have been part of the reason the Bretton Woods agreement couldn't last. In 1971, President Richard Nixon announced a temporary suspension of pegging the U.S. dollar to gold. As we all know now, that suspension became permanent, and our money supply, though legal tender, is merely fiat currency backed by the U.S. government. So goes the government, so goes the value of the U.S. dollar.

Cash, like books, has always been special. What we used to hold in our pockets is now mostly sets of numbers on a screen: we get direct deposits and pay our bills online. Losing the tangibility of money contributes to our disconnection between having and not having it; the difference between the meaning of cash, debt, and credit.

CREDIT

The use of credit and the buildup of debt have different but obviously related histories. It takes credit (the ability to obtain goods before payment) to acquire debt. Whereas the issuing of credit dates as far back as the Age of Antiquity, credit reporting has a unique history that didn't begin until centuries later.

According to Equifax, the oldest credit reporting agency, the first credit "reporting" began in 1803, with a group of English tailors who exchanged information on customers who failed to pay their bills. This was the start of credit reporting agency **Experian** (initially known in the United States as TRW after the purchase of a U.S.-based firm in 1968). By 1826, newsletters like the *Manchester Guardian Society* began publicizing the names of those who didn't pay their debts. In 1899, the Retail Credit Company curated the longest lists—not of deadbeats, but rather of creditworthy clients. Those lists were sold to other business owners, and demand kept growing; new branch offices were opened across the country. This is the company that later would become **Equifax**. By the early 20th century, issuing credit became more and more common and so did the need to know whether customers and clients were creditworthy. According to its website, in 1968, credit reporting agency **TransUnion** began as the Union Tank Car Company. Almost as an afterthought, they acquired the Credit Bureau of Cook County (CBCC) and the maintenance of over 3 million card files of personal data.

Before these three credit reporting agencies became publicly traded empires that dominated the business, they first had to deal with the **Fair Credit Reporting Act of 1970**. This act was designed to protect consumers from inaccurate reporting and bias, and impose a measure of privacy. It also intended to regulate how data on creditworthiness was collected, since it was a much more person-to-person business in those days. By the 1980s, these three credit reporting agencies had business across the country.

According to CreditRepair.com, each of these firms has a particular focus on a certain subset of creditors. But as consumers, their reporting is an opportunity to audit how industry sees us.[3]

Fair Isaac Corporation

Engineer Bill Fair and mathematician Earl Isaac were the original data scientists. In the span of just two years, 1956 to 1958, they went from the idea that data could improve business decisions to pitching and selling their first credit scoring system. What we know as the FICO® score was originally just a tool for businesses,

---

3   "What is a Credit Bureau? Know Their History," Credit Repair, https://www. creditrepair.com/articles/credit-improvement/history-of-credit-bureaus, 2019.

where most of the credit was being issued. It wasn't until 1981 that Fair and Isaac introduced the ubiquitous risk score between 300 and 850 that measured creditworthiness. By 1991, the risk scores were made available to the three credit reporting agencies to bring some sameness to their reports. According to industry trade magazine *National Mortgage News*, in 2013, over 10 million lenders purchased scores from FICO, and so did more than 30 million consumers. In 2017, operating revenue was nearly $1 billion. That's a lot of scores.[4]

DEBT

Though the ubiquitous credit card didn't appear in earnest in the United States until the Diners Club was created in 1950, carrying debt and credit has conceptually been around since the Age of Antiquity. Ancient Greece and ancient Rome began standardizing credit, and it wasn't until the Dark Ages that the world's major religions set out to ban **usury** (charging interest or fees on lending).

In the United States, the advent of Ford's Model T helped to usher in the era of consumers carrying debt. According to Equifax, General Motors Acceptance Corporation (GMAC) was born, allowing car purchasers to get a car with a 35% down payment. The economic boom post-World War II continued the trend of carrying debt; there were new houses to buy and new appliances needed to fill them. The aforementioned Diners Club Card was the first charge card in 1950; in 1958, the Visa card was introduced by Bank of America (then called the "BankAmericard"). Originally, it was launched to facilitate purchases in California,

---

4   Lubove, Seth, "Finance: The boys in the back room," Forbes, May 4, 1998, https://www.forbes.com/forbes/1998/0504/6109042a.html#26de47721511, 2019.

but it became an international charge card by 1974. According to Visa's website, they now operate in nearly every country and territory in the world.

Mortgages

Compared to credit cards, mortgage history is just a little more complicated. Mortgage financing's proper place in a portfolio has been muddled by the desire for homeownership and the marketing of the American Dream by specialized corporate and government interests. In the early 20th century, mortgages were typically five-year interest-only loans with 50% paid up front and a large balloon payment at the end. For people able to afford such a mortgage (*mort* is Latin for "death" and *gage* is Latin for "pledge"), it was a system that worked well. The US Census Bureau has records for housing going back to 1940. The median price for homes in every state (not including Alaska or Hawaii, since they had not yet been granted statehood, but including the District of Columbia) was under $5,000. Adjusted for inflation, the majority were under $40,000.[5]

Regardless, the Great Depression saw to it that by 1935, almost 10% of homes were up for foreclosure. President Franklin Roosevelt's **New Deal** included the **Housing Act of 1934 and 1937**, seeking to solve the crisis of homeownership. The nearly 1 million mortgages that were in default were essentially refinanced, and the Federal Housing Authority (FHA) was created, along with other agencies. FHA introduced fifteen to thirty-year mortgages, lowered down payments, and put amortization of loans in place

---

5 "Historical Census of Housing Tables Home Values," United States Census Bureau, 2019, https://www.census.gov/hhes/www/housing/census/historic/values.html.

so they weren't all interest-only. In 1938, the Federal National Mortgage Association (Fannie Mae) was created to essentially buy those 1 million bad loans, and much later, the Federal Home Loan Mortgage Corporation (Freddie Mac) was created to further expand the market for mortgages to be sold as mortgage-backed securities. Fannie and Freddie specialized in securitizing fixed rate mortgages insured by the FHA and the Veterans Administration (VA). By the 1980s and 1990s, high interest rates soured the market for mortgages in general, so new adjustable rate mortgages (ARMs) started being sold in earnest. These mortgages started off with low interest (payments) and then spiked after a set number of years. This was a toe in the water of alternative financing, and the gradually-relaxed standards of loan purchases by Freddie and Fannie were a foot (an army of feet) into a scheme that could only go wrong...eventually.

Before the 1990s, only 30% of Freddie and Fannie's mortgage purchases were required to come from people below the median income of their neighbors, according to the U.S. Department of Housing and Urban Development (HUD) guidelines. While this was going on, large banks were also luring risky borrowers in with primary/secondary loan combinations that allowed less qualified borrowers to avoid the expense of private mortgage insurance (PMI). By the early 1990s, pressure to create a more inclusive home ownership pool encouraged the administrations of both President Bill Clinton and President George W. Bush to increase the 30% quota of below median income borrowers to as high as 56%. According to the Foundation for Economic Education, Freddie and Fannie "found it harder and harder to find creditworthy borrowers. So, in response...they had to reduce their underwriting standards." Whereas Freddie and Fannie were known for mostly "safe" mortgages, this combination of government quotas, alternative (subprime) lending, and corporate avarice created the perfect storm—the Great Recession of 2008. Effectively, forcing the faux American Dream of homeownership doesn't work for anyone, and bad mortgages nearly destroyed the global economy.

Student Loans

Buying a home with a mortgage used to be the scariest "grown-up" financial endeavor a young adult could undertake. That may still be the case, but now Americans are facing adult debt long before they think of driving around with a REALTOR®. Student loan debt at the end of 2017 totaled nearly $1.5 trillion. For some perspective, home mortgage debt at the time totaled $8.8 trillion.[6] Both are good causes, but neither are good numbers.

The first direct student loan program for the United States was initiated by President Dwight Eisenhower in the **National Defense Act of 1958**. It was created to help subsidize students with skills in science and math, to compete with the talent being created in the Soviet Union. It was a fairly successful program, but for only a couple of years. The **Federal Family Education Loan (FEEL)** program of 1965 was not a direct student loan program; instead, the federal government guaranteed private loans (easier on the federal budget). The budgeting cost nuance of federal guarantees versus direct financing was reimagined in President George H.W. Bush's **Federal Credit Reform Act of 1990** and President Bill Clinton's **Omnibus Reconciliation Act of 1993 and 1997**. In 2008, President George W. Bush enacted the **Ensuring Continued Access to Student Loans Act (ECASLA)**, which gave

6   Friedman, Zack, "Student Loan Debt Statistics In 2018: A $1.5 Trillion Crisis," Forbes, June 13, 2018, https://www.forbes.com/sites/zackfriedman/2018/06/13/student-loan-debt-statistics-2018/#2121546d7310, 2019.

the Secretary of Education the authority to buy (guaranteed) private loans, in light of the financial crisis. This new law made guaranteed loans look a lot like direct loan programs. President Barack Obama's **Health Care and Education Reconciliation Act of 2010** finally repealed the FEEL guarantee programs, and all loans issued after 2010 are direct loans.

CHAPTER 10

JOY OF BALANCE

Banks are intimidating institutions. Like most businesses, they try to make money every year, but unlike most businesses, money *is* their business. Money is a bank's inventory: it's what it sells, and it's what it buys. All other businesses make at least a show of offering some product or service in hopes of a profit; not banks. Banks are loud and proud: money is their business.

So, the idea of beating banks at their business might seem ridiculous. After all, they have been at this game for a lot longer than any of us have been on earth. But the good news is that we don't have to defeat banks to beat them at their own game. We just need to be the one in 300 million people who don't lose, and the banks will be none the wiser. If you're worried about their profits, don't be; they'll be fine.

Joy of Balance is about winning the interest and compound interest game. It's also about growing your net worth by balancing your relationship with debt and cash. In life, it's important to stay right side up versus upside down. To get debt, someone has to trust you, and trust is usually earned before it is given. Anything that's small enough to charge on a credit card is likely better managed just using cash (or a debit card that will immediately take cash from your bank account). Those small purchases are not likely worth the effort of managing the debt. And if you don't manage the debt well, you pay more in interest to your creditors than you earn from your savings. You are dooming your net worth to negative status. That is the opposite of what any of us are intentionally trying to do, but it happens every day. We can't solve the world's problems if our own financial solvency is at risk.

This chapter is about building the habit of maintaining a positive net worth to provide opportunities that go beyond the financial. For many people, their self-worth is closely tied to their net worth. This is a shame, of course; who you are should have little to do with how much money you have. Unfortunately, we learn as early as elementary school how much attention one can get by sporting a new pair of sneakers or a new dress. If I didn't know it before I had kids, I learned it when it my oldest started getting excited to show her teachers her new clothes from Grandma—at four years old. We all crave attention and validation to varying degrees at different times in our life and for different reasons. Net worth is not self-worth, but a positive net worth will eventually allow for opportunities that can bring you joy.

Positive Net Worth

With the exception of 0% credit cards and 0% auto financing, most every other debt is going to charge you interest. If you're not paying interest, odds are you have an amazing credit score (over 800) and you probably aren't carrying much debt. The financial net worth formula is simply the value of all of the stuff you own (including money) less the value of all of your debt. The difference is either a positive (you own more stuff than you owe) or negative (your debt is higher than the value of everything you own).

Since most people don't have the best savings habits, their positive net worth usually comes from habitual retirement savings from work (where they can't touch their money) or the increase in value of their home (over and above the mortgage and other debt). What if I asked you to measure your net worth using only your checking and savings accounts, subtracting your car payment, student loan, credit card balance, and any other money you owe? Would your net worth still be positive?

If it is, you are well on your way to exponential growth. Once you have more cash than debt (excluding a home and mortgage), you are ready for any crisis or opportunity. And it's the opportunities that come our way that make the difference between just getting by and doing very well. It's the difference between existing and achieving your version of the American Dream.

CHAPTER 11

CASH

Whenever I work with a client, I am always interested in how they are using cash. Having cash on hand is one sure sign of financial health. It reflects an ability to live below what your income can afford. Spending below your capabilities is something we have to learn intentionally, because the natural inclination after getting a raise or promotion is to think of the new opportunities to spend that we didn't have access to before. This is, in part, because we are being trained to think of money that way scientifically by the marketers that surround us on and offline (see **Joy of Enough**). We are trained so well that some of us actually believe that money was and is "made to be spent," so we throw caution (and conscience) to the wind! Depending on what we spend on, money can buy a little happiness; but there is a happiness, too, in accumulating financial security, and that comes with the discipline of building up a cash reserve.

Liquidity

The phrase "cash is king" is an old one, making the inference that cash is the best asset you can have. Like banks, cash is "old school," but it works. When there's an emergency, there's nothing more friendly than good ole United States currency. The health of an individual or a business is often measured by how much cash is on hand for this very reason. You can't fake cash: you either have it, or you don't. Cash is easily measured, valued, and liquidated, unlike personal property. This means you can easily take action when there's an emergency or an opportunity in life.

One of my friends went to go see a financial adviser after saving a sizeable amount of money that included $50,000 in a cash account. Sitting with her husband and financial advisor, she told him she was interested in all of his suggestions except regarding the $50,000. She wanted to keep that $50,000 liquid, because just having it made her feel safe. The young adviser attempted to listen, but after nearly an hour of conversation, circled back to that emergency fund and suggested she invest it. My friend took one incredulous look at the adviser, another at her husband—then, they got up and left.

Good for them. Not only was the financial adviser not listening, he was also not giving good advice. Before doing any investing, we all need to have a liquid emergency fund that makes us feel safe.

As a young bank teller, I had a customer who used to budget with stacks of envelopes. There was an envelope for every category of expenses she could think of, even the odd ones that only showed up once or twice a year (for example, she had one envelope for her car's property tax bill and one for vacation). Rather than accumulating money in her checking or savings account, she would add cash to these envelopes on a regular basis, so when the bill came due, she knew the money was available. This is now called the "envelope system/method," and there's even a phone application for it, Mvelopes. This may or may not be the method for you, but the point is that she got used to having cash or not having cash to pay for things, and it detached her mind from using debt as a fallback.

Cash Management

There is, of course, the money-in-a-shoebox method of saving cash. And who can forget the money-in-a-shoe when you're on the beach? The unfortunate drawbacks to these physical methods of hiding and saving money are:

- You might forget where you put the money (when you need it)
- Most people hide money in the same places (where thieves look first)
- You are not earning any interest

Luckily, you do not need to have a bunch of cash lying around the house to get the benefits of having cash. You just want to have funds readily available for any emergency.

The source of most people's cash is their paycheck. Part of the problem associated with trying to build up a bunch of cash is that the quickest way to feel rewarded is to spend it. And as I wrote in the prior section, there are plenty of professionals plotting to have you spend as much money as possible!

Where is the pleasure in spending less than you earn? In the long road towards accumulated savings. If you have never accumulated much cash before—or your parents didn't model it for you—it will feel hard. But that's why this book is called *Joy of Financial Planning*, not the *Pleasure of Financial Planning*. To build up a cash emergency fund, there has to be more money left after your paycheck is spent. The challenge people have creating savings is that there's usually more week than paycheck; even when you *know* you make more than your bills, somehow, the money just disappears! There's only one technique for fixing this problem without a great amount of pain: creating a habit.

Taking Care of You

My dad used to say that there is a little child inside each of us that wants to be taken care of. Finding a life partner to take care of that "little child" is a subconscious goal many of us start working on while we're actually children! Relationships we have with others are predicated on how well they nurture that "little child" in us. But all good parents (and Whitney Houston) teach us that the "greatest love of all is learning to love yourself." It's the same with money: you need to take care of you. Create a habit of paying yourself first.

Creating a habit is the easiest way to fake discipline. Early in my career, I hit the gym every day that I went to work. Friends used to marvel at my discipline, to which I remarked that it was just a habit. You can create a good habit by doing the same thing over and over for five or six days in a row. For example, after you get paid, you could always go online and transfer some money to your savings account. The key here is to decide ahead of time how much money you want to save per pay period and transfer that money to a savings account *before* paying bills. Yes, before paying bills. If you know what your bills (non-discretionary expenses) are likely to be, then you can make your commitment to a savings amount before little emergencies (or non-emergencies) come up. If there's any money left over, spend away!

With the power of technology, you can create an automated habit for your money, rather than even creating the habit for yourself:

- Ask your payroll/human resources person to split your paycheck into checking and a savings account, OR
- Set up an automatic transfer in your online banking account to run on the dates you get paid

By choosing either one of these options, the portion of your income that you are allocating to savings will go into your savings account before it spends much time (if any) in your checking account. After a while, you will form your life around what goes into your checking account, and you won't even miss the money that goes into savings.

Painless ways to increase the amount that goes to savings:

- Increase the percentage going to savings by 1% every six months
- Increase the percentage by half of any raise or promotion you receive

Saving doesn't have to be hard at all. You can leverage technology and painless plans to increase your savings by just putting a few of these steps in place. And you will have taken care of #1 in the process.

Cash in the Bank

It makes sense to have cash in traditional bank accounts, but I also see it in certificates of deposit, money market accounts, brokerage accounts, and retirement accounts. Cash has a place in many types of accounts, depending on your plan. Because most of our money starts as cash, making intentional choices is the challenge of cash management.

In the early 1990s, your basic checking account paid 1% interest. Savings accounts paid around 2 or 3%, and certificates of deposit paid a little more to hold your money for a specific time period. Depending on decisions by the Federal Reserve Chair and the Federal Open Markets Committee (FOMC), bank rates will head up or down, but with federal deposit insurance (thanks to FDIC), much of your money will be safe. FDIC insurance, established in 1933 by the **Banking Act**, currently protects up to $250,000 of your money per bank account ownership category per bank. For example, if you have a single owned account with $250,000 and joint account with $250,000 at one bank, both accounts will be protected under the FDIC.

Because risk and return go together (the more risk, the more return), banks have never felt the need to be too generous with their interest. Terrestrial banks have been the worse in this regard. I can often double a client's interest just by suggesting they move their money from one of the big banks to a similarly FDIC-insured bank account that only exists online.

Like everything in financial planning, knowing the purpose of the resources is important. If you are setting aside money for an emergency (meaning you want it readily accessible), then a bank is a good option. You may as well get as much interest as any bank will give you.

Cash in Your Brokerage Account

Almost everyone has some cash in the account they use for investments, whether that's an IRA, Roth IRA, or plain vanilla online
account where you buy and sell bonds and equities (stocks).
You need enough cash to pay for the transaction fees, so cash is
important. But more than a few times, I have run across client
accounts that had 10, 20, 30% or more of their investment money
in cash holdings. These holdings are often held in accounts that
pay less than 1%, usually less than one half of 1%. If you have
money earmarked for investing, ensure that it's actually invested!
Otherwise, park those funds somewhere you can get closer to
matching inflation.

Cash in Your Life Insurance Policy

One of the selling points for whole life insurance policies is the
build-up of what's called "cash value" in your policy. Rather than
having a life insurance policy with a simple purpose (to pay the
face value should the insured pass away), whole life insurance
policies have become the Swiss Army knife of insurance tools.
Your monthly premium payment goes towards the cost of the
insurance, the costs (and profit) to the insurance company, and
some measure of interest returns to you. (You can get something
similar with other universal life and variable life policies, but, for
example purposes, let's focus on whole life.)

Parking money in a whole life policy used to be quite advantageous in the late 1970s and early 1980s for those who had excess
cash reserves and feared rising taxes. Robert Castiglione, founder
of LEAP, Inc., author of *LEAP: Lifetime Economic Acceleration
Process,* and the inspiration behind books like *Becoming Your*

Own Banker and *Bank on Yourself,* initially made quite a name for himself. With top marginal tax rates as high as 70%, loopholes like overfunding insurance products with cash became the norm. The Tax Reform Act of 1986 put limits on how much an insured person could "overfund" their insurance policy, and that drastically reduced the gap between the advantages and disadvantages of using this tool for cash management. This is because the way you gain access to cash you might be saving in an insurance policy is to "borrow it" from your death benefit. If you don't have to borrow too much, you don't have to pay it back, because the amount you borrowed will just be deducted from your death benefit when you die. Borrowing too much (anything over the premiums you've paid), on the other hand, will trigger a tax consequence.

Whether to save cash in an insurance policy gets muddled with other reasons you may have to buy a permanent whole life insurance policy. Those reasons aside, it's hard to make a case for saving within insurance policies while there are many more simple and liquid tools for accomplishing the same goals.

CHAPTER 11 TAKEAWAYS

Any good bank knows that liquidity is critical to business operations. Cash management for humans (acting like banks) begins with having some cash available just for emergencies. Like insurance, having an emergency fund of available cash will ensure that most emergencies are covered. Using technology to help create a habit of saving makes a nonintuitive process easier.

Where you keep your cash is the difference between maximizing your opportunities (much like a bank) and almost literally throwing money away. The best place for an emergency fund is a high interest, FDIC-insured bank account. Brokerage accounts and insurance policies do a terrible job of returning value on your investment.

Actionable Strategies:

- Use technology to automate cash saving habits (pay yourself first)
- Move excess cash/emergency funds to high interest FDIC-insured bank accounts
- Review your brokerage account statements for excess cash
- Review any permanent insurance policies and compare their value to term

CHAPTER 12

CREDIT

According to Fair Isaac Corporation (the people who create your FICO® credit score), your payment history accounts for 35% of your score. Considering how important credit scores are to receiving credit, it's surprising that the scores have only been around since 1989. Then again, the first credit cards, Diners Club and American Express, were only initially used in 1950 and 1958, respectively. Later in 1958, Bank of America created the first iteration of the Visa card, the BankAmericard. (I know, I like "Visa" a lot better too.)

The whole idea of using credit for small items is a relatively new phenomenon. Buying a house or a car on credit has historically made sense because of the relative size of those purchases. But using credit to buy incidentals, dining out, or a new pair of shoes was invented by Baby Boomers. Regardless, credit scores are used by lenders of all kinds to evaluate whether we will receive the leverage provided by any kind of credit. It is a little confusing to know that there are more credit scoring companies than FICO, which means there are different scorers out there who rate your credit.

PERSONAL EXPERIENCE

When I was eighteen, my dad thought it would be a good idea for me to work while in college. And instead of what might be a typical college job, he thought it would be a great idea to work for a bank. My older sister had worked for a bank while in school, so I was slated to go work for the same one. The only problem? The only open position was full-time. My dad didn't blink—he suggested I take it.

Through twelve-hour days on Monday, Wednesday, and Friday, along with a four-hour day on Saturday, I was able to make forty hours per week work. On Tuesdays and Thursdays, I was a full-time college student, and the other days of the week, I was a full-time banker.

On college campuses in the 1990s, it was pretty easy to get a credit card. Banks were lining up students with new opportunities for debt by giving away T-shirts. Everyone seemed to get one except for me, even though I worked for a bank! So, I filled out an application at work, feeling like they had to give me a credit card.

Well, they didn't.

I applied and got turned down again, and I'd almost given up when a co-worker suggested I ask the district manager of our region to sign off on my application. So, the next time he came through, I asked Mr. David Wheeler (oddly, I still remember his name) to sign off on my application. Mr. Wheeler signed it, and I soon received a $300 revolving credit line on my first credit card.

In a short while, I purchased the five CD, dual-tape deck I had been eying for months. After receiving a tax refund, I figured the best thing I could do was charge the nearly $300 stereo to my credit card—to build my credit—and pay it off with the refund. In my mind, it was a great idea, but months later, I had spent the tax refund and run up my credit card. It took me a bunch of years to get out from under what eventually turned into a bunch of debt. Debt creeps up on you, regardless of good intentions. Had I paid attention to the snowball effect of paying down debt, I would have paid it all off a lot faster.

The life lesson is I was upside down—not only in my finances, but for a while, I was behind in things I wanted to do in life. Paying for dates was a challenging proposition; come to think of it, so was paying for gas sometimes! It took me awhile to learn that controlling my expenses would, by default, control how and when I used (misused?) credit. Like any drug, credit can be a gateway; in this case, to debt.

In my early twenties, it didn't have to be this way. Just because I finally qualified for credit didn't mean I was ready to manage debt. After all, with my first full-time job, I was just learning how to handle cash!

PROFESSIONAL EXPERIENCE

Early on, I had clients who needed help with debt, specifically credit cards. I've also had clients who were challenged by too much cash. Speaking of the latter, one particular client moved from two paychecks per month to just one so it would be easier to balance monthly expenses against one lump sum. He then had to fight the urge to spend his first dollars on entertainment, "before all of the money went away" on bills. So, though one check made things easier to budget, he still had to work on the inside. He had to answer the question, "What makes you feel like you have to spend first versus saving (paying yourself) first?"

We walked through those challenges, and slowly, he was able to save three figures, then four figures, and we built a plan towards him saving upwards of $10,000—five figures!—in a single year.

It wasn't the bills that were holding him back, it was something more personal and nuanced. Thankfully, with a little help, he was able to work through those personal challenges.

My clients who have built up a lot of credit card debt often imagine themselves as the first persons to have done so. I reassure them that over the course of two focused years, their entire outlooks will change. I've done the "snowball method" (see the next section) with clients for paying down credit cards, and it works! One card at a time, balances get reduced, then go away entirely. Just having a plan to pay down the debt is a relief. Actually following the plan makes the day-to-day less stressful. Achieving the debt reducing plan goals—well, that's just euphoric.

Good Credit

Good credit opens you up to good opportunities (maybe great ones). Whenever I see a car ad on television for 0% financing and $0 due at signing, I look for the fine print. And the fine print usually states that it's reserved for their best borrowers. Truth be told, 0% financing can still come with a cost (for example, not getting a discount on the invoice, the free oil changes or whatever). But even if there was no cost, just a great deal, wouldn't you want the option? Well, the only way to get the best options on credit is to have the best-looking credit report and associated credit scores. And the way to do that is to first understand what lenders are looking for and what they are looking at.

Credit Bureaus

For hundreds of years, data on borrowers were hard to come by. It required keeping and sharing data on millions of people. Today, that seems like an easy proposition, but before the 1980s, most data were held in offline paper records in cabinets and drawers. The eventual use of technology by the three major credit bureaus (Experian, Equifax, and Transunion) made accessing data on borrowers a lot easier for lenders. When the Fair Isaac Company (FICO) created a score that could be used to reconcile the data in 1991, evaluating the data became easy as well. Whenever we apply for credit, lenders are looking at one or more of our credit reports—usually your FICO® score.

5 Cs

For most large lenders/banks, the FICO® score is all they need (and likely all the frontline people are allowed) to evaluate when making the decision to extend credit. Smaller banks, credit unions, and other independent institutions may use a combination of the 5 Cs to evaluate creditworthiness:

- Character
- Capacity
- Capital
- Collateral
- Conditions

"If I take care of my character, my reputation will take care of me." Dwight Moody, a Unitarian evangelist, would have made a great credit card issuer (if he'd lived past 1899). In fact, the

character portion of credit evaluation refers to your reputation for paying back debts, taking on reasonable amounts of debt, and sticking around in the same home or job for a few years. (This is where changing jobs annually could hurt you, but not by much.) **Capacity** is merely a reference to your ability to pay. Lenders will ask what you make and verify that number. **Capital** refers to whether or not you're putting any of your money at risk. For example, a friend of mine was having trouble getting a credit card. He asked whether a secure credit card application would make sense; considering he wanted to build his credit, I suggested it would. From the bank's perspective, he was investing capital for credit.

You may notice that borrowing for a car or home will typically incur a lower interest rate for repayment than a credit card. That is because there is **collateral** that makes any extension of credit "secure," because they can always repossess a car or kick you out of the house! The final "C" has to do with market **conditions** of the economy and the potential use of your loan.

Again, most of these 5 Cs are usually wrapped into the algorithms of the FICO® score these days, but if you're working with a smaller lender and can make your case, knowing these 5 Cs just might help you get some credit.

CHAPTER 12 TAKEAWAYS

Good credit is easy leverage in a world that wants you to engage in commerce. It is easy to overexpose yourself to the temptations of credit, but a well-managed credit score can lower your costs by hundreds or even thousands of dollars on large purchases like cars and homes.

Actionable Strategies:

- Go to Annualcreditreport.com to receive your free annual credit bureau reports
- Check to see if any of your credit cards offer a free FICO® score
- Walk through the 5 Cs to identify where you can improve your FICO® score

CHAPTER 13

PAYING OFF DEBT

Debt is exactly the opposite of cash. It's an obligation that, at some point, you will have to pay. It can force you to work when you would rather not, live in a home you would rather leave, and suffer situations you cannot change. At the same time, debt can be an alternative way to leverage your good reputation and more specifically, creditworthiness. So, is it good or is it bad?

The answer is easier than it seems—debt is bad! Why would you want to owe somebody money? Why would it be a good thing to need leverage? Wouldn't it be better if you actually had the money you needed to buy what you wanted? Of course. So, if you don't have debt, you don't need it and you certainly don't need to want it. But if you already have debt, there is a joy in getting rid of it.

Accumulating debt can happen slowly or all of a sudden. For many of us, it happens slowly, often through small charges on a credit card that don't all get paid off every month, or over the course of earning a college degree. For others, it happens quickly, through a large purchase or a medical bill that can't be paid. Getting rid of debt takes great habits, some of which you may not have had when you got into debt in the first place! It requires income, of course, but it also requires making the sacrifices you couldn't make along the way to accumulating that debt. Paying off debt may also require your creativity, which could make becoming debt free more like solving a puzzle; and, if you're anything like my sister-in-law, puzzles can be fun!

Avalanche Method or Snowball Method

Both of these popular methods for reducing debt will give someone in debt a couple of things they haven't felt before: control and progress. Most responsible people I know, including clients, will try to pay a little extra on all of their debts each month. This is not a recommended strategy. Go online, and you will find advocates for either the avalanche or snowball method to help reduce that overwhelming feeling associated with a large number of debts.

The first step, after reviewing all of your balances, minimum payments required, and interest rates, is to prioritize the order with which you will pay them off. In both methods, your strategy is to pay the minimum amount required by all of your creditors except one. You choose one debt to effectively "pick on." All of your attention and extra money you set aside for debt will go towards paying off one debt fast. After that first debt is paid off, in however many months, you take the amount you had been paying to that debt and add it to the amount you were paying to the next debt in your order of priority.

The avalanche method takes an academic approach to the order. It suggests paying off the higher interest debts first. Of course, this makes sense, because the higher interest is hurting you more financially. What this doesn't take into account is your highest interest debt may be a student loan for $90,000, and your lowest interest debt may be $1,000 on a credit card. Paying down $90,000 of interest may take a couple of years, while the $1,000 debt may be taken care of in one or two paychecks.

Why does this matter? Well, the advocates of the snowball method take a more behavioral science approach. The thinking is that paying off that $1,000 credit card in a couple months gives you an early "win" in your debt reducing commitment, and that win could be the encouragement that keeps you on your plan for the longer-term debt payoff.

I tend to agree with the thinking behind the snowball method, but have had clients who favored the avalanche method for its mathematical advantage. Whichever method you choose, they will both provide a sense of control and real progress.

Earn More Money

Maybe your debt situation is a result of overwork and inattention to details like the interest rates on credit cards. If you've been working really hard, now is a great time to ask for a raise. When the federal government wants a raise, politicians have to take the unpopular stance of raising taxes or fees on citizens. It rarely happens, because opposing politicians will accuse them of mismanaging the people's money and run against them. This is not your situation! If you ask your employer for a raise, you will not have an opposing employee "run against you" for your job. You will get either a "yes," a "no," or a "maybe." Any raise you receive can be earmarked toward paying down more debt using the snowball or avalanche method. If you are in sales and have an extraordinary month, reward yourself with something fun with a small portion of your "extra" cash flow, then take a chunk out of your debt with the rest. If there are no options for earning more money at work, then take advantage of the gig economy that allows any of us to efficiently earn money on the side.

There are multiple ways to earn an income; when you have debt, the key is giving that new money a job, and that job is paying down debt. Again, try not to get lost in the debate of good debt versus bad debt. In this book, we're discussing how to pay off debt, period. If you get through your credit cards, student loans, your car loan, and all you have left is your mortgage, start paying that down too. Debt is not evil, but it is not great, it is not fun, and when you have enough cash, it doesn't need to be a part of your life. The lower your debt, the more control you have over your choices, your current life, and your future.

Viewer Discretion is Advised

If you've ever watched someone put together a puzzle, you probably noticed their focus and attention. My sister-in-law Shandra will first make sure she can see everything at once by pouring out all of the puzzle pieces onto the table and flipping them right side up. You can do the same with your debt statements. You can print them all out and put them on a table, or at least log in to all of them online, with a different tab for each account. Once you can see them all, they (hopefully) become less intimidating. Even if you are only concerned about or only have one big, fat bill, take a close look at it. See its nuances and its contours: identify the interest rate, the balance, and the minimum payment. Try to calculate how they come up with the minimum payment (typically about 2% for credit cards) and read the boxes that may estimate how long it will take to pay off.

Once you've gotten to really know your debt, take a deep breath. They are just numbers. Before you do any paying off of debt, know your options. Refinancing is an option, whether it's mortgage, car, or credit card debt. This option is available to people with great credit scores.

Other Options for Reducing Debt

If you have lost your job or ability to work, you may be forced into asking your creditors to reduce your debt in a **negotiation**. If they agree to give you some debt relief, the agreement may still be reported negatively on your credit report, and, in turn, negatively affect your credit score. A low credit score may hurt your ability to receive additional credit in the near future. This is the second-to-last resort when dealing with your debt.

The absolute last resort is filing for **bankruptcy**. Bankruptcy is a financial status, and it's all a court proceeding. You go to court, speak with a judge and explain why there's no way you could pay back the money you owe. Just think about that. I have known people who have filed for bankruptcy, and it is a difficult step to take emotionally. If you do take that emotional journey, you will be served well to learn as much about the process as possible.

There are two types for individuals: **chapter 13** and **chapter 7**. Chapter 13 will give you the option of keeping all of the things you have purchased and working through a plan to pay back what you can over a specific time period. It's considered a "reorganization" of debt, which is a relief, but expect this history to stay in your virtual credit file/credit report for seven years. Chapter 7 bankruptcy is a whole other level that will likely require you to sell some of your things to pay back some of your debt. This could include your car and your home, depending on the latest exemption amounts. As you might expect, taking this kind of action to reduce your debts is a serious legal and financial matter. This will be reported to the three credit bureaus/reporting agencies and will remain in your credit file for up to ten years.

If you have your income and your health, negotiating debt reduction and/or filing bankruptcy need not be on your radar. Those are the extreme options. I purposely sandwiched those between refinancing and these next strategies that merely require your consistent effort: I really don't want you to think about these options if you can otherwise avoid them.

IN FOCUS: Student Loan Debt

I remember visiting George Mason University for orientation. My dad marched upstairs to the finance department; on the wall, I could see clear as day the price for two years versus four years of college. They had the poster for two years because many students transferred from Northern Virginia Community College, which had a large campus within the same county (Fairfax).

I don't remember talking to the financial counselors, and though we walked back downstairs to the orientation, I don't remember a word of the student welcome. All I began to realize was that my parents were not paying for college, and I would be responsible. And now the decision: pay for four years of university, or two years of community college, then transfer? I did what was logical and right for me, registering to begin my college career at Northern Virginia Community College.

That long-term financial planning decision provided a lot of joy the year I made my last student loan payment for my eventual alma mater, George Mason University. I'd like to think I saved myself at least two years of loan payments; in fact, I probably saved three or four years of payments.

Student Loan Types

As you evaluate incurring a student loan or paying one back, it helps to understand the difference between public and private student loans. **Private student loans** operate a lot like regular loans, with strict guidelines including a credit check, unsubsidized interest rates, and fewer guidelines for negotiation (should you need to negotiate your repayment plan). **Public student loans** offer "fixed interest rates, income-based repayment plans, loan cancellation for certain types of employment, deferment (postponement) options, and interest rate reduction based on repayment method."[1]

With all of those features, the William D. Ford Federal (Direct Loan) Program offers many advantages. If only there was one type! In fact, there are four types of direct loans:

- Direct Subsidized – up to $5,500 depending on grade level
- Direct Unsubsidized – up to $20,500 depending on grade level
- Direct PLUS
- Direct Consolidated

Direct subsidized loans are the most common, as they are earmarked for undergraduates with financial need. The "subsidized" part comes from not accruing any interest while attending school at least part (half) time. There is a lifetime limit on these loans per person. **Direct unsubsidized** is meant for a greater universe of students (with or without financial need). These loans can also be used for graduate school, but not being subsidized, interest

---

1   More information can be found at StudentLoans.gov

is always accruing and at a higher rate than subsidized loans. The **Direct PLUS** loan is for parents on behalf of children. Parents have to qualify through a credit check, and this loan can go up to any amount needed to cover tuition over the direct loan needs.

I often talk with parents about any one of these three loans as options to use if trying to save for retirement or pay down other debt while also wanting to pay for their kid's college. The good news is they can keep their promise to their kids (and themselves) by funding their retirement until their child graduates, then repay the loans on their behalf. An added benefit is incentivizing the kids to graduate or face the wrath of paying off those loans themselves!

Direct Consolidated loans are a complex choice. Though a person with student loans may get solicited for a "consolidation loan," most private consolidation loans come with a fee (similar to the fees for refinancing your home). StudentAidEd.gov emphasizes that there isn't a fee for going through the federal programs for consolidation, but there may be drawbacks. Like any combination of loans, you may refinance lower rates for a higher rate just for the benefit of having one payment. Academically, that may be the wrong thing to do, but for some people, having just one payment feels better. Walk through whether you are giving up any loan forgiveness or payment reduction options if you choose to consolidate federal loans. These are the areas where you may lose in an otherwise good situation that public federal consolidation offers.

Student Loan Repayment

Teaching as an adjunct instructor at American University in Washington, D.C. has given me real-life perspective on how students feel about student loan debt: They hate it. And we tend to ignore the scary things we hate. As a result, the students have no idea how to pay back all of their student loans.

There are many options for paying back federal student loans, which is great for the borrower (even though it can be confusing). I'll try to simplify those options here.

There are three **traditional repayment plans**:

- **Standard Repayment**: a ten-year plan where you pay the least amount of interest
- **Graduated Repayment**: an up-to-ten-year plan where payments start low and increase
- **Extended Repayment**: an up-to-twenty-five-year fixed or graduated plan (higher interest)

The first two plans are available to all borrowers, while the extended repayment plan is only available to borrowers with a minimum of $30,000 of direct loan debt. Many people who borrow will, unfortunately, find themselves in the $30,000 plus category; if so, they may want to look at the income-driven repayment plans.

There are currently four **income-driven repayment plans**:

- **Pay as you earn (PAYE)**: maximum payments are 10% of discretionary income
- **Revised pay as you earn (REPAYE)**: payments are 10% of discretionary income
- **Income-based repayment (IBR)**: payments are 10% or 15% of discretionary income

- **Income-contingent repayment (ICR)**: payments are lesser of 20% of discretionary income or a fixed twelve-year payment plan

All of the income-driven repayment plans are eligible for **Public Service Loan Forgiveness** (PSLF), which may or may not trigger a taxable event depending on current federal law. Your discretionary income may include your spouse's income; it's calculated by taking the difference between your income and either 150% or 100% of the poverty line for your state.

IN FOCUS: Mortgage Debt

The vast majority of us don't buy homes in the traditional sense: we borrow homes from banks and promise to spend the next fifteen to thirty years of our lives purchasing them from the banks. Paying for a mortgage is not just a mechanism for what we traditionally call "home ownership," it is a lifestyle. Mortgage payments, similar to rent, are typically the largest household bill, but unlike rent, they are a much longer commitment of payment. This commitment starts at the very beginning of your new relationship with a bank and is determined by how much of a down payment you have invested.

Conventional loans require a 20% down payment that immediately provides leverage in the form of equity for the bank that holds your mortgage. With that 20% investment, your desire to walk away from the commitment of paying the bank back is reduced dramatically. For example, a $500,000 home will require a $100,000 (20%) down payment. Not many people are willing to walk away from a $100,000 investment, so making the mortgage payments on time becomes a focal point of daily life. It affects the job you take, the hours you work, and indirectly, the hours you actually spend in the house. Patrick Holland, vice president at direct mortgage lender Embrace Home Loans, says,

> For most individuals, buying a home will be the largest financial undertaking in their life. Discussions with a true mortgage professional that will take all obligations into account is essential. Go into home ownership with a proper education about what to expect so you can make the mortgage part of the financial plan.

He is right, because once you have made a commitment to carrying a mortgage into home ownership, you have added a new long-term relationship to your financial life.

Government-backed loans allow borrowers to reduce that initial commitment to 3.5% of the home value (with excellent credit), or as low as 10% of the home mortgage with much lower credit scores (between 500 and 579). These Federal Housing Administration (FHA) or Veterans Administration (VA) loans come with their own sets of qualifications, restrictions, and increased amounts of paperwork. Suffice it to say, not everyone qualifies. Receiving a government-backed loan may also require paying additional monthly costs, namely **Private Mortgage Insurance** (PMI) or **FHA Mortgage Insurance**. Both types of insurance are designed to cover the banker if you default on your mortgage, since that initial investment was so much smaller. The cost of PMI or FHA mortgage insurance will depend largely (again) on your credit score. Ask your mortgage banker to help you determine what the best value is for your investment.

Another question to ask for planning purposes is how you might eventually remove the extra cost of mortgage insurance from your monthly payment. Traditionally, PMI is cancellable upon reaching the 20% equity threshold in your home, while cancelling FHA mortgage insurance may require refinancing the entire loan. Again, what you choose at the beginning of your loan's life may determine your life, for years. Patrick Holland says,

> *No one mortgage is right for every situation. Having options based on short- and long-term financial goals can allow for flexibility and planning. This is a crucial part of the mortgage discussion when buying a home. Know your options and make a sound financial decision.*

Mortgage Payments

Your monthly mortgage payment is typically referred to as **PITI**: Principle, Interest, Taxes, and Insurance. The principle and interest refer to the loan you signed up for and the associated amount of interest you are paying on the principle for the loan term. The taxes here are the property taxes typically paid to your city or county. The insurance is the homeowner's insurance that protects your home from damages. Unlike car insurance, homeowner's insurance may not be required in your state, but it will likely be required by your mortgage lender (to protect their collateral for your loan).

The total amount of your PITI is calculated by your mortgage banker or loan officer to help determine whether you qualify for a mortgage in the first place. This calculation is called a **front-end ratio**, and if the total PITI payment falls below 28% of your monthly gross income, you are likely to qualify for the loan. If a more expensive home would break down to a PITI payment that is higher than 28% of your gross monthly income, you are more likely to be disqualified from that mortgage. This is why, for planning purposes, I suggest visiting with a mortgage banker or loan officer before you start looking at houses online or with a REALTOR®. It would be heartbreaking to fall in love with a $700,000 house only to realize that you can only qualify for a loan that would squeeze you into a $500,000 home.

Escrow

Paying the taxes and insurance for your home along with your debt service is actually a unique setup. A car is a similar (though much smaller) purchase, but your car loan only includes the principle and interest. You pay the property tax and car insurance separately. With a home mortgage, you set up what's called an **escrow account** with your lender, where the property taxes and insurance payments accumulate until due. Whether you have to use an escrow account rather than paying those tax and insurance costs separately depends largely on the lender's requirements. Whether you want to pay those costs separate from your mortgage payment depends largely on your ability to set aside funds in savings to pay those bills (especially the property tax bill). You can lose your home to the state for not paying property taxes! You could lose your house to a fire, and if you aren't paying your homeowner's insurance, you will not get reimbursed to rebuild your home. If that happened, would you keep making mortgage payments? Scenarios like these are what lenders are protecting against when they require an escrow account.

Adjustable Rate Mortgages

One way people overcome being disqualified for a mortgage loan on a too-expensive house is to apply for an **adjustable rate mortgage (ARM)**, which allows for a lower interest rate for a determined number of years, then jumps to another market-based rate at the end of those years. For example, you could have 4% or 5% loan on a seven-year ARM, but then in the eighth year, have to pay the prevailing interest rate of 6% or more, depending on market conditions. (After seven years, the interest rate could be lower in this scenario, but it more likely will be higher.) So, that would leave you with a PITI payment that maybe you couldn't afford. ARMs have been abused in the past, notably during the 2008 financial crisis. Features to look for, if using an ARM, are caps on the interest rates over the lifetime of the "adjustable period," and it helps to be certain of at least one of two things:

- You plan to sell your home well before the rate "adjusts"
- You will be able to afford the new loan rate if you can't sell your home

An adjustable rate mortgage can be a great tool for circumventing limits the mortgage industry might place on your goal of owning a home, but buyer beware: those limits are there to protect you.

Paying Off the Mortgage

If you have a fixed rate mortgage and mortgage rates go down, most savvy shoppers will contact their mortgage lender or an outside loan officer to **refinance** the loan.

Refinancing at a lower rate allows the borrower (you) to pay down the loan faster with the same outlay of cash, or to lower your cash outlay while resetting the time it takes to pay off your loan. Most borrowers choose the low hanging fruit of the ladder. They will take a thirty-year mortgage that they've been paying for five or six years and reset the timeline to thirty years for the benefit of a lower payment. Depending on life circumstances, lowering the monthly obligation might be the best thing for that borrower. Others may see the academic opportunity of just lowering the rate and paying off their loan quicker or more cheaply. For example, a thirty-year mortgage loan with a $3,000 PITI (payment) that's been paid for ten years may be refinanced to a $200 lower monthly PITI payment. Rather than saving that $200, the borrower may keep paying $3,000 for the remainder of the balance; with a lower fixed interest rate, it will certainly take less than the remaining twenty years to pay off the loan. What works best for each family depends on their situation in the other areas of financial life.

Refinancing isn't without its own costs. Besides seeing that optional lower PITI payment, it will be important to consider some of the same **closing costs** you would pay with a brand-new mortgage. Closing costs typically include application and origination fees, title fees, fees for lawyers, fees for credit reports, and even postage! When making the decision to refinance for saving purposes, ensure that you are *actually* saving.

An alternative to refinancing can well include making extra payments to principal, as long as the other parts of your financial plan are satisfied. You will want to call your lender so those extra funds are used as you intended. The big benefit of this method? There are no new fees to consider! Just remember that paying off a mortgage will take years, and if the other areas of your financial life could better use those extra funds, it's not so easy to "take it back" out of the illiquid asset of a house.

CHAPTER 13 TAKEAWAYS

There are many ways to pay down debt once you make the decision to do what it takes. Methods like avalanche or snowball help to create momentum for paying down debts that inspire you to keep going, even when your personal goals take a while. Sometimes earning additional income through a raise at work or a side job is an option for directing new money at reducing debt.

Other options for reducing debt in general include negotiating for lower payments, longer terms, or lower interest rates with creditors. If nothing else works, bankruptcy is an option, but if possible, make it the last of the last resorts.

Student loans are a special kind of debt. They can't yet be dismissed in bankruptcy, but federal direct loans offer multiple ways to repay student loans. Student loan debt consolidation should be done with careful attention to detail, because some repayment options may be lost.

Mortgage debt is likely the largest debt many of us will encounter. There are guidelines for qualifying for a mortgage. Your ability to pay your loan back quickly is mostly determined the day you sign the documents for your new mortgage loan. Making extra payments or going through the process of refinancing can help to reduce your loan repayment schedule more quickly once there is extra cash available in your financial plan.

Actionable Strategies:

- List all debt that you currently service (balances, interest rates, and minimum payments)
- Decide the order of payoff priority based on the avalanche or snowball method

- If you have student loans, walk through the seven repayment plan options
- If you have a mortgage, discuss the cost/benefits of refinancing with a loan officer
- Instead of mortgage refinancing, consider making extra payments when possible

JOY OF
BALANCE

Summary

It is difficult to change the world when you can't afford to spare change. Just having cash available is a difficult concept for some people. They are either used to owing money or having it all invested. There is a beauty in the discipline of accumulating cash, actually increasing your purchasing power, and not buying anything. Set a target to put aside three to six months' worth of expenses in a high interest (usually online) savings account. When you have saved the money, every once in a while, go in to look at it—and do nothing with it. Then go about your day. It will change your relationship with money.

You can take advantage of that change once your debt is under control. To see where you stand with your debt management, go to AnnualCreditReport.com to receive a free copy of your credit reports from TransUnion, Equifax, and Experian. Review these reports for inaccuracies and/or differences. You may also choose to go to a website like MyFICO.com to receive your credit score and just become aware of what others are saying about your ability to manage debt. Then, take it upon yourself to count how many months it would take to pay off your debt at your current pace or using the snowball or avalanche methods.

Having cash when no one else does leaves you wide open to take opportunities. On a basic level, you can buy things when they go on sale: clothes, cars, homes, stocks, etc. On a more advanced level, how many times have opportunities come your way that you've had to pass up because you didn't have the cash? These could be opportunities that aren't just "nice," but that could be life-changing. You don't have to miss out on those. Pay off as much of your debt as fast as you can, then start building up your "opportunities account." Famous English businessman Sir Richard Branson (yes, he's also been knighted) is famous for having said, "Opportunities are like buses—there's always another one coming!"

When your bus comes around, I want you to be first in line at the bus stop.

A Final Word on Balance

Greek philosopher Aristotle's thoughts on morality could be summarized as, "Excellence is a habit." I believe the rewards of discipline are often first discovered through the habit of doing the right things. This is a balance we can strike in our communities after we have done the hard work for our own families. Striking the right balance between cash and debt is a necessity in modern society that we can achieve with awareness and intention. I see a future where reason and policy demand that great sums of debt are no longer common for individuals or countries. I see a future where the wealthiest nations assist the poorest of nations, not out of charity, but out of responsibility for our fellow men and women. As our 35th U.S. President once eloquently said, "If a free society cannot help the many who are poor, it cannot save the few who are rich." I agree.

STRATEGY IV

JOY OF
SAFETY

Risk Management

"An ounce of prevention is worth a pound of cure."
~Benjamin Franklin

CHAPTER 14

BACKGROUND & HISTORY

The earliest history of insurance goes back to the 14th century. It began as marine or maritime insurance for cargo crossing oceans, mostly from Europe. The idea was to transfer risk from the merchants to somebody—anybody—else. At its heart, that is all insurance promises: a transfer of risk, presumably from you to an insurance company. But in practice, it is a transfer of risk from you to other insureds who pay premiums.

Life and property insurance as we know it came centuries later, thanks in large part to the Age of Enlightenment in Europe. The Age of Enlightenment was a progressive era of science and reason and began the separation of church and state. Insurance requires the skills of actuaries (or, as I like to call them, "the first data scientists"), and you want your insurance company to take on risk based on science (and math) rather than belief.

The first life insurance company in the world was founded in London in 1706, the Amicable Society for a Perpetual Assurance Office.[1] In America, Benjamin Franklin is credited with

---

1   This company is still active, as Aviva, today, and has an extensive and fascinating archive that can be accessed publicly through https://heritage.aviva.com/.

starting the first insurance company in 1752, after Philadelphia's devastating fire at Fishbourn's Wharf in 1730. The Philadelphia Contributionship for the Insuring of Houses from Loss by Fire was the first of many insurance companies we have today.[2] Most of the popular life insurance companies we know today were founded in the 19th century—think of companies like New York Life (1845), MetLife (1868), and Prudential (1875). The differences seemed to stem mostly from whether they were "mutual" companies (paying profits to policy holders) or "public" companies that shared profits and were beholden to shareholders. Property insurance companies seemed to sprout in the early 20th century: Allstate (1931), Liberty Mutual (1912), Progressive (1937), and GEICO (1936).[3]

The taxation of benefits, specifically life insurance benefits, has been a subject of some controversy over the years. Because life insurance benefits are generally not taxable, permanent policies that allow for a savings component provide a shelter for income taxation. How much shelter should be allowed was the question— until the **Tax Reform Act of 1986** under our 40th United States president, Ronald Reagan. This legislation limited the amount of cash savings that could "build up" in a life insurance policy without threat of nullifying the tax benefits. Life insurance is still useful for creating liquidity or "cash" when there is little available, but it is a much-reduced tax shelter for savings.[4]

Before there was health insurance, there were social groups that pooled their own funds, without the help of an insurance

2   "History," The Philadelphia Contributionship, https://1752.com/about-us/history/, 2019.

3   Beattie, Andrew, "The History of Insurance," Investopedia, June 25, 2019, https://www.investopedia.com/articles/08/history-of-insurance.asp, 2019.

4   Graetz, Michael J., "Tax Reform 1986: A Silver Anniversary, Not a Jubilee," TaxAnalysts, October 21, 2011, http://www.taxhistory.org/www/features.nsf/Articles/066C3B71D4C8F8CA85257930006459EE?OpenDocument, 2019.

company, to take care of each other's medical bills. (Over and over again, I am struck that insurance, at its core, is a social contract among neighbors far and wide.) The first hint of true prepaid medical care came in the form of mariner or seaman insurance. In 1798, the **Act for the Relief of Sick and Disabled Seamen** was signed by our 2nd US president, John Adams. The law created the Marine Hospital Service and a mandatory 1% tax on privately employed sailors, who were enabling commerce at an important time in US history. There was no group policy for sickness until the Massachusetts Health Insurance Company of Boston was formed in 1847. The Franklin Health Insurance Company of Massachusetts created the first accident policy in 1850; sickness and accident insurance were precursors to the health insurance policies we know today.

The 26th US president, Theodore Roosevelt, and the 32nd US president, Franklin Roosevelt, both tried and failed to initiate national health insurance (in 1912 and 1934, respectively). FDR instead just created unemployment insurance, workmen's compensation, and oh, Social Security.

Hospital plans, first started by a group of teachers in Dallas, Texas, began to expand during the Great Depression. By 1937, those plans were combined by the American Hospital Association (formerly the Association of Hospital Superintends) as the Hospital Service Plan Commission. Their logo was a blue cross, which is half of the Blue Cross Blue Shield many of us have come to recognize generically as health insurance.

The Blue Shield comes from the doctor part of the plan. The American Medical Association, which did its part to oppose national healthcare by encouraging state and local prepayment plans, were worried that the Blue Cross folks would start covering physician costs. To thwart the possibility of fee restrictions out of their control, they combined the state and local plans into what we now know as Blue Shield. After World War II, employers began offering health insurance in lieu of higher pay, and the IRS (to this day) allows employers to deduct the cost of health insurance.[5]

The reimbursement of healthcare costs to doctors and hospitals has vacillated between a "cost plus" fee-for-service approach to highly complex "managed care" options that have done nothing to reduce costs. Advances in science only increase the cost of care and contribute to the increased cost of the insurance. But it's cheaper than paying out of pocket!

Over the years, the use of insurance has served as an important wealth management strategy for business owners, property owners, workers, widows and orphans. In the following chapters, we will review the many options for transferring risk of loss to a pooled community of fellow risk takers managed by an insurance company.

---

5   Quadagno, Jill, "Why the United States Has No National Health Insurance: Stakeholder Mobilization Against the Welfare State, 1945–1996," Journal of Health and Social Behavior 2004, Vol 45, https://ssa.uchicago.edu/sites/default/files/uploads/JHSB04ExtraQuadagno.pdf, 2019.

CHAPTER 15

SHARED RISK

In general, insurance is the shared distribution of risk. In exchange for your money, an insurance company will sign a contract that says they will cover your risk of loss. In practicality, insurance agencies are pooling the risk and the annual premiums (payments) of thousands of other customers to cover your risk of loss. Buying an insurance policy of any kind is making the decision to spread your risk across a pool of other people who also buy insurance policies. Who are those people? It doesn't matter to you, but in reality, they are your tribe that will protect you, should you come to any harm. The insurance company is merely the conduit for their protection. So, thank you insurance companies: You are making communities great again!

The insurance companies are good at doing the math (statistics) to know how much in payments, or "premium," they should charge to cover their clients' emergencies and still make a profit. They have people called actuaries who calculate the probability of each policyholder suffering a loss that will cause the insurance company to pay a benefit. Their statistical analysis makes it so "the house" (the insurance company) wins in the long run (or makes a profit). My accounting professor used to say, "No one knows when you, in particular, are going to die, but an actuary could calculate the mortality rate of the people in this room to the second." My accounting professor was a little dramatic, but, in all practicality, he was right. Actuaries make the insurance game work. As long as there is enough money left over after your emergency to cover everyone else's emergency, pay for the expenses of the insurance company, and cover a certain profit, everyone's happy.

Some insurance coverage is legally required by the government or your profession, so most people have that kind of coverage. That's a trap. Health insurance wasn't legally required personal insurance; then, after the **Patient Protection and Affordable Care Act** passed in 2010, it was. Then, after the **Tax Cut and Jobs Act of 2017**, it wasn't. Does that mean you'll never get sick or spend a night in the hospital? Without a law requiring life insurance, will anyone die with people depending on them? Since there is no law requiring liability protection, are you exempt from becoming the subject of a personal lawsuit? The answer to all of these ridiculous rhetorical questions is of course not. This chapter is about managing the risks of living (and dying), the risks of numerous kinds of emergencies that you can't afford with an emergency fund. These are risks you can transfer to a community of fellow policyholders managed by insurance companies, some of which have been with us since the 18th century.

The seven strategies continue with risk management, because (much like Maslow's hierarchy) after food, water, and shelter, safety is the next important human need. If you can't protect against losses associated with your property, your reputation, your health, or your death, then there's not much need for the rest of financial planning.

I started the official part of my financial planning career at an old, reputable firm called New York Life Insurance Company.

The management team who doubled as my trainers were highly committed to the business of selling insurance. It was there that I learned a lot about a category of financial planning that is basic in concept, but complex in implementation. **Joy of Safety** has eight topics of its own, but experienced and licensed life, health, property, and casualty insurance agents would read this section and say that we are just scratching the surface. And they would be right. You can be introduced to these topics in this book, but truly learning them will take years of study and experience. The purpose of these chapters is to give you a foundation of knowledge that you can bring to all of your meetings with insurance agents (in person or on the phone).

Sharing risk with insurance is the oldest, most proven, and least expensive kind of leverage you can buy. Making the conscious decision to share your risk with others is the first way to protect yourself and your family, and to reclaim the legacy you imagined.

CHAPTER 16

LIFE
INSURANCE

Life insurance helps to reduce the financial consequences of death. You are going to be missed in many personal and spiritual ways by the people that know, admire, and love you. But you don't have to be missed financially by the people who depend on your income.

When you get married and have children, you typically make a lot of promises, spoken and unspoken. The promise life insurance helps you keep is, "You will have my financial support for the next thirty or forty years." You are like a machine that prints money every year. Maybe you "print" $100,000 or more every year, and you estimate that with raises and promotions, that number will grow higher annually. Over twenty or thirty years, that's at least $2 or 3 million of financial support to your family. If all goes as planned (i.e., you live and are gainfully employed), you might earn that $2 or 3 million dollars that will benefit your family. And during that time, you may pay off a mortgage and save for a college fund and the so-called retirement years. If things don't go according to plan (i.e., you die unexpectedly), there's life insurance. Life insurance can be used as a bridge between where you are financially today and where you hope to be in twenty or thirty years.

Now, there are competing philosophies around life insurance. Some believe life insurance should be used as a forever gift, meaning you keep paying for a policy for the rest of your life. Appropriately, these policies are called "whole life" or "universal life" insurance. These policies not only require you to keep paying a monthly premium (depending on how they are designed), but they typically have you paying a little more each month than you actually need to pay for one month of coverage. The extra amount is often accumulated as cash in these policies, and can serve as a "forced savings" technique.

In a world where there are not only competing philosophies but also competing priorities, I don't see our generation appreciating a tool that "forces" you to do anything. Many of my clients compare temporary (or term) insurance to the permanent insurance options, and though many are in the accumulation phase of life, they choose the temporary insurance. This is the bridge option that allows them to close the gap between where they are now financially and where they aspire to be in ten, twenty, or thirty years. Along the way, they choose to keep available the savings that would have been sent to the insurance company for the higher cost of a permanent policy. You should choose what seems appropriate for your family's goals and your personal behavior. Some people appreciate forced savings—like getting a big tax refund at the end of the year—but some people do not.

My favorite thing about life insurance is how powerful it can be, should the worst emergency happen—someone you depend on financially dies unexpectedly. Most people consider death and dying scary subjects. I agree. It's an unknown, a topic, as my dad used to say, that God didn't let us know about. Only after someone close or someone famous dies do we really stop and think about what it means. And especially if it's someone close, our society seems to think the best course of action is to get over it. You never get over the death of a close loved one; you just learn to carry the pain. Imagine the feeling of falling, but never hitting the ground. After a while, you just get used to the feeling of falling, knowing you will one day hit the ground; until then, you live.

Insurance as Leverage

I tell my clients that if people depend on you financially and you save $100 per month, at the end of the year, you will have $1,200. If you died, that's what your beneficiaries would get (assuming the proper estate planning paperwork was completed). Alternatively, if you pointed that $100 per month to a term life insurance policy and you are reasonably healthy and under fifty years-old, you could pass along anywhere from $250,000 to $1,000,000 to your beneficiaries. The same $100 set aside, but an entirely different result.

I heard it said a few times when I worked for an insurance company that the majority of wealth transfer happens through life insurance benefits. What's striking to me is how much of that "wealth" is accessible even to someone who might consider themselves in the lower middle-income bracket. If our generation is going to make a dent in the chasm between what our parents could have achieved and what we hope to offer our children, then life insurance may end up playing a role. We need our entire careers—and second careers—to earn the income we'll need to stay afloat in this economy. We will need even more savvy to earn more than our needs and achieve our unique versions of the American Dream. On the off chance our lives are cut short before we can earn a lifetime of income, life insurance benefits will help us keep our promises to our families and to our causes.

PERSONAL EXPERIENCE

Soon after I got married, I thought buying some life insurance would be the next adult thing to do. This wasn't because I was a financial planner at the time (I wasn't), but I thought I had seen somewhere on TV that it was a responsible thing to have as a married person.

Not knowing that there were specialists in the field, I went to someone who I considered to be a financial adviser, but, in fact, was more of an investment adviser. The difference was not in his title, but his expertise. When I asked about life insurance, I was given a list of a few companies with a few different rates and a few different terms to choose from. I picked the one priced in the middle. A few years after that experience, I was hired by a life insurance company and learned about all of the options I hadn't been given. I learned about how much I could have qualified for, what my true options were, and what I wasn't effectively presented. I began to learn that not all "financial advisors" are the same.

Today, I pay a little over $100 per month for two insurance policies to share the risk of losing my life early with the insurance company. My two policies are for $500,000 each: one was originally a twenty-year level term, and the other with no guaranteed premium rate, which started out cheaper, but grows in price annually. I would definitely purchase the same amount of coverage again, but I might have designed it differently (now that I know more about my options). Insurance premiums have continued to decrease because life expectancy has gotten longer. Like everything I share in this book, my policies are just an example. Life insurance rates especially have many factors that affect what you pay.

PROFESSIONAL EXPERIENCE

The bank is the oldest financial institution, and the first one many of us come into contact with as young adults. The next oldest financial institution is the insurance company, and I worked for one of the best. New York Life Insurance Company is the old guard, having started their company in 1845, just ten years after this country was granted a life insurance charter. My first opportunity to work for this venerable firm came in 1998, about a year after I graduated college and started working in accounting. I didn't accept the opportunity then, but many years later, in 2013, the timing was right. At New York Life, I learned about a wealth management tool, life insurance, that I'd thought was pretty straightforward, but turned out to be multifaceted. Early on, I wondered why I hadn't heard of "whole life" insurance policies or "income annuities" before. By 2013, I had worked in accounting, banking, staffing, and even run for United States Congress—but I still had a lot to learn!

Over the two and a half years I worked there, I fell in and out of love with insurance. I finally got to the professional distance phase when I left the firm to start my fiduciary wealth and time management firm, the Jason Howell Company. With the option to sell insurance or instead sell advice and refer the implementation to others, I chose the latter. Now, without receiving commissions for insurance products, I am happily calculating coverage for my clients and referring them to independent licensed insurance agents.

Many of the clients I work with are in the "accumulation" phase of life, meaning they have both protecting and saving to do. I typically recommend they separate their death benefit needs from their savings goals. This will manifest in a high amount of (death benefit) term life insurance while allowing them to pay off debt, save, or otherwise repurpose hundreds of dollars.

Michael Feinberg, a Chartered Financial Consultant® and area vice president with Arthur J. Gallagher & Co., says,

> *Often, protection needs are at their highest when available funds are at their lowest—at the outset of a promising family and career, when there are mouths to feed, a mortgage to pay, and often decades of income being relied upon. In these situations, high face amount, 20-30-year level term insurance will give you the most bang for your buck and not leave you uninsured during the prime of your career.*

How Much Life Insurance Do You Need?

I can't know that, but I can share with you one way I work it out with clients. One way to calculate life insurance needs is through something called "Human Life Value." You calculate this by taking your salary, discounting how much you spend for personal needs, and multiplying it by the number of years your dependents expect you to work. You then calculate the present value of those future cash flows (your salary discounted for your absence), and that's probably how much insurance you need. In fact, if you really wanted to get into the weeds, you could adjust for inflation, which is essentially the future pay raises your dependents/family would also miss out on.

For example, if new client Jane is a forty-five-year-old who makes $100000 with twenty-two years until she retires at age sixty-seven, then her total salary for the next twenty-two years would equal $2.2 million ($100,000 multiplied by 22). But this wouldn't account for salary increases over those twenty-two years, nor would it account for the cost savings of her absence.

So, I choose a discount percentage, typically 30%, and establish a cost of living increase over the life. That would look like 70% of $100,000, or $70,000, and a 3% increase per year. The present value of that amount is approximately $1.1 million. This is less than the approximately $2.2 million Jane would have earned, had she lived, but this accounts for Jane not being around anymore. Added to that, we used a gross salary in this example, so the $1.1 million is fairly conservative, in that it's a little higher as a potential death benefit than necessary. When I make a recommendation to a client and their insurance agent, I usually round down or round up to the nearest $100,000 or even $500,000 of coverage. I've learned that buying life insurance is a little like buying fruit; cheaper dollar-for-dollar if you use round numbers.

There are different ways to analyze how much you need, but I don't find them to be worth the effort. For example, there's the "financial needs approach," which estimates your immediate expenses as a lump sum and your ongoing expenses based on an estimated investment return from a lump sum investment of your life insurance benefits. It is wonderful arithmetic, but in many ways, more calculation than is necessary for a number that will likely be wrong. Life insurance doesn't have to be complicated. The underwriters are calculating what you qualify for using a modified earnings multiple/human value approach, and that method will get you close to what your beneficiaries will need. Working through the application process with an independent insurance agent you can trust will take you the rest of the way towards a final benefit amount.

How Much Does This All Cost?

Life insurance costs will depend in large part on three factors: your age, your health, and your desired death benefit. Regarding your age and health, neither tend to get better (typically, we get older and more out of shape as time goes by), so life insurance is always "on sale" today. The third factor, how much you need, depends on a calculation we made in the previous section.

You will see advertisements on television for Select Quote that usually begin with, "A forty-year-old man just got hundreds of thousands of life insurance death benefit for less than a dollar a day!" What they don't say in the ad is how long that forty-year-old man is covered. (It's on the TV screen, but you have to look for it.) Usually, the man is covered for a ten-year term. That means, after ten years, that rate they offered on TV (a rate that's impossible to compare, because the only factors we have are age and gender) will go up drastically. So, let me add a major fourth factor to the cost of insurance: how long you would like to be covered. And, of course, this doesn't take into account the higher costs of buying permanent insurance, i.e., insurance that will last at least until age 100 and may have a savings component. Those prices can be hundreds of dollars more per month, because you pay for more than *just* the insurance.

The least expensive life insurance tends to start with what you get from your employer. Your benefits package may include a flat $50,000 term policy or some multiple of your earnings as a death benefit. For example, if you earn $100,000 per year, your employer may pay a death benefit of $100,000 (1x) or $200,000 (2x) to your beneficiary on your behalf. In this scenario, your employer is the owner of the policy, you are the insured, and whomever you designate is the beneficiary. Oftentimes, an employer who offers such a benefit for free will also offer you additional coverage if you pay for some of it. Talk with your human resources representative for details.

There's no way to predict how much life insurance will cost without knowing your age, your health, your desired death benefit, how long you would like it to last, and whether you would prefer to have a forced savings component. But those are the major factors that insurance companies, with their underwriters and actuaries, measure when offering you coverage.

CHAPTER 16 TAKEAWAYS

Not everyone who *can* sell you life insurance knows a lot about life insurance. How long the insurance is in place makes a big difference. It can be used as a bridge to a future time when you have similar resources saved up. Consider using the "Human Life Value" approach to calculate how much death benefit your dependents should expect. This factors your earning potential, which is approximately your income multiplied by the number of years you expect to keep working.

Every one of you has a life that matters to maybe 1,000 other people. Life insurance will not prevent you from dying or even dying young, but it will offset the financial burden of your passing for these people that care about you. By how much is up to you.

First, talk to your employer about how much life insurance coverage you have and how much money it would take to buy some more. Then, talk with an independent insurance agent (one not affiliated with a firm that advertises on TV) and compare what they could offer to what you can buy from work. An online way to compare is to search for life insurance; you'll see links to NerdWallet.com, PolicyGenius.com, or SelectQuote.com.

Actionable Strategies:

- How much life insurance do you need? You can use a simplified "Human Life Value" approach of multiplying your income by the number of years you intend to work
- Compare your estimated life insurance need with how much you are getting from work
- Ask your HR folks how much it costs to add additional life insurance coverage

- Contact an independent insurance agent who has access to multiple insurance carriers to request a quote
- Compare the value of an additional independent insurance policy with additional insurance you can buy from your employer

ID PROTECTION & RESTORATION

I used to love the *Dukes of Hazzard* when I was little. Bo and Luke Duke were my favorite anti-heroes (somehow, they could make a car jump in the air and land without crashing). The show was fairly repetitive: Bo and Luke would do something to irritate Boss Hogg, and Sheriff Roscoe P. Coltrane would chase them. Sheriff Coltrane would get close to catching them and Enos (of, "Enos, you dipstick") would somehow screw up the arrest. The episodes I hated the most would vary from the formula by having some people impersonate the Duke boys and commit a real crime. It would take a full episode (sometimes two) for the Duke boys to clear their name. Considering that I would cry during commercials, waiting an entire day to watch how a case of stolen identity got figured out was torture.

Having your identification stolen can pose many risks to your personal finances. It's also a heck of a waste of time trying to prove you are who you are to the institutions you depend on: banks, the Social Security office, U.S. State Department, etc. Unlike other categories of risk management, you have both prevention and cure options in this category.

PERSONAL EXPERIENCE

Generation X may have been the last generation of college students to write their Social Security numbers on papers and exams. It's hard to believe now, but I remember doing that on my freshman and sophomore assignments. My, how the world has changed since the pre-internet early 1990s!

Now, I guard my Social Security number fairly well; I don't even have it in my wallet (yes, I used to carry it in my wallet). I carry my ID and credit cards there, of course, but I don't even keep my wallet in my back pocket. (It ruins pants and makes it too easy for pickpockets, I think.) I'm part of a small percentage of people who pay for an ID protection service. (I really do it because it's tied to some other legal protection perks that I wouldn't have otherwise.) Most of the IT people I speak to believe in the benefits of paying for credit monitoring or alerts; some say our IDs have already been stolen anyway.

PROFESSIONAL EXPERIENCE

I usually talk to clients about the option of purchasing ID protection service from a company that offers restoration services. These services can help with the costs of recovering your ID and whatever money was stolen. Most of the time, if money was taken from your bank account or charged to your credit card, your banks will reimburse you, but it's nice to have a service that may cover the cost of an investigator or attorney.

I caution clients about their social media accounts, especially how they document new purchases or when they plan to travel. Becoming a little less transparent in these areas can help to protect the physical safety of your stuff.

Passwords are also an important piece of the pie. I suggest something that my IT friends recommend, which is some sort of password manager. Password managers, like 1password, Dashlane, and LastPass, can take the responsibility of managing a bunch of passwords away from you. Besides the relief, it will also make it a lot harder for someone to guess and steal your passwords. The hardest thing for me is the idea of essentially giving up all my login info to one company, but that's what the IT folks (i.e., the folks who deal with stolen passwords and electronic security breaches all the time) recommend.

Prevention

Besides purchasing one of the ID protection services that promises to protect your identification, there are a number of things you can do to reduce your risk:

- Don't just write down your Social Security number when asked to on forms. I remember writing down my full Social Security number at the top of my papers and exams in the early 1990s to "verify" it was from me. Looking back, it seems crazy. Our professors could have stolen many, many identities, but thankfully, that rarely (if ever) happened. Keep your Social Security number to yourself as much as possible. There's no real reason to keep your Social Security card in your wallet (if you even know where it is).

- Speaking of social, be wary of your use of social media. None other than Kim Kardashian, one of the queens of the medium, learned the hard way that broadcasting your location can get you into trouble.[1] If you're going out of town, think very hard about whether that's information to share with everyone who has access to your social media profiles. Remember that listing your favorite movies, books, your dog's name, etc. are great tips for the wrong people trying to guess your passwords.

- Review your credit history at least annually—it's free. You may have access to a credit score with one of your credit cards, but seeing the entire report is something you can get for free from each of the major credit reporting agencies: Equifax, Experian, and Transunion. Just go to AnnualCreditReport.com to get yours. I often suggest people pull their credit reports in January, since it's the easiest time to remember. You could also use your birthday as a reminder. "Hey, I'm forty-five! It's time to check out that credit." Or something like that.

- Consider initiating a "credit freeze," which will prevent all access to your credit report unless you personally get rid of the freeze. If monitoring your credit reports annually isn't enough, this will supposedly lock it down from all applications for credit—even your own. If you like to sign up for department store cards (perish the thought!) to receive that 10% discount on today's purchases, a

1   Schnurr, Samantha, "Ambush, Gunpoint and Robbery: A Timeline of Kim Kardashian's Traumatic Week in Paris," E! Online, October 3, 2016, https://www. eonline.com/de/news/799296/ambush-gunpoint-and-robbery-a-timeline-of-kim-kardashian-s-traumatic-week-in-paris, 2019.

credit freeze will cause you a lot of hassle at the counter. But if, as is recommended, you apply for new credit infrequently, this method will serve you.

- Keep records of your debit card, credit card, driver's license, and passport numbers in a separate safe place. There used to be an impressive American Express commercial in the 1980s that sold new customers on the idea that if you lost your wallet while travelling, they could replace your ID and credit cards while you were away. What a great service! I suppose now that everything's connected, giving your banker a Social Security number will give you some access, but without some other ID (which may have been lost with your credit cards), the burden of proof is on you.

- Sign up for mobile alerts and/or fraud alerts. You can get mobile alerts every time there's a transaction on your account—no big deal. A fraud alert is a much bigger deal, because you sign up for it with the credit bureaus (Experian, Equifax, and Transunion). A fraud alert stays on for seven years. Unlike a credit freeze, if someone applies for credit, they won't be immediately denied; instead, they'll have to go through some extra steps to prove their identification. Whether you need to pay for this fraud alert service depends on your state's rules and whether someone has already stolen your identity.

Cure

Should your data be breached in any way, the Federal Trade Commission has a forty-page report to help walk citizens through how to react.[2]

Some highlights include:

What to do right away:

- Call the department that handles fraud for whatever institution was part of the breach and let them you've been hacked, or, as the FTC puts it, "someone has stolen your identity"
- Freeze your accounts and change your password
- Place a fraud alert on your credit reporting bureaus like Equifax, Transunion, and Experian (when your identity is stolen, fraud alerts are free)
- Go to IdentityTheft.gov and follow the prompts to create a report
- Take your identity theft report and make another report with the police

What to do next:

- Start repairing the damage
- Close new accounts at each business where accounts were opened in your name
- Work with the businesses to remove false charges on your accounts

---

2   "Identity Theft: A Recovery Plan," Federal Trade Commission, https://www. consumer.ftc.gov/articles/pdf-0009_identitytheft_a_recovery_plan.pdf, 2019.

- Work with the credit reporting bureaus to correct your credit report

In everything you do, take notes: who you spoke with, when you talked with them, and what they said. Your identity is your reputation, and though this will take work if it happens to you, it's worth getting your reputation back. Though most financial institutions promise to reimburse clients for any losses incurred, the timeline for those reimbursements may vary. In addition, a loss of proof of identification can make it difficult to receive new proof of identification.

Contracting with an ID protection company may not cover all security breaches of organizations that have record of your ID, but they may assist with credit and identification restoration. This kind of risk management is about protecting your money and your time. Having a "friend" at the time of ID theft can be reassuring. Many of these vendors provide $1,000,000 of coverage expenses associated with regaining your identification. Some also promise to reimburse you for fraudulent charges, but typically your bank will do that anyway (though reimbursement times can vary).

CHAPTER 17 TAKEAWAYS

Your personal identification may have already been stolen, and is likely available on whatever the dark web is supposed to be. It's difficult to keep up with hackers, but there are things you can do to not help them. Protect your Social Security number by not sharing it unless it's absolutely required. (You will know if you don't fill in the blanks automatically and your doctor or dentist comes back with the form.) And with social media, decide carefully how much you are willing to share versus how much you just want to follow. There are over a billion people on Facebook alone. Lack of your data won't hurt their ability to sell their database. Monitoring your credit report at least once a year, perhaps in January, is a great habit. Better yet, putting a freeze on your credit by requesting one from all three of the credit reporting agencies will take credit fraud almost entirely off the table for would-be hackers. Lastly, if your data is breached and used, take immediate action. Report the breach to credit bureaus, the Federal Trade Commission, and file a report with IdentityTheft.gov. It's your good name and you need to protect it.

Actionable Strategies:
Before something bad is done with your ID or data:

- Safeguard your Social Security number by...
  » Not leaving your Social Security card in your purse or wallet
  » Not writing it down just because there's a space for it on a form (use the last 4 digits)

- Initiate a credit freeze. Contact each credit bureau and request a free freeze

- Protect your data. Limit sharing your location, favorite books, CDs, and artists on social media
- Sign up for mobile alerts. Contact your banks and insurance companies to ping you
- Make copies of your driver's license, passport, credit and debit card numbers
- Create complicated passwords or use a password/encryption service
- Sign up for one of the ID restoration (protection) services

And if your ID or data has already been compromised:

- Call the fraud department for whichever firm (i.e., bank) lost money and let them know
- Initiate a credit freeze (since you probably didn't earlier)
- Go to IdentityTheft.gov to report your identity breach.
- File your report with the police. It seems weird, but will help your case later
- Clean up. Work with institutions to close false accounts and confirm your ID

CHAPTER 18

MEDICAL INSURANCE

I think health insurance should be called "life insurance," because you're trying to protect your life. And what's now called life insurance should be called "death insurance," since you're trying to protect against death. Alas, I guess "death insurance" would be a little harder for insurance agents to sell.

Medical insurance is on again/off again as legally required coverage (depending on who's president of the United States). Legality aside, medical expenses (pre-retirement and post-retirement) have the potential to become the largest expenses within a household budget. Comprehensive medical (health) insurance coverage allows for expensive medical procedures and preventative medical visits to manage the costs of healthy living. Finding a place in your budget for medical insurance coverage makes sense (and likely dollars).

For the longest while, health insurance was just something we got at work. Little did I imagine how controversial it was and would become in my lifetime. It's easy for health insurance to not "be a thing" as long as we're connected to employers that offer it (either directly or through a family member). But health, like death, is an equalizer. More people go bankrupt because of a lack of health insurance than almost any other cause. Even though losing a job ranks high on the list of reasons for bankruptcy, the concurrent loss of medical benefits for some can be financially catastrophic compared to the loss of their income.

Our human status is what empowers and limits us at the same time. When something goes wrong with our bodies, our desire to repair it will take first priority. Practically speaking, this health maintenance is another category where some prevention is possible.

PERSONAL EXPERIENCE

Because I started working full-time at eighteen years old, I had my own health insurance coverage early in life. I was lucky enough not to get sick very often, so I mostly accrued sick leave at work. I did visit the doctor for an annual physical, and I saw my dentist every six months. These preventative measures were fully covered by medical insurance plans, so I was fortunate. By the time I became a full-time entrepreneur, I was a married man, so attaining medical coverage was as easy as having my wife add coverage to her medical plan at work.

As the years have gone by, group plans available to employers (which I have now become) have been getting more attractive. Going forward, I will need to compare what my wife's employer offers to what I can purchase on the open market.

PROFESSIONAL EXPERIENCE

Health and medical insurance are not usually topics clients expect to spend a lot of time on with their financial planner unless they are near or over age sixty-five. Currently, as you approach age sixty-five, you'd better have a solid understanding of the rules around Medicare (and all of its parts). But what if you are well under the Medicare age (as most of my clients tend to be)? My clients are usually given access to a range of options through their employers, including such ominous acronyms as HMO, PPO, and HSA. Deciphering between the benefits of employer-based health coverage plans takes time (which is a good thing, because that means there are options). If you don't have access to employer-based medical coverage through your own employer or that of a spouse or a parent, then you are left comparing plans on the state or federal healthcare exchange.

Typically, I will ask to review the medical care policy from my client's employer and go through the deductibles, co-pays, and maternity/paternity care coverage options. When working with a married couple, I will walk through benefits offered by each spouse to determine whether they should maintain separate coverage or combine. When young children are involved, the cost of family coverage can vary widely between plans offered to each spouse. Most employer-based plans are **managed care** plans (plans that create a discounted financial relationship between the insured and a defined pool of medical practitioners). You recognize managed care organizations in the form of Health Maintenance Organizations (HMOs), Preferred Provider Organizations (PPOs) and Point of Service (POS) plans. **HMO plans** require you to work with a general practitioner (family doctor) first, who will see you and make a recommendation for a specialist in the shared network of medical practitioners. **PPO plans** are typically the more expensive option, but they are popular because you can go outside of the network of medical practitioners and still be reimbursed (albeit for a lesser amount). This plan works well for people who have had a set of doctors for years and really don't want to change those just because they changed employers (or their employers changed insurance providers). **POS plans** work kind of like a hybrid of HMO and PPO by requiring a general doctor referral before seeing a specialist, but allowing you to go "out of network" for a small increase in cost. The final plans I typically see are the **High Deductible Health Plans (HDHP)**.

As of this writing, parents can maintain coverage on adult children under the age of twenty-six. That decision often depends on whether their children have jobs that offer medical coverage. Wherever I can find savings for clients matters, and reducing coverage from "family" to "married" is an easy place to look.

Prevention

By the time we're forty, we start noticing the things we didn't do well with our bodies. For example, I'm still managing a rolled ankle that got hurt playing basketball twelve years ago. I didn't have it looked at until a year after the injury, and as of today, I've never been consistent about the rehab; hence, it still hurts sometimes. Healthcare needs can dramatically affect post-retirement life plans, but healthy living begins decades before.

How you nourish and train your body will affect your lifestyle. Some of the most prevalent diseases in America, like pneumonia and arthritis, are hard to predict and protect against. Others, which attack the cardiovascular (heart disease) and endocrine system (diabetes) are preventable and affected by our lifestyle. You may contract a disease or have an accident that comes out of nowhere, but just like in other parts of financial planning, in health planning, it makes fiscal sense to control the areas you can.

That said, we will all need health coverage sooner or later, so the purpose of this section is to highlight what you should look for. Health/medical insurance (much like other forms of risk management) is not designed to cover every single injury. It's meant to cover the health-related emergencies you can't afford. In fact, the debate around which things are covered was and is a major point of contention between those who supported the **2010 Patient Protection and Affordable Care Act** and those who did not. Medical science, no matter how much we abuse our bodies, will likely keep us alive longer than we expect. Quality of life is what we have to worry about.

If you're like me, you don't look your age. Something about the Boomer and previous generations generally seemed to look more "adult" than those of us in later generations. Besides grief, the fastest way to "look old" is to lose your health. There are only a few promises I made to myself as a child and young adult:

- Workout at the gym on a regular basis
- Save comic books for my children
- Save a kitchen drawer for candy bars exclusively

The first two promises I kept; the third, I broke (I'm still getting over it). Working out has given me another category of goals to target at random times in my life. There's no reason to look your best when traveling with your in-laws on vacation, but I use the ten days I spend with them annually as a reason to get in the best shape of the year. Restricting sugar intake or waking up my workout routine is a positive shock to my lifestyle. It reminds me of youth, which is typically associated with health, which is something I'd like to maintain.

Cure

The most drastic use of medical insurance is for unexpected emergencies. Long-term (or I should say long-earned) diseases like heart disease or Type 2 diabetes can creep up on you over the years. A terrible car accident can happen in a moment. A sudden diagnosis of cancer can change a life forever. In these cases, having medical insurance coverage can mean the difference between solvency and bankruptcy.

According to the 1986 **Emergency Medical Treatment and Active Labor Act**, all hospital emergency rooms are required to examine (and typically provide care to) patients, regardless of their ability to pay. A 2008 *Washington Post* article titled "Equal Treatment for the Uninsured? Don't Count on It" describes the subtle and not-so-subtle differences in care depending on whether patients are covered by an insurance policy. (Notably, this article was written before the 2010 **Affordable Care Act**.) Though there will undoubtedly be more changes to the healthcare system by the time you read this book, it strikes a professional services chord when the articles quotes a physician saying, "No other professionals—lawyers, plumbers, accountants—provide uncompensated services to one-fifth of their clients."

The lesson is that you *could* get care without medical insurance coverage, but why risk your physical and fiscal health? In the United States, we have some of the best health-related technology in the world and some of the best educated health professionals. As of 2018, we have no better mechanism for paying for the services of medical professionals like nurses, radiologists, endocrinologist, and doctors than with medical/health insurance.

What Do I Look for in Medical Insurance Coverage?

The easiest thing to look for is how much of a deductible you'll have to pay before the insurance will kick in: the higher the deductible, the lower the monthly premium. Some insurance companies have a maximum "out of pocket" cost, after which medical insurance coverage kicks in for the rest.

The amount you pay for visits, whether they are emergency room, urgent care, specialist, or regular office visits, makes a difference. If pregnancy is in your future, either directly or indirectly, taking a look at the cost of delivery will be an important step in your baby-planning journey.

Insurance that will work best for you and your family will depend on a few important factors:

- Whether your favorite doctor will be covered 100% or only partially
- How much of the prescriptions you are on will be covered
- Whether you have a medical condition that requires frequent trips to a specialist

There are other factors, but these will be critical when open enrollment comes along and you are asked to choose between the alphabet soup of HMO, PPO, POS, or even EPO (Exclusive Provider Option) plans.

CHAPTER 18 TAKEAWAYS

Whether legally required or not, health insurance is the kind of protection that is not worth skipping. The younger you are, the more powerful you feel, but medical emergencies are too common not to leverage the protection of millions of other insurance plan participants. Like most insurance coverage, the least expensive and highest value is typically found in a group plan that can be offered at work. (So, where you work has an important role to play in your medical coverage.) Perhaps not-so-coincidentally, the two largest causes of personal bankruptcy come from medical expenses and job (income) loss.

When evaluating health insurance, consider plan types and which will work best for you:

- Health Maintenance Organization (HMO) requires you to choose a primary care physician from their list and seek his/her recommendations for specialists. These plans are typically lower cost, but you have to work within their network of doctors.

- Preferred Provider Organization (PPO) gives you a choice of "in-network" or "out-of-network" doctors, but the in-network doctors are less expensive. Regardless, you don't need a referral to see a specialist. Your monthly premium will cost a little more.

- Point of Service Plans (POS) are similar to PPO, but encourage you to go through a primary care physician for recommendations to specialists (or pay more for out of network doctors).

- High Deductible Health Plans (HDHP) trade a lower monthly premium for a greater contribution to your deductible before the benefits kick in. If you have a long time until retirement and are relatively healthy, this can be a good option. This type of plan also allows you to invest in a Health Savings Account.

- Health Savings Accounts (HSAs) are portable savings vehicles that can be used to save money that is earmarked for medical care any time in the future.

Actionable Strategies:

- Talk with your doctor about the benefits of reducing your sugar intake
- Talk with your doctor about your ability to engage in aerobic and anaerobic exercise
- Have your doctor conduct an annual comprehensive physical
- Have your dentist conduct a cleaning once every six months (x-rays once per year)
- During open enrollment, ensure your preferred medical providers are priced in-network

CAR INSURANCE

Insuring a car involves more than protecting the property. It also includes protecting against damages, injuries, and potential lawsuits that may result from using the property. Your car insurance has liability or lawsuit coverage, which protects you from car accident lawsuit; the question is how much.

A general or "umbrella" liability policy is an additional layer of liability coverage for lawsuit damages that are higher than your car coverage. It also provides coverage for attorney's fees or other defense costs for frivolous lawsuits that can still cost you money (even if you win the case). You will typically purchase this kind of policy through the same company that has your car insurance. You know the names of the companies that offer home and auto and liability/umbrella insurance. (They are the ones that advertise on TV all of the time.) You probably have at least one policy with one of these firms. Talk to your agent about the benefits and what it might cost to add layers of protection.

PERSONAL EXPERIENCE

I have never been too interested in reading my car insurance policy. When I was younger and on my parents' policies, I was just happy they were "taking care of it." As I got older, I was just happy to get a "good deal" (not that I knew what that was). When I became a financial planner, I started reading policies for clients and asking questions about my own.

My networking group included a property insurance expert who worked for Liberty Mutual. He was kind of a genius when it came to property and casualty insurance. He eventually offered me a unique policy, where the liability coverage for the humans (me, my passengers, and anyone I might hit) was the same for the property, per accident. In my case, that number is $500,000. This is the same number for any uninsured motorists' accidents, people who may hit my car, injure me or my passengers, and not have their own coverage. My car coverage for two older cars is just under $200 per month.

PROFESSIONAL EXPERIENCE

New clients are often surprised that I am interested in seeing their car and home insurance policies. But these polices are critical to protecting their long-term financial plans, so even though I don't get paid to sell them insurance, I have an interest in recommending the right coverages. This is what clients pay for when they hire me for advice.

If you own a car, you have legal requirements for insurance coverage. But those requirements are the minimum standard, which do more to protect others than protect you or your family. Through a secure software program, I let my clients attach their car, home, and liability policies for review. For car insurance, I will look to confirm there is enough liability coverage to withstand the high end of a lawsuit, typically $250,000 per person or $500,000 per accident.

How Car Insurance Works

Reading a car insurance policy is not high on most people's bucket lists, but after reading a few, I've found that they can be quite interesting. Your car insurance policy has a Declarations Page ("DEC page," if you'd like to know the industry nickname). Besides your name and address as "the insured," you will also see your coverage details.

Choosing a car insurance plan is more than deciding between full coverage for your car and someone else's in an auto accident or just "liability" coverage, in case you don't care about fixing your car and just want to satisfy the law. Personal Auto Policies (PAP) have four standard parts:

- Liability Coverage
- Medical Expenses/Payments
- Uninsured Motorists
- Damage to Your Car

Liability Coverage

In the accounting world, "liability" is an important term. It speaks to what you owe. In the insurance world, it's a term to describe how much protection you will receive from the insurance company should you "owe" someone lots of money after losing a negligence lawsuit. Here, the insurance company is promising to cover not only the lawsuit, but also your legal costs. Not a bad deal, but they will only pay up to the limits you've selected in your policy. Now, stay awake here, because it's interesting.

The bodily injury liability is meant to cover the costs associated with you getting into an accident, injuring someone in the other car, and getting sued. When I look at policies for clients, I see most of them cover $100,000 of liability per person and $300,000 per accident. As the cost of a broken leg (or worse), and lawsuits for accidentally breaking someone's legs have increased, so has the recommended liability coverage. Instead of the typical $100000/$300,000, good agents now recommend liability coverage of $250,000 per person and $500,000 per accidents (or $250,000/$500,000).

In addition to bodily injury, you will also see property damage liability, which is meant to cover the cost of damaging someone else's car. The default I see in the Washington, D.C. area is $50,000. That's a big number for a typical car accident, but that's if you're just bumping into another person's car. As humans, we also have the capacity to run into lampposts, buildings, homes, and to total other cars. Most major cities have a large number of luxury vehicles which, if totaled, could cost at least $60,000, if not over $100,000, to replace. The cost of increasing coverage from $50,000 to $100,000 in property damage liability will likely not be significant when it comes to your monthly premium. What you might see on your Declarations Page is a combined set of numbers like $250K/$500K/$50K, with that last number representing the property damage. You may also see one number that covers the total amount of liability. Just be sure you have an amount that makes sense for where you live and for your net worth.

Medical Expenses/Payments

This part of the policy can either be quite beneficial or not that useful, depending on your state and your medical insurance. It is meant to cover medical expenses (or even funeral expenses) incurred by you or your passengers or family members driving your car.

So, the first question I would ask is: Isn't this what my medical insurance is for? Yes, but it depends on whether your medical insurance covers you for auto accidents. Also, maybe your medical insurance does cover you, but there's a co-pay or deductible—this coverage would take care of those bills. Normally, I see clients have coverage amounts between $5,000 and $10,000 on this line item.

Find out whether your medical insurance covers car accidents or accidents. Also, some "no-fault" states require personal injury protection (PIP) insurance; you may be required to use that coverage before touching the medical payments portion of your car insurance. (No fault states include: Florida, Hawaii, Kansas, Kentucky, Massachusetts, Michigan, Minnesota, New Jersey, New York, North Dakota, Pennsylvania, and Utah.) Consider the rules of your state and the limits on your medical insurance as you make decisions about the medical expenses/payments portion of your auto policy.

Uninsured Motorists

Uninsured motorist bodily injury sounds like it covers a lawsuit stemming from an uninsured motorist getting hurt—it's not. It's designed to cover costs for you (insured), family members, and any of your passengers that get hurt by an uninsured driver or a hit-and-run driver who is at fault. This ensures that everyone is covered, even if the somewhat small percentage of people driving around without car insurance run into you. This coverage pays what the other person's insurance would have paid, had they been adequately insured. I typically end up recommending similar amounts of coverage here as I do for liability coverage: $250K/$500K.

Damage to Your Car

Don't forget about your own car. Because car insurance is legally required in just about every state, the easy thing to do is get the minimum coverage required to satisfy the law. All that does is protect other people instead of protecting you, your family, and those who trust you (your passengers).

In this section, you have two coverage options: collision and comprehensive. Collision will cover damage to your car if you are in an accident, regardless of who is at fault. Of course, if it's not your fault, then the other person's insurance will pay for the damage to your car. Comprehensive covers losses that don't stem from hitting other cars, like hitting a deer, storm damage, breaking a windshield, etc. Protecting your car no matter what will, of course, drive up the cost of your overall insurance, so managing the use of a deductible is something to discuss with the insurance agent.

Your deductible is how much you have to cover before any insurance covers your car's damage. Typically, the higher amount this is, the lower your insurance premiums (payments) are. Most deductibles I've seen have been $500. That's probably as much of a payment you want to fork over, should you get into a car accident, but if you have a savings account that allows you to afford more, like $1,000, talk to your insurance agent about how much that could reduce your premium.

Gap Insurance

This supplemental insurance is designed to cover the risk that you might total (suffer a total loss or theft) your car while you still owe more money to a lender than the value of your car. This will often happen because your car depreciates faster than you can pay down a loan (especially for a new car). If you own your car "free and clear," don't worry about gap insurance.

Gabriel Cruz, an agent with a large insurance carrier says,

> *Gap insurance is good if you are upside down on a car loan. So, if, for example, you rolled a previous loan into a new one, you are, of course, going to start out owing far more than the car is worth. In that case, gap coverage is a great move. Never get gap coverage from your auto financier. It is always a fraction of the cost when done through your insurer.*

What Does All This Typically Cost?

The biggest factors that will affect what you pay for car insurance on an annual basis are your age, driving record, the type of car you're insuring, and your credit score. (Yes, I said your credit score. What fascinates me about financial planning is how inter-related everything is.) In this case, your credit score is used to help evaluate how you are likely to drive. If your car insurance costs more than a couple hundred dollars per month, you better have an expensive car, have a bad driving record/credit score, or be under the age of twenty-five. If you can't say yes to any of those, you might want to compare prices.

CHAPTER 19 TAKEWAYS

Car insurance is only boring if you never have to use it. It can get quite interesting when you actually have a car accident, and it can drastically affect your life if you are sued due to an accident. Your finances may survive losing a lawsuit with the right coverage. This is when purchasing the minimum required doesn't help you achieve your goals. Knowing that there are so many car accidents on a daily basis—and how distracted we all are—car insurance is necessary for protecting your long-term financial goals.

Actionable Strategies:

- Increase your liability coverage to at least match your net worth
- Confirm that your medical insurance covers car accidents
- If you live in a "no-fault" state, invest in a personal injury policy (PIP)
- Increase your uninsured motorist coverage to protect yourself and passengers
- Evaluate the cost of increasing your deductible to afford comprehensive coverage

HOMEOWNER'S INSURANCE

As with car insurance, reading your homeowner's insurance policy is not the most fun you can have on a weekend—but it's important to protect where you sleep every night. If you're like most people, the majority of the things you own live there too, and the most important people in your life live with you and visit you at your home. You not only want to keep your possessions safe, you also want to ensure that you are safe from financial loss in case the people who visit your home are accidentally injured. Like car insurance policies, homeowner's insurance coverage is usually sold as a combination policy that insures your physical home, the property inside, and some of the liability you might face due to a lawsuit. To be more specific, most basic homeowner's insurance policies have a standard (or basic) set of "perils" that they cover. (Insurance companies define **perils** as any event that causes a financial loss.) Policies either name all of the perils they cover or specifically name the perils they will not cover.

PERSONAL EXPERIENCE

There are many reasons why a person living in a home wouldn't pay attention to homeowner's insurance. When I first became a homeowner, it was because my father had divorced and needed another co-signer for the mortgage refinance. When we later sold that house to buy a more expensive one (in the run up to the financial crisis, no less), I was again added as a co-signer (dragging my feet the entire way). I never read the policy; luckily, we never needed to use it.

I aspire to become a homeowner, but as of now, I rent a town-house with my family. We have renter's coverage for personal property loss up to about $25,000 and liability of about $300,000. We have some coverage set aside if we are unable to live in our home and incur expenses (like meals, hotel costs, etc.). That amount of coverage is $5,150. Like most insurance, that's one I hope to never have to use (especially with two kids). There are add-ons to my renter's policy that are similar to what can be added to a policy for a home you own: electronics coverage, credit card forgery, sewer backup, and a personal articles policy (for named items, like my wife's engagement ring and art). I added an electronics policy to cover my phones and laptops. The neat thing about this policy is that it's $4 per month while I was paying $12.99 for each cell phone in my house (mine and my wife's). If you bought the insurance on your cell phone, chances are the vendor is Asurion and chances are awfully good you are paying more than $12.99 per month per phone. I know this because the day I decided to increase my coverage with my now friend at Liberty Mutual, was the day I received notice that the price for Asurion was going up to $15.99 per month (per phone). They made it easy. Much like general liability insurance, my "electronics" policy was only offered to me because I had a relationship with Liberty Mutual. Those ads on TV about discounts and perks for singing up for multiple policies with one carrier? In my experience, they've been true.

All of this protection currently costs $220 per year.

PROFESSIONAL EXPERIENCE

I request very specific information from my new clients about their homeowner's (or renter's) policies, but I give them an out—if they just send me their policies, I'll read them. I normally just receive the declaration page, which shows me the categories of coverage they've signed up for. What I tend to look for is whether the value of their home, as estimated by the most recent tax assessment, is equal to the coverage they would receive from their insurance company, should it be completely destroyed. Sometimes, I'll see that the coverage has a good estimate of what it would cost to rebuild the house based on market value, and other times, I'll see the coverage includes the cost of rebuilding the land. Which is impossible. So, a key here is to ensure my clients aren't paying for the expensive value of the land, but only for the structures they are actually trying to insure.

One named peril I might have them add to their policy is water and sump pump back coverage, since most basic policies don't automatically cover that. No basic policy covers the cost of a flood from a natural disaster (more on this topic later), but if a toilet backs up and causes your basement to flood, water backup coverage could be well worth the extra monthly payment.

How Homeowner's Insurance Works

To begin to understand how homeowner's insurance works, it helps to read the many parts in your homeowner's policy. If you give it a skim on the declaration page, you will find coverage separated by letters, typically coverages A through F:

A. "Dwelling" refers to the amount of coverage for the physical structure of your home
B. "Other structures" refers to detached structures like a garage or pool
C. "Personal property" refers to the property in your home
D. "Loss of use" includes any additional expenses incurred when living away from your home
E. "Liability" refers to coverage to protect against lawsuits brought on by other people
F. "Medical payments" refers to payments you make to others for minor injuries

Dwelling

Coverage A, dwelling coverage, may be the easiest to understand. The number here signifies how much you will be reimbursed should your home be damaged or destroyed. The complicated (and critical) part is *how* your home was damaged, because that also determines whether you will be reimbursed. Most home-owners are sold a basic policy where the perils are named, so you know exactly what is covered (for example, fire, lightening, volcanic eruption, smoke, explosion, etc.). If your homeowner policy is "open perils," than it will list what's excluded instead of what's covered. For your home's structure, you may have a broad policy that will cover almost any kind of damage, but for the other sections, it could be "named perils" or more limited.

How much coverage you need for your dwelling is calculated based on the value of your home. (Whether it's the market value or the tax assessed value all depends on what the insurance agent relied upon when writing up your policy.) Take a look at the "additions" portion of your latest tax assessment. This line item refers to what was built on the land you live on. This is what dwelling is supposed to cover—essentially the cost to repair or rebuild your home if damaged or destroyed. If it's a home built within the past forty years or so, the replacement value will be pretty darn close to the market value (or, at least, it should be).

Your insurance agent might have a harder time figuring out coverage for a really old or ornate home, when the cost to rebuild is higher than the market value. Your "additions" tax assessment could be close to the market value, but still not equal the cost to rebuild the entire structure if it was destroyed.

If you are concerned about the true cost to rebuild your house, the most accurate test is to hire a home inspector. The home inspector will look at the outside and the inside of your home to make an accurate assessment of its value. You can then use that assessment to increase or decrease your dwelling coverage.

Of all of the categories on your homeowner's insurance policy, dwelling is the one that does what you would expect—protects your house and keeps you physically safe.

Other Structures

This coverage keeps any structures on your property that are not attached to your home safe, like an unattached garage, shed, pool, special landscaping, etc. (Note that the ground isn't insured; just the landscaping and pools are covered here if they are "in-ground." Above-ground pools will more likely be covered by the personal property portion of your policy.) The amount of coverage is limited to 10% of the dwelling coverage, so that makes the dwelling coverage all the more important. If your agent sells you $500,000 of dwelling coverage, then your other structures will be limited to $50,000. That may be enough or it may not; knowing how the numbers work will help you plan ahead!

Personal Property

I have always found this coverage quirky. Personal property is general coverage to protect your stuff if it's lost, stolen, or damaged. The blanket coverage amount is limited to 50% of your dwelling coverage amount. It even covers your stuff if you are not in your home, or if someone else's stuff is in your home and gets destroyed. The quirky part is that seemingly anything that would be really valuable is typically excluded or limited in this policy. So, if you have a $500,000 house, your default personal property coverage is $250,000. But your pets (or any animals) are usually excluded, as is rented property. The protection for other common bigger ticket items is severely limited: any cash you have lying around ($200), jewelry ($1,500), silverware and guns ($2,500). What else would you likely spend, in this case, $250,000 on?

The answer is things you wouldn't ever think of, like your bed, your fridge, or your dining room table. You aren't covered for wear and tear, but if it's destroyed by fire, you're covered.

Loss of Use

This coverage reminds me of the auto insurance coverage of a rental car when you "lose the use" of your car while it's being repaired. The last time I had a fender bender and had to rent a car while mine was being repaired, I didn't want to give it back! For homeowner's insurance, this coverage will help you pay for a hotel while you are displaced and any other normal living expenses that being put out by the loss of use of your home costs you (most notably, the ability to cook). You are limited in total to 20% of your dwelling coverage. In the example, if your dwelling coverage is $500,000, your loss of use coverage will total $100,000. Knowing that, can you stay at the Four Seasons, dining on caviar while your home is being repaired? That's not likely, but check with your policy and your insurance agent.

Liability

It's scary to think about hosting a party for friends, or one of your kid's friends, and someone getting hurt—badly. Lawsuits are almost always at least six figures, and when you're planning for the future, your emergency fund does not usually take potential lawsuits into account.

Lawsuits are the primary concern of the liability coverage portion of your homeowner's policy. It covers you and your fellow family members (residents) for personal liability due to neg-ligence. If someone comes over to your house and cheers for the New England Patriots while they destroy your favorite NFC football team, insurance is decidedly not going to cover you if you beat them up. But any accidental injury or property damage that a person incurs will more likely be covered. Everything I have ever read states that this coverage is restricted to a minimum of $100,000, but most policies I see are two or three times that amount. With medical costs ever increasing and the ubiquitous "pain and suffering" that personal injury attorneys are adept at outlining, it seems like anything less than a couple hundred thousand dollars is putting your net worth in jeopardy. If you lose a lawsuit and don't have enough coverage to pay the judgement, the remainder comes from you. Even as a renter, I have $300,000 worth of coverage in this area, and that's not including my supplemental coverage.

Medical Payments

Medical payments is the smallest amount on your declaration page because, in part, it's meant to cover smaller claims. For example, you are covered if someone trips on your steps and sprains a wrist. You are also covered if you are playing sports at a rec center and cause someone to roll an ankle. The key thing about this coverage is whether you are at fault or not, the policy will still cover you. Even though the amounts vary, I often see policy coverage here under $10,000.

Renter's Insurance

These plans are a lot like homeowner's insurance, except there is no coverage for the structure/building you live in. Like most insurance, there is often a deductible (in my case, $500) before any coverage kicks in. But, like homeowner's, there is loss of use coverage in case you have to stay someplace else if you can't stay in your apartment for some reason. There is personal property coverage for your things that are damaged in your home, but there is usually a limit for personal belongs damaged or destroyed outside of your home. My renter's insurance policy is where I added the electronics coverage.

CHAPTER 20 TAKEAWAYS

Protecting the safety of your home encompasses more than just the outer structure. With homeowner's insurance, you are also protecting most everything inside your home and safeguarding your emergency fund, should you be embroiled in a lawsuit. A safety tool that travels with you even if you're not at home is a smart one to have. If you own a home, you have coverage, but you may be overinsured or underinsured, depending on what you worry about happening the most. If you are worried about something that homeowner's insurance can keep safe, then call your agent to get it protected. You have bigger concerns than worrying about a lawsuit from trip and falls or a toilet backing up. Save your mental energy for bigger things.

Actionable Strategies:

- Compare the six categories mentioned here to your homeowner's policy
- Compare your annual home tax assessment "additions" value to the dwelling coverage; if there's more than a $100,000 discrepancy from the assessment, call your insurance agent
- Compare your liability coverage in your homeowner's policy to your car policy
- If you have flood insurance, set aside the cost of what could be a large deductible
- Consider the value of water and sump pump backup coverage as an addition
- Consider the value of electronics/home computer coverage as an addition

CHAPTER 21

LIABILITY (UMBRELLA) INSURANCE

Insurance is a "just in case" financial tool: Just in case you incur a loss, you want to leverage the payments of other policy holders to reimburse you. Umbrella insurance is extra liability insurance, and like all insurance, you hope you never need to use it. But it is there just in case the liability coverage you already have with your homeowner's (or renter's) and/or car insurance isn't enough to cover your loss.

PERSONAL EXPERIENCE

The first time I bought extra liability insurance must have been through a friend who was selling property and casualty insurance at a business networking event. He either did a good job or a bad job selling it, because I bought it, but I didn't really know what or why I was buying it. All I knew was that I trusted his expertise and it was better than having a relationship with an 800 number. He got me on the path to automatically paying for an umbrella policy whenever I switched carriers, so by the time I learned what an umbrella policy could do, I already had it.

Years later, at that same networking group, some of our members were sued for not letting a new member in. This being a volunteer business networking group, the lawsuit had little grounds, but few of those defendants had umbrella policies. Without such a policy and with the threat of having to defend themselves, they did the smart thing and each hired lawyers. Unfortunately, each of their lawyers cost them an up-front charge of $10,000 for the retainer. This is a charge that an umbrella policy would have saved them. This was one case where the supplemental insurance of umbrella policies actually stands out as primary: a lawsuit having nothing to do with either homes or cars. Through my friends, I learned an important lesson that I now share with my clients.

PROFESSIONAL EXPERIENCE

Most financial planners and advisers I know spend little time on property and casualty insurance. Traditionally, those policies didn't fall under the purview of my colleagues because plainly, they'd never sold them. What's fascinating about this industry is that most of the expertise offered is traditionally tied to the time when the products were sold, whether that's life insurance, stocks, or mutual funds. Even so-called "comprehensive financial planners" may skip the importance of home, car, and liability insurance out of career habit! As the phenomena of fee-only, fiduciary advisers/planners grows, you will hopefully see more professionals taking tools they have had to study through the

CERTIFIED FINANCIAL PLANNER™ programs, for example, into account, even though they do not get directly paid for it.

I ask my clients to send me their car, home, and separate liability insurance policies if they have them. This gives me an opportunity to review and total the amount of liability insurance coverage they currently have. If they are underinsured, I'll send them back to their insurance carrier to buy some more. It's a call that their insurance carriers love to receive. No, I don't get compensated to sell insurance, but I am compensated to give the best advice possible, and umbrella policies are part of keeping my clients safe.

How Umbrella Policies Work

You can't buy extra liability insurance unless you have liability insurance to start with. You have liability insurance built into your homeowner's/renter's policies and your care insurance policies.

Where do you buy an umbrella policy? Typically, the same insurance carrier where you have your car insurance. From an insurance carrier's point of view, the underlying liability coverage with your car insurance is a high-water mark for any particular lawsuit to overcome before the umbrella policy would have to kick in.

Logically speaking, most large lawsuits likely come from car accidents. We are far more likely to get into a car accident that causes bodily harm then for our house to get us into trouble (or our networking groups, for that matter). Perhaps this is why the insurance carriers typically require you to have your car insurance with them before they'll issue a supplemental policy. This allows them to set the requirements for liability coverage through your car insurance policy, hopefully ensuring that you never use your umbrella policy at all. For example, if the liability coverage built into your car insurance policy is $500,000 per accident, you would have to be sued (and lose the lawsuit) for over $500,000 before any extra liability protection is used by your umbrella policy. Obviously, if you lose a lawsuit of more than $500,000, you would be in real trouble. Uncommon as that is, the risk of the insurance companies having to pay out of the umbrella policy is fairly low. And that allows them to keep the costs low.

MOST PEOPLE FOCUS ON THE MINIMUM, LEGALLY REQUIRED PROTECTION (INSURANCE); THE WEALTHY FOCUS ON SAFETY AND PROTECTION OF THEIR ENTIRE FINANCIAL PORTFOLIO.

How Likely Are You to Get Sued?

We all face at least a minimum risk of being sued because we live in a country that allows personal lawsuits. Your level of risk depends on many factors associated with your level of affluence, but also with your financial management. Your risk goes up if you own a:

- Home or multiple homes or farming land
- Swimming pool, trampoline, or other dangerous apparatus
- Car with multiple drivers or expensive cars in general
- Animal [like a pet, horse(s), or other]
- Business
- Seat on a board
- Public profile (or if you participate heavily on social media)

Insurance that is legally required will force you to defer some of this risk to insurance companies, but many of the risks on the above list may not be covered unless you have a personal liability policy. Make a list of your risks and make a decision about umbrella coverage with the help of a qualified independent insurance agent (and hopefully a competent fiduciary adviser).

What Does This Typically Cost?

As all of the insurance commercials have burrowed into our brains, "bundling" as many of your insurance needs with one firm will usually provide you with the most discounts. I have my car, renter's, and umbrella policy with one firm. I pay monthly, which isn't the cheapest option (paying annually is usually cheapest, but it doesn't fit my cash flow needs). In my case, my renter's insurance is cheaper than my liability insurance, which is $38.25 per month ($459 per year), purchasing an extra $1,000,000 of liability coverage for my family. I have known people to pay under $200 per year, but they were usually homeowners who had their policies with the same firm.

CHAPTER 21 TAKEAWAYS

We live in litigious times, and the cost of healthcare is seemingly always rising. That combination puts your financial safety at risk if you at all interact with other people (or if your pets do). **Most people focus on the minimum, legally required protection (insurance); the wealthy focus on safety and protection of their entire financial portfolio.** Insurance is part of that portfolio, and an umbrella policy serves an important role. For a few hundred dollars per year (or less), you can usually layer on another $1,000,000 of liability protection. On the off chance you are sued and held liable for more than the protection afforded by your other policies, you can be covered.

Actionable Strategies:

- Estimate your net worth to determine exactly what you are protecting
- Contact your car insurance carrier and ask if your coverage qualifies for extra liability coverage
- Estimate the cost of an umbrella policy with your insurer (equal to at least your net worth)

CHAPTER 22

DISABILITY INSURANCE

Disability insurance is coverage that protects your income, but only up to a certain amount and for a certain period of time. Life insurance helps you keep your promises even if you die; disability helps you keep your income even if you live (but happen to be disabled). If you get hurt so badly that you can't work, and you have used up your sick (and vacation) days, disability insurance will continue to provide some income. The amount of income depends on how long you are hurt, whether you had any pre-existing conditions, and, of course, how much you make when you're not hurt.

You can buy these kinds of policies through an insurance agent, but you may have access to this coverage through your job and not even realize it. **Short-term disability** insurance coverage is designed to last for a short period of time. After you file a claim, the payments don't kick in until after the "elimination period," the amount of time outlined in your policy before benefits begin (usually weeks, not months). When the payments do begin, the benefit percentage will also depend on your policy (usually 80% of your monthly income). These payments can go on for a few months, but for a short-term policy, not much longer.

At 80% of your income, you're not only going to be hurt physically, you're going to be hurt fiscally as well (you see what I did there?). This is where an emergency reserve of savings fits well. Supplementing your disability benefits with savings can keep your monthly budget the same, assuming your expenses aren't reduced by your injury anyway. Some people who don't have a short-term disability policy through work may choose to "self-insure" by just saving up a few months of salary. If they get hurt, they can use sick days, vacation days, and savings to take care of their budget for any leave without pay (LWOP) days at work.

Long-term disability insurance typically has a longer elimination period (usually ninety days or more). This is also income protection coverage, but in case you are disabled for more than a few months. It will keep covering you for possibly years—read the terms of your policy—but at a benefit percentage closer to 60% of your income.

If you are so badly injured that you can't work, 60% of your income is better than 0% of your income, but it's still a drastic financial strain. The statistics can be misleading on how likely you are to get injured and for how long. Disability insurance agents, for example, do a great job quoting how likely, statistically, you are to suffer a job-threatening work injury. Whether they are true is tough to know. None of these insurance policies are tools you want to need, but they are all available to protect what's important to you.

PERSONAL EXPERIENCE

I don't have disability insurance. As an entrepreneur, there's a great argument for having some protection for my income, since I'm the one driving most of the new business to the firm. Part of me considered getting a policy before finishing this book (you know, to present the image of the perfect financial planner versus the real person that I am), but it's more important for you to know that even financial planners don't buy every tool.

That said, my wife does have it. Each time Jennifer went on maternity leave, she used a mix of short and long-term disability coverage to supplement her time away from the office. Combining vacation, disability income coverage, and sick leave gave her the maximum time available for the start of our two daughters' lives.

When I ran for Congress in 2012, an irate business owner approached me, upset about prospective hires who were on public disability insurance, allegedly without being qualified. As an employer, one of his interview screening questions was, "Have you ever been on disability?" If your answer was "Yes," you were out the door. Considering the stigma that can go along with public disability, it's a wonder anyone survives the experience.

PROFESSIONAL EXPERIENCE

Whenever I work with clients, they remain the kings and queens of their money. My job is to provide advice, expertise, and context for their personal situation based on working with clients who face similar challenges. Considering that, I have opinions about some of the financial tools available, and I share those with my clients. When it comes to disability insurance, the best way to get it is through work. I ask my clients what they know about their work policies, and depending on how much they have, help them plan a certain amount of cash emergency funds.

Disability insurance could more easily be called "income insurance," since it is meant to replace your income should you become unable to work due to sickness, injury, or, for example, pregnancy. Some of my clients don't have disability insurance through work; then we have to do the tough math to see whether paying a monthly disability premium for $100,000+ earners is worth the coverage.

I have read (and often heard quoted by disability insurance salesmen) that the risk of an injury that would cause you to miss work is higher than the risk of premature death. The inference is that if you're going to recommend life insurance to adults in their thirties or forties, then you should definitely recommend disability insurance. This kind of coverage makes my list of recommendations on financial plans, but usually in the form of talking to a third-party insurance agent and subsequently making a cost/benefit decision based on their unique situation.

Private Disability Insurance

Most people that have either short or long-term disability coverage receive it through a group policy at work. If you pay all or a portion of the policy premiums, then the percentage that's covered by the premiums you pay is applied to any payout you might receive if you are disabled. For example, imagine paying $50 per month for a policy at work as the entire cost of the monthly premium. If you are injured and the benefit is $2,000 per month, none of the $2,000 would be taxed. Alternatively, if your employer pays that $50 on your behalf, then the entire $2,000 will be taxed as income. On the one hand, you may not care either way because you are usually taxed on regular income, but considering that the $2,000 is likely a percentage of your gross income, every dollar you could take home counts.

The vocabulary is important in policies like these, because it is not as familiar. You may see someone collect on a life insurance policy in the movies, but disability insurance benefits aren't mentioned much on TV.

One of the key terms is "**elimination period**." This phrase holds the key to understanding how much of disability insurance benefits work. Short-term disability usually pays about 80% of your income to you, should you be unable to work due to a disability. There might be no elimination period, meaning that as soon as your claim is filed, you can start collecting benefits. With long-term disability, there may be a 90 to 180-day elimination period, meaning you have to wait three to six months before you can collect any benefits. Considering this reality, you will want to have a backup income plan for those first few months.

Short-term disability was designed to serve as that backup plan in the insurance world. In the financial planning world, a healthy savings account serves as that backup plan. Have you ever heard that you should have three to six months of expenses for an emergency fund? This is where it would come in handy.

What's unique about the integrated science of financial planning is that there are multiple ways to achieve goals. One could "self-insure" with an emergency fund of any size, if only you knew how much you'd need. In the case of short-term disability insurance, since the policy limits are typically about ninety days of coverage, setting aside an emergency fund rather than paying a monthly premium may make the most sense for people. Long-term disability coverage has the ability to extend for years, even until retirement. Even though long-term disability coverage usually covers about 60% of lost wages due to injury, a ten or twenty-year income insurance policy is hard to set aside in savings. Some people, depending on the cost of the coverage, may choose to go ahead and buy a long-term disability policy. If you do make that investment, discuss the difference between "own occupation" and "any occupation" with your insurance agent.

The former allows you to claim a disability check if you can't do your current job, and the latter only pays a benefit if you can't do *any* job—big difference! You want to be covered if for any reason you can't do your job.

What Does This Typically Cost?

Disability insurance covered by your employer is the cheapest. Whether it is free or you are asked to support some of it (typically $25-$50/month), exploring the benefits offered through work just makes sense. Whether you need to supplement anything you get for free will depend on the elimination period, the benefit amount (what percentage of income the policy will pay), and whether the price you pay could go up in later years.

How much a disability policy costs, especially a long-term disability policy, depends on your age, your job, your gender, and the amount of income that's being covered. A rule of thumb that you'll see online is that a policy will cost 1% to 3% of your gross income per year. So, if you have a $100,000 salary, expect to pay $1,000 to $3,000 per year.

Public Disability Insurance

The Social Security Administration also provides disability benefits for at least one year if you become totally disabled before retirement age. It's a pretty high hurdle and not as common as injuries covered by employer-sponsored or third-party disability insurance coverage.

Note that there are two kinds of disability coverage through the Social Security Administration (SSA):

- Social Security Disability (SSD)
- Supplemental Security Income (SSI)

There is a medical disability qualification process, regardless of which type a person is applying for. SSD benefits are based on work experience and compensation history. Individuals will need to have worked for five out of the last ten years to be eligible at all under SSD. Since everyone's pay history is different, an individual's personal benefit will always vary. SSI is needs-based, so that amount is fixed, but it is also income and wealth tested. Most people reading this will be excluded from this coverage, since in 2018, the Substantial Gainful Activity (SGA) income limit for someone who wasn't blind was $1,180 per month, and the amount of wealth/money an individual could own was $2,000 ($3,000 if married) as of 2019.

Notably, all disability insurance offered through the Social Security Administration is long-term disability insurance. If you are interested in short-term disability insurance, you have to get it in the private market.

CHAPTER 22 TAKEAWAYS

Disability insurance should really be called "income insurance," because it keeps your ability to receive income safe. These policies never cover 100% of your income, so even if you have one, should you go on an excused extended leave—for example, due to illness, injury or pregnancy—you will need to reduce your expenses or cover the difference with personal savings. The cheapest way to have this kind of protection is through work. Private disability insurance was not typically designed for total disability for longer than the short-term (ninety days or less) or long-term (six months to a year). Public disability insurance through the Social Security Administration is meant for people who have incurred "total" disability for at least one year.

Actionable Strategies:

- Look up your benefits package at work and review your disability policy options
- Rework your budget to live off of 80% of your income (for a short-term disability)
- Rework your budget to live off of 60% of your income (for a long-term disability)
- Identify the difference of an "own occupation" vs. "any occupation" policy
- Discuss purchasing disability policies outside of your employer with an independent agent
- Review what counts as "total disability" according to the Social Security Administration

LONG-TERM CARE INSURANCE

Long-term care, also called "custodial care," is coverage for home care and/or nursing expenses, usually delivered as people get into their eighties and nineties. People usually go "on plan" (use the policy benefits) when two **activities of daily living** (ADLs) become difficult. ADLs include the basics, like bathing, toileting, transferring, feeding, and dressing. There is an order to when we learn these activities as children and, ironically, we can lose our capacity to complete them in that same order. A severe enough injury can cause anyone to lose one or two ADLs, but these policies are typically offered to people with chronic illness or disability. Some people with disposable income decide to share this risk with an insurance company by buying a policy while they are younger. If you do buy this in your thirties or forties, however, adding something called an "inflation guard" may cost you more, but ensure that your future benefits increase with the cost of inflation over time.

Long-term care insurance pays for skilled nursing or unskilled caretaking. Medicare does not cover long-term care unless you are in a skilled nursing facility, and then only fully for twenty days. After 101 days, patients pay 100% of the costs. Considering most people who go "on plan" can be using it for three years or more, planning for long-term care is a must.

Humans are like fine wine: as we age, we get more robust, textured, and nuanced. Unfortunately, our skin does the same, but we usually just call those wrinkles. Our society doesn't do a great job honoring the elderly, and much like death, chronic illnesses and disability are things that many of us would just like pretend only happen to other people. Healthcare is hard enough to manage when we are in our primes; when we get older and disabled, it is harder still. And that's just tough to think about.

As individuals, there are things we can do to preserve our dignity at what might be the toughest stage of our lives (or that of our parents or spouse). Like other kinds of insurance, there are opportunities for both prevention and cure.

PERSONAL EXPERIENCE

At the ripe old age of sixty-five, my father passed away. (I know, that age was neither ripe nor old.) Unfortunately, my older sister passed away before him, only two years prior. *Psychology Today* magazine says grief can overwhelm the body with stress hormones, leading to stress cardiomyopathy. In other words, even though my father's cause of death on the death certificate said heart disease and diabetes, he really just died of a broken heart. The two years between my sister's death and his scripted my roller-coaster experience with caregiving. The physical work wasn't the hard part—the emotional was. How do you manage your mind when someone you grew up respecting, fearing, and following, now needed to respect, fear, and follow doctor's orders (that you are responsible for enforcing)? How do you enforce those when the strong and confident parental figure you knew is at times weak and vulnerable, and other times frustrated and fiercely angry at his situation? You deal with it one day at a time, is how you do it, and it is, emotionally, one of the hardest things I have had to do in life.

My dad did not have a long-term care insurance policy, and as a result, no subsidies for professionals to come in and help. That said, his ADLs that would have qualified him for plan benefits went in and out. Sometimes he could feed himself and sometimes he couldn't (or wouldn't). It was a tough time, and even now, it's hard to write about. Suffice it to say, as a former caregiver, it would have helped to have help.

For about six months, my dad was in and out of the hospital. During his final hospital stay, I was cautioned that having a professional caregiver at home would be necessary. I actually thought this would be good for my dad—someone different for him to talk to.

I still remember the day I was called back to the intensive care unit (ICU). It was a Sunday, and my dad had been in the rehab center of the hospital. Over the prior week, he had fallen, been rushed to one hospital's ICU, then the regular care, then another hospital's rehabilitation center. On this particular Sunday, I felt comfortable enough to leave him alone to sleep. I went home to mow the lawn, get a shower, and just as I settled to watch the Lakers in the basketball playoffs, I thought to call the hospital. My dad was a thirty-year Lakers fan, and I wanted to tell his nurses to turn the TV on for him when he awoke. When I called, they told me he was back in the ICU. I rushed back to the hospital, where I was told he'd had a mysterious (and apparently incurable) infection. He died just a few days later.

The tragic reality of being a caregiver is that you're serving someone who may never recover. And you know it. Despite "knowing," I wasn't ready for my dad's death. It took a while to sink in. I haven't recovered from that experience. I haven't "gotten over" my father's death. But I have learned to carry "it" (whatever "it" is.) And I hope my clients hear my experience in my voice and see it in my eyes when we discuss this topic.

PROFESSIONAL EXPERIENCE

I learned about long-term care insurance through a life insurance company. In my state (commonwealth) of Virginia, the life and health state licensing exams used to be taken at the same time. Licensing varies by state, and I believe that now in Virginia, you can take the life insurance licensing exam separately from the health insurance portion. That's too bad, because neither section was too hard and it opened me up to new opportunities early in my career to have both licenses. The license to offer long-term care insurance was one of those opportunities.

During my group training, the instructor explained that buying long-term care insurance for herself was the best present she could give her children. No longer would she have to worry about becoming a burden to them when she aged into needing assistance. She would instead have a professional perform the care, while her children managed that care at arm's length.

I have worked with people who could and could not qualify for these policies. With each, the strategy for healthcare planning remained the same—ensure that the client would not run out of money. I don't sell these policies now, but I address the purpose of these insurance plans with my clients and help them identify where the cost could fit in their budgets. Their next step is to work through the application process with an independent third-party insurance agent, who provides the real numbers that the client and I can try to incorporate into their overall financial plan.

Prevention

Long-term care is meant to help people with both chronic illness and disabilities that lead to loss of ability to perform normal activities of daily living. What we can do while we are able is pay more attention to doctor recommendations and preventative care during our mid-lives. In our thirties, forties, and fifties, our bodies change, but our minds still assume we are as capable as we were in our twenties. At peak performance, we probably are, but we will need to put in more effort to maintain that ability and to recover. That maintenance includes bringing a consciousness to how we feed ourselves, how much we sleep, and how much physical activity we do and with what intensity. I can only hope that eating in moderation and working out consistently might help delay or even prevent my need for assistance in my later years. I won't know until I get there. I do believe that working with your doctor on your personal situation could give you useful guidance for the kind of preventative maintenance you could use for yourself. But that only speaks to physical decline.

What scares insurance companies the most is mental decline. Studies have been proven and disproven about activities you can use to put off diseases like Alzheimer's and dementia. Do crossword or Sudoku puzzles help with prevention? How about learning another language? Surprisingly, the most commonly known ways to slow down the onset of Alzheimer's or dementia is to exercise, eat well, and get some regular sleep. The Alzheimer's Association also recommends maintaining social connections and avoiding head trauma.

Cure

Retaining care assistance in your older years will be expensive—emotionally, physically, and financially. Since chronic illness and/or disabilities more likely catch up with you towards the end of your life, those "expenses" are shared with family members who feel responsible for your care. Social safety net programs like Medicaid only kick-in after all of your assets are spent down, ensuring that you are in the worst possible position before receiving care: disabled and broke. State-based programs or State Partnership Programs work with an existing long-term care insurance policy to protect the amount of wealth you can retain while receiving Medicaid.

When purchasing an individual long-term care policy, you are generally buying access to a pot of money that will be used up whenever you need to go "on plan." Getting access to these benefits will depend on the details of the policy. Some details include where the policy will allow you to receive care, like a nursing home, assisted living, or just at home. You also will want to check whether the care can be provided by licensed professionals—referred to as "skilled care"—and/or non-professionals, like someone who could just pick up your groceries or keep you company. You could have a daily limit of how much you can spend, or a monthly limit. For example, you might have a daily limit of $100 per day that you could spend on assistance, or a monthly limit or $3,000. If your option is either, you will have more flexibility over how many times someone can come see you and still receive payment depending on how much it actually costs that caregiver per visit. Some policies may even allow for you to pay for family members to visit you.

What Does This Typically Cost?

Long-term care insurance works by undergoing a medical, typically cognitive screening, and then working out how big of a pool of insurance benefits (money) you would like to create. For example, if you wanted to spend $3,000 per month for a benefit period of six years, you would have payments estimated for a $216,000 policy. The cost for that kind of a benefit depends on a lot of factors, especially your age. Since most people won't go "on plan" until their eighties, if you buy a policy in your forties, you will pay much less than if you wait until your sixties. These insurance policies are usually sold when clients are in their fifties and sixties, and are usually in the hundreds of dollars ($200 to $800) per month range, depending on health and options.

Where Can I Get This?

Independent insurance agents/brokers sell long-term care insurance policies. When insurance agents get licensed, they usually take both the life and health state examinations together. Selling long-term care insurance relies on the health portion of the exam, along with other continuing education. An independent agent can survey multiple insurance agencies to see which organization can serve your particular needs the best.

You may also be offered a hybrid insurance product that protects against the downside of dying before you get a chance to use the plan. For example, some insurance companies and their agents focus on a whole life insurance/long-term care hybrid policy that allows the insured to build up cash value that can later be used for long-term care needs. Should the insured die before going "on plan," at least a beneficiary will receive proceeds tax-free. This also gives the insurance companies a way to mitigate the growing costs of offering separate long-term care insurance versus the life insurance policies they have much more experience in cost planning.

It may seem counterintuitive, but we want the insurance companies to make a profit on these and other policies so they stay in business. Medicare does not cover long-term care unless you are in a "skilled nursing facility," and then only fully for twenty days. (After 101 days, patients pay 100% of the costs.) So, if the government won't take care of you and the insurance companies can't afford to say in business, then we are left with our retirement savings accounts to cover our care. After your savings are spent down, then you may qualify for Medicaid, a joint federal-state program designed for low-income individuals. There are ways to mitigate spending down all of your retirement savings before receiving benefits from Medicaid (for example, state partnership programs), but Medicaid facilities are no one's first choice for care.

Historically, there were many more insurance agencies offering long-term care insurance products than there are now. It just got too expensive and the actuaries did a poor job of estimating the costs. If you plan to use an insurance company to defray the risk of needing assistance in your old age, start talking to the very best-rated insurance agencies, who have been around for over 100 years and are expected to be around for hundreds more. You know these firms: they advertise every day (especially during sporting events, for some reason). Independent third-party insurance agents will typically have access to multiple highly-rated insurance firms. Ask one to work with you on not only your options for a plan, but also your options for an insurance firm to work with.

Self-Insurance

Purchasing any insurance policy is a decision to leverage the resources of an insurance company to offset the risk of loss you face. In the case of long-term care insurance, the risk you are trying to protect against is spending all of your money on extended care when you've lost your ability to independently function. Long-term care insurance is not legally mandated and is an oft-ignored risk management tool because:

- People incorrectly assume the government will take care of them with Medicare
- People assume their children will take care of their needs (without consequence)

Neither of the above assumptions are true. Because medical costs continue to rise, the ability to project how much long-term care might cost for someone who needs daily (or ever hourly) care is difficult to estimate. Suffice it to say, it already costs thousands of dollars per month for nursing home care, and those costs are outpacing inflation.

That said, if you build a financial plan that allows you to set aside hundreds of thousands of dollars, you can "self-insure" this risk. Two people making a few hundred thousand dollars per year and living below their means can accumulate a healthy amount of retirement assets, which could indeed be set aside for long-term care. There's just one important question to answer if this is your scenario: Would you want to?

CHAPTER 23 TAKEAWAYS

We will all face long-term care needs. It will begin, perhaps, with watching your parents take care of your grandparents, or with you taking care of your parents. It will eventually be something you face personally. How you plan for these events will determine the lifestyle you will live when you are at your most vulnerable. The best cure is prevention, if possible. Some of us are genetically predisposed to some ailments, no matter what we do. But that shouldn't stop us from trying to reduce the effects of diseases that will limit our lifestyles as we age. Long-term care provides a safety risk that is likely the most expensive we will encounter— more than an expensive car accident or even lawsuit. Taking steps to plan for the likely events of your age include managing your physical, mental, and spiritual health. It also could include keeping your friends and family close.

Actionable Strategies:

- Watch your head. If you need a helmet, the activity is probably not worth the long-term effects
- Talk with your doctor about your optimal diet and level of exercise annually
- Decide who your true friends are and find ways to spend more time with them
- Discuss the insurance options you have with an independent third-party insurance agent
- Decide whether your financial plan can allow for self-insurance and if you prefer that option
- If you have parents or older people you love, spend time with them while they're healthy

JOY OF SAFETY

Summary

The idea of sharing risk has been around for centuries. It began with what was considered "big business" in the 14th century: the maritime industry. Like many good business ideas, it eventually trickled down to consumer applications.

The ability to share risk with your neighbors through an insurance company is an invaluable tool for achieving your life's ambitions. Life is consistently surprising. The only thing we can count on is change—sometimes good and sometimes not-so-good. Having insurance policies keeps the other parts of our portfolio safe: our emergency cash savings, our income, our health, our cars, our homes, and even our reputations.

Putting these protections in place frees you to go after the other areas of financial planning that provide additional leverage. The wealthiest people remain that way because they understand the hierarchy of financial planning and they understand leverage: Spend a little to protect a lot. I know, it's not fun to spend money on safety or protection. What if you don't use it? Well, if you don't have to use insurance, congratulations—it's the best money you ever "wasted!"

Risk management is the "eat your vegetables" part of financial planning; the joy comes later. If the surprise emergency happens, it won't disrupt your life as much as others expect it should. Your life is too important to be financially disrupted by emergencies you can't afford. That's why you buy insurance—to offset the risk of your important life being disrupted. You need to make it to the other side of your goals and dreams before you leave this planet. Your family needs you, and your community needs you to be successful.

A Final Word on Safety

None of these risk management products compare with the safety of the tribe that was common comfort well before even the oldest insurance companies. A combination of having people who care and modern insurance tools make for the best "coverage," whatever generation you live in. We can create that "kinder, gentler" society that our 41st US President referred to in the early 1990s just by being *there* for each other. And if that example travels across these United States, and across the oceans, then perhaps we can create the country and world imagined by our 35th US President, where "the strong are just and the weak secure and the peace preserved." That's the vision of safety I wish for; that could endure.

JOY OF LEGACY

Estate Planning

"You may delay but time will not."
~Benjamin Franklin

CHAPTER 24

BACKGROUND & HISTORY

Estate planning goes back centuries, but the idea of inheriting your family's stuff probably goes back to the caveman days. It's a history so rich it could take up volumes, but, alas, you don't have the time to read it (and I don't have the time to write it). Suffice it to say that you'll find history of inheritance documented from Ancient Rome, Ancient Greece, and likely whatever holy book you ascribe to. You will find the Greek, Latin, and Italian phrases turned into words we know in English as legal terms. It is fascinating, if you are impressed by the origin of things.

Patriarchy is markedly pronounced during the early years of estate recognition. In the old world—before the United States of America was a "thing"—families did the inheriting (especially land). If decisions were allowed by the government or royalty, they were only made by males, and even those decisions had conditions (for example, the recipients must not have been slaves, adopted, or in jail). You may recognize the oral wills from the Christian Bible in both the Old and New Testament. Again, even there, you'll notice that the inheriting is done by family.

The most significant law to modern day estate planning is the **Statute of Wills** enacted by England's Parliament in 1540 (before it became Great Britain). This one law was the first to articulate the possibility of divvying up an owner's land and leaving it to someone of their choosing upon their death. This could all finally be done through a written will. This was a big deal, because the prior law in place (**Statute of Uses**) made it impossible to divide up land to give it away upon your passing. Prior to the Statute of Wills, unclaimed land just went to the Crown, aka King Henry VIII. Then and now, wills are required to be in writing, signed, and witnessed. Of course, the exact details depend on where you live (i.e., which state).

Why does all of this matter? Because the right to pass property to others is the most fundamental part of estate planning; unfortunately, many people get this confused with estate tax planning.

Federal Estate Taxes

The federal estate tax has been imposed, repealed, and reduced since the 18th century. Early on, the history of federal estate tax planning followed closely with the wars that dot U.S. history. It goes as far back as 1797, when it began as a stamp tax to raise revenue for the Navy. Much later, the costs of the **Civil War** inspired the **Revenue Act of 1862** and the first "legacy inheritance tax." It wasn't really until the Industrial Revolution that the political atmosphere inspired a true legacy tax on the newly concentrated wealth of the industrialists. Naturally, once "the wealthy" were singled out, our first heated political debates began about who should be taxed, why and how.

The **Revenue Act of 1916** brought on the modern era of federal estate tax, later termed the "death tax" by many politicians.

The Center for Budget and Policy Priorities, a progressive think tank in Washington, D.C., suggests that policymakers created the modern-day estate tax as "a backstop to the income tax."[1] Their inference is that up to 55% of estates that get taxed are based on increases in the value of stocks, art, and real estate that had never been taxed in the first place.

Estate taxes are not a big deal for most people anymore. Estate planners used to sell their services as mostly methods for reducing the tax burden at death for even the moderately wealthy. They would offer this as an opportunity to pass down as much wealth to the next generation—and as little to the US Treasury—as possible. During much of the 20th century, it became cheaper to give away money while you were alive than wait for the "death tax." At the time, there were no gift taxes while you were alive. If you gave away money, homes, and land while people could thank you, you received two benefits: lots of appreciation and little-to-no taxes!

Eventually, the **Tax Reform Act of 1976** equalized the rates of estate and gift taxes by providing a framework for what's called "lifetime gifts" through a single exclusion amount. Brilliant!

Beginning in the 21st century, the history of the estate tax has become something you really needed to keep up with. An entire generation of professional estate attorneys spent the first fifteen years of their career trying to help moderately wealthy families avoid the federal estate tax. Now, much of that expertise is important to less than 2,000 tax returns per year. The Tax Policy Center (TPC), a joint venture between the Urban Institute and the Brookings Institution, provides models and statistics to policymakers about tax policy. After the **Economic Growth and Tax**

---

1   Huang, Chye-Ching and Chloe Cho, "Ten Facts You Should Know About the Federal Estate Tax," The Center on Budget and Policy Priorities, October 30, 2017, https://www.cbpp.org/research/federal-tax/ten-facts-you-should-know-about-the-federal-estate-tax, 2019.

Relief Reconciliation Act of 2001 (EGTRRA), which raised the estate value exclusion amount to $1 million, the TPC's analysis states that 50,500 returns were subject to federal estate tax that year. By 2009, that exclusion amount was raised to $3.5 million, knocking down the number of tax returns that paid a tax that year to 5,700. The **American Taxpayer Relief Act of 2012** extended the life of a previous exclusion amount of $5 million, which further reduced the taxpayers affected to 4,100.

The **Tax Cut and Jobs Act of 2017** increased that exclusion amount yet again to $11.4 million per tax payer, and married couples (when the survivor is a U.S. citizen) can pass an unlimited amount of assets without incurring a federal estate tax. If both spouses pass away, their collective estate would have to be worth over $22.8 million to trigger federal estate tax. Out of about 240 million tax returns, less than 3,000 will have to pay estate taxes upon their death, and as few as 1,900 in 2018.[2]

If estate attorneys focused solely on those 3,000 (or fewer) tax-payers for business, they would go broke! Instead, estate attorneys rightly focus on the multi-million client opportunity, building estate plans for the vast majority of us who need one.

State Taxes at Death

A discussion about estate taxes would not be final without mention of state-based estate taxes. The Tax Foundation, a Washington, D.C. based think tank, last reported in 2017 that fourteen states and the District of Columbia still have an estate tax, while six

2   "Key Elements of the U.S. Tax System," Tax Policy Center, https://www. taxpolicycenter.org/sites/ default/files/briefing-book/ key_elements_of_the_us_tx_ system_1.pdf, 2019.

states levy an inheritance tax.[3] Maryland has both kinds of taxes upon death. The rate of states dropping their estate taxes has sped up, especially as the federal government has raised their exemption higher and higher. It becomes a competition: who wants to die (or live) in a state that has a high tax, when they could just as easily live in one of thirty-six others? Though many states have an exemption of $5.49 million (the previous exemption amount for the feds), some states have a lower exemption amount. Attorney Ryan Brown of Arlington Law Group in Arlington, Virginia says that two of those states include "Oregon, with a $1 million limit and a 16% tax, and Pennsylvania, which taxes every estate, with rates dependent upon the relationship between the decedent and the beneficiaries (as of 2019)." Which state has what is changing all of the time, so for a current list, seek out Nolo.com or the TaxFoundation.com, or just see an attorney licensed in the state that you live (or plan to move to).

Digital Estate Planning

The Uniform Law Commission (ULC) is a little-known nonprofit, nonpartisan, unincorporated association of state commissioners from each of the United States (including the District of Columbia, the Commonwealth of Puerto Rico, and the U.S. Virgin Islands). It's the nation's oldest state governmental association, comprised of attorney volunteers, typically appointed by each state's governor.

Among many duties posted on their website, the ULC "strengthens the federal system" by providing consistency to laws, rules, and procedures from state to state. They also "keep state law

3   Walczak, Jared, et al., "2019 State Business Tax Climate Index," The Tax Foundation, September 26, 2018, https://taxfoundation.org/publications/state-business-tax-climate-index/, 2019.

up-to-date by addressing important and timely issues." And what could be more timely than digital estate planning?

In 2014, the ULC drafted a piece of digital asset legislation called the **Uniform Fiduciary Access to Digital Access Act** (UFADAA). The acronym is long enough, so I'll summarize that the spirit of this legislation was to allow any executor or personal representative of an estate to have full access to a decedent's digital estate. Full access meant every social media account, every email address, every digital file, and every login. Both privacy groups and large technology corporations protested this possible invasion of privacy and blanket overruling of all Terms of Service Agreements.

Since the ULC is a volunteer body that effectively makes suggestions, states have to decide to adopt legislation that the ULC proposes. Only Delaware adopted the UFADAA as state law, meaning a revision was inevitable. Enter the revised UFADAA, aptly titled the Revised Uniform Fiduciary Access to Digital Access Act (RUFADAA).

RUFADDA allowed for more nuance in the instructions for digital estate keepers. For one, it provides for the use of online repositories that have been created to document who has access to which digital assets. There is a three-step hierarchy that highlights the nuance in this revision:

- Online tools can empower a particular person who, in turn, can control a digital asset
- Regular estate planning documents can empower a particular person to control a digital asset
- Terms of Service will control the digital asset if the above conditions are not met

Even with the hierarchy in place (more than forty states have adopted RUFADAA as of 2019), executors may still have to petition the courts to outline why access to a digital estate is pertinent to settling the traditional estate. It's a high bar, but at least there are rules in place that privacy groups, industry, and more than forty states can agree upon.[4]

Posterity & Charity

Whether or not you are wealthy, you will leave something behind. Even longer ago than the genesis of estate planning, there was likely the inherent idea of making sure your family remembered you. Today, many of us will leave digital trails for future generations to behold (like it or not).

Perhaps as old as the concept of posterity is the idea of charity. Like inheritance, the concept of philanthropy has recorded history dating back to the Greeks and Romans. In the United States, the **Revenue Act of 1913** exempted charitable organizations from paying taxes.

---

4   Wibberley, Ryan, "You Should Have An Estate Plan For Your Facebook Account," Forbes, June 3, 2018, https://www.forbes.com/sites/ryanwibberley/2018/06/03/you-should-have-an-estate-plan-for-your-facebook-account/#7c40b0e1764f, 2019.

JOY OF LEGACY

Whenever I have a speaking opportunity, I ask the audience members to raise their hands if they have an estate. Invariably, less than 20% raise their hands. Then, I let them know the bad news: unless they are immortal, they will all eventually have an estate (when they die).

For a second, everyone in the audience thinks, "I could be immortal. Am I immortal?"

I know whenever I hear "everyone," my first gut reaction is, "Not me!" You probably do the same thing.

"Do you have an estate *plan*?" is the question my audience members often think they are answering (and most people do not). The lack of an estate plan is a byproduct of old thinking that only rich people needed a plan for their loved ones after they die. This old thinking stems from a time when an estate plan was mostly designed to avoid taxes.

In fact, planning for your "estate" is a professional way to say "making it easy for your loved ones to deal with the financial mess you would have otherwise left behind." Reconciling all of that is quite the task if there are no rules or instructions to follow. That is what an estate plan provides: rules of the road according to your wishes (even after you are gone).

Estate planning also tends to lump together medical directives and powers of attorney to create instructions in case you are mentally or physically unable to manage your medical or legal affairs. If you are alive and need assistance with paying your bills or cashing your checks, who's going to do it? If you are in a dubious medical situation, who decides when to turn off the machines? Estate planning attorneys typically coordinate drafting legal documents to ensure that when these things happen, what you want to happen gets done.

The alternative to identifying a medical power of attorney, for example, is relying on whomever your state or your hospital deems to be your closest relative. That person will make the final decisions; unless, of course, there are multiple "closest relatives" who choose to fight about those decisions. Is that possible in your family? Similarly, when there is no "last will and testament" after a death, the rules for who receives your assets are set by state law, and an "administrator" (typically from your family) must volunteer to administrate your estate to distribute money, pay off debt, and handle guardianship of your children. It's all very serious and very adult.

This process of "administration" is part of a court process called **probate**. The probate process involves the county court, typically where the person died. When there is no last will and testament, as in the example above, the administrator and the county court work together to properly distribute assets. The probate process takes time, money, and detail orientation. It is a terrible administrative task to handle at likely the worst time in a beneficiary's life. Estate plans are designed to reduce or eliminate the requirement to go through this process.

Estate plans include documents that outline how you want your assets distributed (a will); how you want your medical care administered (advance medical directive or living will); who you want to make medical decisions on your behalf (medical power of attorney); and who you want to handle your financial affairs should you become mentally incapacitated (financial power of attorney). There are, of course, techniques used to defer or avoid taxes and the probate process (such as a trust you create during your lifetime) that a licensed attorney is in a more appropriate position to discuss. But there are basics that people old enough to be in our generation—especially if there are kids involved—can make right to feel good about what's being left behind.

Estate planning is also called legacy planning. What kind of legacy are you building for the future to remember you by? You are probably doing amazing things and would prefer that the last impressions of you aren't overshadowed by mistakes with your estate that could have been avoided. This chapter is about avoiding those mistakes. You will find that some of those mistakes are avoidable for free, while others will require an attorney. For your legacy and to protect the American Dream for the ones that come after you, it could be the best money you ever spent.

PERSONAL EXPERIENCE

I had the unfortunate duty of administering my older sister's estate when she died over a decade ago. She did not have a will. She didn't have a lot of money, but she also didn't have a husband or children. In Virginia, when there are no children and no spouse, the next people in line to become beneficiaries are the parents. Our parents didn't talk much and had split up when we were very young; all of a sudden, I was the point person for divvying up her estate between the two of them. What a predicament! Before I could take the opportunity to grieve, I had to work with the county and my divorced parents to reconcile her estate. It took me almost three years to get it all done, which sounds like a long time, considering her financial life was not very complex. What took so long is I just didn't want to do it, which I believe is the case for most people forced into administering an estate. Things would have worked out differently if my sister, even though she was still a young adult, would have prepared for the day she might die. Free will substitutes, or better yet, an estate plan built by an attorney, would have saved a lot of stress.

When I began writing this book, I remembered the last step I had taken towards getting my family's estate plans in place. I had owed an estate planner colleague of mine a phone call to follow up from our last meeting (before my kids were born). The funny thing is that I'd brought a check to that long ago meeting to get started with my estate plan, but instead of taking it (or even asking for it), he opted to wait until I'd identified a **trustee** (a trustee is identified when you create a living trust). Unfortunately for me and my family, that was just what I needed to postpone getting it done. So, not many people are perfect in these areas—not even me. After I had some friends read a draft of this book, I was cheerfully encouraged (guilted) into getting my estate plan done before publishing. Note: If you find yourself sitting across the table from an estate planner, just give them the check and get it done.

PROFESSIONAL EXPERIENCE

The beginning of a client conversation about estate planning begins one of two ways:

- "Yup, we took care of that…" OR
- "Yes, we need *all* of that!"

For the latter, there's no doubt that any couple responsible enough to hire a financial planner has probably been talking about the need to put together an estate plan, but just never really got around to it. Once you start "adulting" enough to get married, have kids, and buy life insurance, it feels like you've done a lot already (and you have). But estate planning is the capstone to any preparation you have done or will do for your kids and/or your favorite charity. That's because when I talk about estate planning for my clients, I'm also talking about charity, posterity, and legacy. Before we get to estate planning, we've already touched on family values while alive; now, I focus on what their estate will say when they leave life behind. What do they want their family name to have meant to society?

The big financial planning question is whether they philosophically believe in leaving a financial legacy or whether they'd prefer to "die broke," as Stephen Pollan suggests in his books, *Die Broke* and *Live Rich, Die Broke*. Personal circumstances and beliefs may drive either decision; since I'm meeting most of my clients well before their anticipated expiration date, I let them choose and plan accordingly.

What I do impress upon them is how much they can do today, for free, to avoid or at least limit the probate process. We discuss how their home is titled, whether all of their accounts are jointly owned with right of survivorship, and how to add payable/transfer on death provisions for the accounts that are not. Retirement and insurance accounts typically (but not always) require clients to choose a beneficiary, so the only possible problem is whether their beneficiary preference has changed. We also discuss the more modern field of digital estate planning, including making plans for social media accounts and passwords. If their kids are younger, I'll ask about whether guardians have been chosen; if they're over eighteen, I'll ask whether the kids have medical directives and financial powers of attorney in place (just like their parents).

I am not a lawyer, so I qualify some of my recommendations as personal opinion rather than advice and always suggest they confirm my assumptions with advice from an estate attorney licensed in their home state. Having gone through the probate process personally, what I was most surprised by was how much easier it could have gone had any preparation been done. It's this ease I give to my clients by helping them communicate about a topic that, for most people, is hard.

Your Estate

As I said at the beginning of this section, most people don't realize that they actually have an estate. Understandably, the word "estate" does sound like a sprawling home you would normally see during the opening credits of 1980s era prime-time television soap operas like *Falcon Crest* or *Dallas*. The first image that comes to mind is a large home, with columns bookending a large door, a huge lawn out front, and a hotel-sized pool out back. Wouldn't it be grand if we all had that? Unfortunately (or fortunately?), what we do have is a life. The bundle of things we own in that life, of varying material worth, at the end of our living days, is called an estate.

Calculating the value of your estate is not much different than calculating your **net worth**. Your net worth is the sum of all of the things you own minus all of the money you owe. So, in a simplified example, let's say Jennifer owns her home valued at $500,000, a car worth $20,000, has about $100,000 saved up between retirement and savings accounts, and clothes and miscellaneous electronics worth approximately $10,000. The total value of what she owns is worth $630,000. If she owed $400,000 on the house, $15,000 on her car, and $5,000 worth of credit card debt, then the total value of what she owes is $420,000. This would mean that Jennifer's net worth is $630,000—$420,000, which equals $110,000. One big difference between net worth and estate value could be life insurance. If Jennifer had a $100,000 life insurance policy at work, and she died, the $100,000 may also be added to her estate value. This is where final estate value can get a little tricky, but it matters mostly if you are getting close to the estate tax exclusion amount for federal or state estate tax planning purposes. As you will read in this next section, most of us are not.

Estate Taxes

As mentioned earlier, the **Tax Cut and Jobs Act of 2017** increased the exclusion amount for the value of estates being taxed to $11.4 million per tax payer (as of 2019). And married couples (where the surviving spouse is a U.S. citizen) could long pass an unlimited amount of assets to the survivor. Out of about 240 million tax returns, less than 3,000 will have to pay federal estate taxes upon their death. This does not take into account inheritance or estate taxes limits, which may be far lower in your state. This is why an estate attorney, licensed and experienced in your particular state, is the best person to turn to for advice on this subject.

Living

Estate planning is as much about life as it is about death. Most people might assume that it's just the lives of those left behind, but estate planning is set up to protect your life while you are alive as well. Should you be become incapacitated, temporarily or permanently, physically or mentally, estate planning is there.

There are a lot of terms in estate planning, but none more confusing than the **living will**. No, it isn't a tool to give away your money while you are alive, but it certainly sounds like it! A living will is actually not a will at all, but rather a legal document that lets everyone know what kind of treatment you would like (or not like) in case you are terminally ill and not able to communicate your wishes verbally. Another term that means the same thing as living will is "**advance medical directive**," and that's the term I'll use going forward to avoid confusion.

You can create instructions that will protect your wishes, especially when it comes to do not resuscitate (DNR) rules, when you can no longer protect yourself. Like everything in estate planning, the rules around this vary by state. The advance medical directive can tie pretty closely to a **durable health care power of attorney,** which designates someone you choose to make medical decisions on your behalf (even if you're not terminally ill). This person can also be called a health care representative; you might even see "health care proxy" or "surrogate" terminology.

You'll read online that you don't need a lawyer to designate someone or even put your wishes down on paper; in fact, your doctor and most state departments of health will have forms. It is a document for your life, but it serves as a legal document that explicitly dictates what medical treatment you'd like in case you are unable to make those decisions yourself.

You have probably heard of a regular (financial) **power of attorney,** which is used to give someone the power to act on your behalf for legal and financial matters. Here, I'll give a nice example. What happens if you've planned a vacation to Tahiti and the closing day for your new home in Virginia gets pushed to the middle of your vacation? No need to cancel that vacation; you could empower someone, for just the transaction, with a power of attorney to act on your behalf. The power of attorney (POA) designation in general authorizes someone—not necessarily an attorney/lawyer—to act on your behalf in a number of situations.

Whether it is a financial power of attorney or health care power of attorney, giving someone the legal authority to act on your behalf is a big deal. POAs can be general or (more commonly) limited. A general POA would give an agent you designate legal authority to act on your behalf unless you die or become mentally incompetent. If the general POA is "**durable,**" then the authority can remain up until death, even if you are incapacitated. More commonly, POAs are limited for a specific act or acts or time frame. For example, I have limited power of attorney on my client's investment accounts to trade on their behalf and withdraw my fees for as long as they are clients. I don't have general authority to withdraw funds just anytime or forever (and my clients are happy about that).

Again, all of these "living" documents are legal documents, subject to laws that vary by state. And this is why I always suggest speaking with an experienced estate attorney who is licensed in your state before making any final decisions.

CHAPTER 25 TAKEAWAYS

Unless you are immortal, you will have an estate when you die. Unless you are one of 3,000 individuals who have an estate value above $11.4 million (or couples with estates over $22.8 million), you will not likely have a federal estate tax liability under the **Tax Cut and Jobs Act of 2017**, which extends until 2026. There are many states that have an estate or inheritance tax, so discussing your situation with an estate attorney licensed in your state is the best way to find out how you may need to financially prepare.

Wrapped into estate planning are contingencies for living without the capacity to make decisions independently. Note that legal decisions can be made in your absence and medical decisions can be made according to your wishes, even if you are incapacitated—temporarily or permanently—if you plan ahead with the proper documentation.

Actionable Strategies

- Calculate your estimated estate value as you would your current net worth, but add your estimated death benefit from life insurance to get your taxable estate
- Document a detailed list of all of your assets (including estimated value)
- Document every life insurance policy, its value, and location of the paperwork
- Ask an estate attorney, licensed in your state, about state-based estate taxes
- Work with your estate attorney or doctor to draft a "living will" (advanced medical directive)
- Identify someone to become your agent under your durable health care power of attorney

- Tell your executor where your will is located or register it with your local county
- Update your list of assets (and life insurance policies, if applicable) annually

WILL SUBSTITUTES

What scares a lot of people from getting their estate planning affairs in order is the necessity of meeting with an estate attorney. Attorneys are intimidating because of all of that legal knowledge! The power suits, walnut desks, and cuff links don't help either. Oh, and the fact that they charge money for advice is reasonable, but still a little off-putting.

There are things you can do to protect your estate wishes free of charge. None of this can be considered advice, but rather information you can apply to your life situation. I typically share this information with my clients and I will also share it here.

When it comes to distributing assets, the name of the game is **probate**. As mentioned before, probate is a legal process, typically managed by courts in the city or county where the person died. The court oversees the transfer of assets from the decedent's estate to their beneficiaries to make sure it's done correctly and fairly. The definition of fairly, according to state law, usually means to pay off any debts of the estate, then distribute the remainder equally among all appropriate beneficiaries. To put your own stamp on this process (and opt out of the default rules of state law), a lawyer can assist with the drafting of a legal will.

Will substitutes can be a good intermediary for some assets that can make probate unnecessary (or at least limit its scope). For example, a joint bank account can serve as a "will substitute," because when one person dies, the status of the account remains— the living co-owner does not have to do anything to get hold of the money in the account. Alternatively, for a single-owned account, you could add a "Transfer on Death" provision that allows your intended beneficiary to access the account without having to go through any of the probate process. In addition, property Joint Titled with Right of Survivorship (JTWROS) allows the "joint owner" to continue owning the property without changing title. Attorney Brown says that, "Many states also have a special joint title for spouses called Tenancy by the Entireties (TBE) that includes survivorship and protection against the creditors of one spouse (but not against creditors of both spouses)." Retirement accounts like IRAs and 401(k)s, along with life insurance accounts, often require beneficiaries listed upon opening. Named beneficiaries automatically escape probate (as long as those beneficiaries survive you, of course).

Not Will Substitutes

Some people conduct a search online and find scores of well-funded websites that will sell you legal documentation after filling out a few online fields. The benefit? You don't have to visit a lawyer and you pay hundreds, if not thousands, of dollars less. The downside? Online sites can give you a document, but only a lawyer can give you advice. And only a licensed lawyer in your state could read through whatever documentation you received from an online site to verify that it was correct for your intended purposes (so you're back to talking with a real-life lawyer).

As a fiduciary, I can't confidently recommend any of these sites to my clients, and if I met you in person, I probably couldn't recommend them to you. Granted, I've noticed recently that you can talk with a real-life lawyer on the phone with some of these services, like LegalZoom, but as a non-lawyer, it's hard to feel confident with a document you won't be alive to dispute. Online solutions are no substitute for a lawyer.

Talking through your personal, likely nuanced situation with an experienced professional who is licensed in your state is the best level of confidence you can have when putting these documents together. That said, people (including lawyers) are fallible, and evaluating the expertise, experience, and emotional intelligence of the estate planner you hire is important. I discussed the advent of online solutions with attorney Ryan Brown, and he suggested,

> *Rather than working with a lawyer that does a DUI on Monday, a "slip and fall case" on Tuesday, and a will on Wednesday, find someone who dedicates a majority or all of their practice to estate planning. As with a good financial planner, a competent and experienced lawyer can use their experience with many other clients to provide you options and help you make the best decisions for your family situation. Furthermore, the tax advice you receive from an estate planning attorney, even if it is for income and capital gains tax and not estate planning purposes, may save more money than what the attorney charges to prepare your plan.*

CHAPTER 26 TAKEAWAYS

Most everyone would like their loved ones to avoid the judicial process of probate after their death. Will substitutes allow the deceased to transfer property without enduring the probate process. Simple examples are joint accounts, joint title, naming beneficiaries, and transfer on death provisions. Will substitutes are not attorney substitutes, nor are online programs an equivalent substitute for hiring an estate attorney licensed to practice in your state.

Actionable Strategies

- Correct your named beneficiaries on any insurance policies, retirement accounts, etc.
- Add transfer/payable on death provisions to all individual bank or brokerage accounts
- Confirm the validity of any documents or advice received by non-attorneys

CHAPTER 27

PAYING AN ESTATE PLANNER

There are few professionals that are as powerful as attorneys. Doctors are up there, with their whole "life and death" thing, but as far as people who wear suits, attorneys carry a lot of social status. As much as we don't want to have to deal with them, somewhere along the lines, we will have to deal with legal issues. An attorney is a good friend to have.

Perhaps your first attorney experience is with an estate planner. Besides passing the bar exam at least once and being licensed in your state, a good estate planning attorney is a specialist. There are generalist attorneys who could manage multiple subject areas, but for something as serious as your life and your death, I would pay the premium for someone who specializes in estate planning every day. I mean, it's just a relief to know it will be done correctly (perhaps even the first time).

Wills

Your life expectancy might be in the eighties or nineties, but life doesn't always go as expected. We don't plan because we expect life to follow a straight line, we plan so we can recalibrate when our plans take a wrong turn. Most people are familiar with the **will** from television. It's the document that does two or three important things:

- Outlines how you want your personal belongings distributed
- Identifies who should do the distributing
- Names guardians for any minor or disabled children

Without this particular estate planning document, your estate is effectively unplanned. Anything that is not already designated to someone through a will substitute technique will be beholden to state rules regarding "intestacy," or an **intestate estate**. What that means is the state laws where you died will determine who gets what. (Note that this will also be the situation if you draft a valid will, but no one knows how to find it.) You will also have died intestate if your will is considered invalid because you didn't follow the rules of your particular state for drafting and signing a valid will. In each state, there are rules around:

- Whether you can handwrite your will
- How your will must be signed

If you want your will to be valid, it pays to pay for the process of a creating one. An estate attorney can walk you through the steps to ensure:

- It is written legally for your state
- It is placed somewhere that it is typically found
- It is updated or reviewed at least bi-annually

Trusts

Most people think that estate plans are just for rich people; hopefully after reading this, you disagree. If there's one document that sounds like it should be reserved for the 1%, it is the **trust**. But in reality, a trust is just another tool created for a specific purpose. Actually, I should say a trust is a tool created for many purposes. Here are the most common reasons people create a trust:

- To avoid probate
- To keep their estate private
- To maintain control of their assets after they die (or are incapacitated)
- To reduce estate tax or income taxes

The reason you can avoid the court process called "probate" with the use of a trust is because you create a new entity with a trust document, which requires a **trustee** to administer (or distribute) your assets for you. This keeps your estate private, because instead of someone going through your local county procedures (probate) to manage your estate through public records (and/or court process), your appointed trustee will handle things directly with your beneficiaries. Your trustee will also help you maintain some control after you're dead and gone, because before you die, you can give that trustee instructions on when distribute assets and when not to. For example, if you have a million-dollar life insurance policy and name your trust as the beneficiary, you can include instructions that says to pay your kids that million dollars over time or after college graduation, when you think they might be better equipped to handle the money. You could also stipulate more specific instructions for use of funds, like housing, healthcare, or educational expenses.

Luckily, you don't have to memorize the kinds of trusts that are available; you only need to know what you are trying to do for future generations, charities, or people you care about. A key distinction between trusts are whether they are **revocable** or **irrevocable**. Revocable trusts are made while you are alive, and you are allowed to change any aspect of them until you die. But when you die, even revocable trusts become irrevocable, because you are no longer alive to change them. An irrevocable trust is also made while you are alive, but none of the terms can be changed once the paperwork is drawn up. You give up all "incidents" of ownership. Why would anyone create a tool that they can't change? Because they are able to permanently remove the assets they put into that trust from their estate. Removing an asset—like a house or a large sum of money— from a person's estate may make sense for liability protection, or in some cases, to reduce a tax burden. Make sense? Since an irrevocable trust is so much more "final" than any of the other tools, take the time to do some long-term planning and carefully consider your options with an estate attorney licensed in your state before committing.

A few more terms you want to be familiar with are grantor, trustee, and beneficiary. A grantor is a person who creates a trust. That person can choose who the trustee will be to administer the trust. The trust creates a legal obligation for the trustee to take actions as specified, for the benefit of the beneficiary. Who's the beneficiary? Whomever the grantor decides (spouse, kids, charity, etc.).

To put it all in context, trusts are most commonly used when people have one or more of the following issues:

- You have a taxable estate (either at the federal or state level)
- You have large taxable (non-Roth) retirement accounts
- You have beneficiaries with disabilities (e.g., disabled adult child), substance abuse problems, problems handling money, or with long-term care needs (e.g., a grandma in the nursing home)
- You own real estate in multiple states (without a trust, your estate will have to go through probate in each state where you have real estate)
- You are at or nearing retirement age
- You are remarried and have children from a prior marriage, different beneficiaries than your new spouse, or significant income or asset disparity with your spouse

When it comes to trusts, there are many flavors. Which trust will best benefit your family (or whether using a trust will benefit them at all) is truly under the purview of an estate attorney, licensed and familiar with laws of your state. No matter what your wealth level, privacy and control may be worth the time and expense of putting together trust documents, but talk to a locally licensed estate attorney before using any of the popular online services (or taking the advice from a book like this).

Digital Estate

Not everyone I know owns real estate, but nearly everyone I know has digital assets, i.e., online property. Notably, this property acts a lot like a timeshare, except you "own" a space on someone else's server just like you "own" the opportunity to reserve time on some corporation's vacation property. Unlike timeshares, it's fairly difficult to maintain a (technologically efficient) social life without social media profiles, bank and billing passwords, email accounts, cell phones, computers, and cloud storage. Unfortunately, as soon as you die, this stuff can just "live" out there forever.

Modern law firms and new tech startups like Everplans.com, FinalRoadmap.com and Yourefolio (to name a few) are smartly investing in this relatively new area of estate law. Most states have a coalesced around the **Revised Uniform Fiduciary Access to Digital Assets Act** (RUFADAA) that specifies the level of control that executors, trustees, power of attorneys, and custodians have over your digital assets. For example, the Google platform provides a "trusted contact" you can choose to:

> *Take control of what happens to your Google Account if you're unexpectedly unable to use your Google Account, such as in the event of an accident or death.*

> *Decide when Google should consider your account to be inactive and what we do with your data afterwards. You can share it with someone you trust or ask Google to delete it.*

Google Terms of Service

With Google, you can decide who gets access and to what, exactly. You can also outline how long before your "trusted contact" is notified of your inactivity. For example, "After 3 months of inactivity we'll contact you one month before your time is up." If you've set up another person to receive your "Recovery Email," then you've kind of started this process of preparing your digital estate, at least in regards to Google. It will help the process go much more smoothly if you let that friend or family member know you selected them.

Without formalizing this in your will, you could also just:

- Make a list of all of your digital property and passwords
- Use a password organizer like 1Password, Dashlane, LastPass, or the Mac OS Keychain that you can share
- Store this information in a secure place, but somewhere your digital executor can find it
- Take time to decide what you would like to do with your digital property

Your views on whether you would like to keep your social media profiles up for posterity or take them down may change over time. Like everything in planning, the point is to practice creating a plan and reviewing your plan, so that you always have the most current one available when needed.

CHAPTER 27 TAKEAWAYS

Do-it-yourself estate planning is a nice idea in concept, but unlike most other services you may choose to in-source (tax preparation, investment management, lawncare), if you screw up your estate plan, you won't be around to fix it. Hiring an estate attorney licensed and experienced in your state to help prepare your will and/or your trust is the best assurance you can give yourself and your family that things will work out.

Creating a trust during your lifetime (a living trust) may provide benefits including avoiding probate, estate privacy, and additional control. Your digital estate is another consideration that modern estate planners are beginning to service. Passwords, social media, online and offline storage are now important parts of most people's estate planning.

Actionable Strategies:

- Contact an estate attorney licensed in your state for an initial consultation—many firms offer them for free
- Be sure to discuss the cost/benefits of using a trust versus just a will
- Identify all items in your digital estate and make provisions that are known

CHAPTER 28

GIVING

In October of 2006, *The Economist* reported on a study by the National Institute of Neurological Disorders and Stroke. In their aptly titled article, "The Joy of Giving," they wanted to understand the neural basis for unselfish acts—essentially, "Why do we do nice things?" It turns out that donating engages a part of the brain—the mesolimbic pathway—that usually gets animated to reflect the love between a mother and child, or even romantic partners. The "good" feelings associated with donating are hardwired into humans.

Mother Teresa described generosity simply by saying, "Everything that is not given is lost." Or, as an estate attorney might say, "Everything that does not have proof you gave it to someone else gets lost in probate." There's just a real joy in giving things away, whether you are alive while doing it or planning to after you have passed away.

Charitable giving is usually associated with the very rich and the very old. When I ran for Congress in 2012, I ran against a very similar stereotype in the image of traditional candidates: usually people who were old and/or rich. But just as you don't have to be old and rich to run for federal office, you don't have to be old or rich to give now or plan for generosity later in life. There are thousands of individual causes that can make good use of your resources—time, talent, or treasure. (In this chapter, the focus is on donating treasure, but in the **Joy of Time** chapter, you will read about the joy of giving time and talent.) Supporting causes (and especially tax-exempt charitable organizations) is part of what can help give you purpose and extend the impact of your wealth and your life.

Starting with your local community and spiraling out further is a wonderful way to start giving. The panhandler on the street corner or busker in the subway are part of a menagerie of people we pass by every day that we want to help, but how? What is the most effective way?

My expectation is that there are both short-term and long-term remedies for the people and causes that could use our financial resources. The cognitive dissonance of deciding what is "right" in each case encourages some people to do nothing, in fear of doing what others might consider the wrong thing. But what if you could work with professionals in philanthropy to put together a custom plan for charity in your budget today, for lifetime gifts, and continued giving after your life? Many organizations, even the large ones, will allow you to promise a certain amount and pay it over time. This way, you don't have to feel like your $50 or $100 is too small to make a difference. You could aspire to a dollar amount that makes sense to you and work your way up to it over a year's worth of paychecks. Your place of worship already does this, your alma mater probably does this, and organizations like community foundations do this as well.

Nikki Jerome Ouellette, associate director of advancement and alumni relations for George Mason University (my alma mater) in Fairfax, Virginia, says, "You can start a scholarship that would be used in the current year for as little as $5,000. An (ongoing) endowment can be created for $25,000." Kelly Blanks, chief philanthropy officer of the Community Foundation of Northern Virginia says, "You can start a scholarship or a 'donor advised fund' as long as you can get it up to $25,000 (scholarship) or $10,000 (donor advised fund) respectively within a year of opening the fund. And minimums are waived for funds opened up for memorials."

Donor Advised Funds (DAF) are charitable giving programs that are run by financial institutions (like brokerages) and public charities. You can donate once, throughout your lifetime, or make irregular contributions to these funds over time, even if you're not quite sure where you'd like the money to go. As a vehicle for charity before or after your death, you can work with the program manager to help decided where you want to "grant" your donations (at once or over time). Imagine setting up a fund that you can contribute to over the next twenty or thirty years. And you could ask your friends to contribute as well. After two or three decades, that fund could be quite significant, enough to change the direction of one or even many lives.

Donor advised funds come in many different flavors and have many different rules. Whether you work with a community foundation or financial institution like Fidelity Charitable, discuss your options with their representatives, your attorney, and your tax professional.

Over the course of your life, these donations could be personally advantageous as well for claiming tax deductions (see a licensed CPA for details). And the older you get, working with a state licensed attorney who specializes in estate law will give you and your family an opportunity to give on, live on, and add more value to whatever legacy you leave behind.

Posterity

Whether you want to leave a legacy to charity or pass along the assets in your estate to family members, you can and should be able to do just that. Two financial tools that are beneficial in navigating your intentions after your passing are life insurance and various types of trusts.

Many people have most of their wealth tied up in property. You can donate stock, mutual funds, real estate, and even the required minimum distributions (RMDs) of your Individual Retirement Account (IRA).

Without proper planning, it's very easy for arguments to break out among people who inherit property of any kind (especially real estate or securities). What if one beneficiary wants to keep a stock or a home for old times' sake, but the other wants to sell it for the cash? Life insurance is used in these cases (by the person who has died) to mitigate these arguments by "liquifying" the estate. Upon death, the life insurance policy provides plenty of cash, and instructions can be made in the will or trust to preserve the house while gifting cash to another beneficiary without all of the hassle. Besides passing along the values of your family, you can pass along some peace at the worst time of your family's life (losing you). Digital estate solution Everplans has a great tagline for making life easy after you are gone: "Leave a legacy, not a mess."

There are many ways for a family to use a trust vehicle in estate planning. In the case of posterity, trust vehicles ensure your wishes for distributing your wealth (i.e., when and how) are legally enforced after you pass away. You can determine, while alive, which instructions you would like to implement now and which are reserved for later. For example, Emma has set aside $1 million of life insurance for a minor child (Alex) in case she dies too young. If Emma dies before Alex turns eighteen-years-old, Alex will receive $1,000,000 at the ripe old age of eighteen-years-old. If, on the other hand, Emma works with an estate attorney licensed in her state, she can create a trust that puts stipulations on that $1,000,000; Alex first has to graduate college, and even then, he can only take out $50,000 per year until the account is exhausted. This would allow her to her guide Alex financially, as best she might have if she were alive.

Some family members may set up a **family trust,** which is no more than a derivative of a revocable or irrevocable trust where the beneficiaries can be multiple family members.

Some people use trust vehicles to set aside some money for family, some for charity, and also to save on taxes (if the estate is large enough where that's a concern). If your legacy will be fulfilled not only by setting aside some money for a family member but also by funding a charity, then an estate attorney may recommend one of many **charitable remainder trusts**. The spirit of these trusts is to irrevocably pay a specific amount of money to a beneficiary for a specific amount of time, then give the rest to the charity. Similarly, a **charitable lead trust** pays to a charity first for a period of time, with the remainder then going to a non-charitable beneficiary. The benefits and mechanics of these kinds of trusts are best explained by a licensed attorney, but know that there are many options in the world of posterity.

CHAPTER 28 TAKEAWAYS

Our brains enjoy giving. Philanthropy through community foundations or other already established organizations is easier than it used to be, and you don't have to be a multi-millionaire to start a scholarship or donor advised fund. You can create instructions for a one-time gift or ongoing gifts that begin while you are alive or after your death.

Gifts to charity can also be made in parallel to bequeathing assets to family (it doesn't have to be one or the other, family versus charity). Using life insurance can help to "liquify" an estate, providing cash where needed, and to donate undisturbed property as you intended. The use of family trusts, either revocable or irrevocable, can assist with posterity. And charitable trusts remain a popular option for a hybrid approach.

Actionable Strategies:

- Contact your local community foundation, place of worship, or alma mater for giving options
- Decide what percentage of your estate you would like to bequeath to family
- Decide what percentage (or amount) of your estate you would like to donate to charity
- Work with an estate attorney licensed in your state for creating any trusts

CHAPTER 29

WHAT DOES ALL OF THIS TYPICALLY COST?

The cost of preparing estate planning documents can vary quite a lot. You will see online services offering a whole package of items (will, powers of attorney, revocable trust, etc.) for under $1,000. They are great deals if they work. If you are going the online service route, at least have it reviewed by a local estate attorney with expertise and experience drafting estate planning documents in your state.

Each estate planning document can be purchased à la carte; in a popular metropolitan area, each will typically cost anywhere from $300 to $1,000. What I mean to say is if you are buying just a will or just putting a durable healthcare power of attorney document in place, you can expect to pay less than $1,000.

Most estate planning attorneys offer a package price for all of the estate planning documents your family could use. In the Washington, D.C. area, local attorneys will charge between $1,500 and $4,000 for an estate planning package that, beyond the basics, may include one trust document. If you end up putting together multiple trust documents, it's not uncommon to spend upwards of $10,000.

Warren Buffet is quoted as saying that, "Cost is what you pay and value is what you get." An expensive attorney may or may not be worth hiring over a less expensive one. Evaluate them based on their level of experience in your state, whether they work with families like yours, and perhaps most importantly, whether they ask you LOTS of questions.

JOY OF LEGACY

Summary

We will all have estates. Legacy planning allows us to take the wealth we have accumulated and provide instructions for who and how others will benefit from the spoils of our labor, skills, and experiences. Estate planning gives us the opportunity to have a definitive form of life after death on this earth. Because we must one day leave the realm of the living, planning to help those who are left behind is nothing short of a kind gesture at the end of a life well-lived.

These days, there is a lot of available technology that is useful in assisting attorneys with the arduous task of compiling all of your documents, passwords, and even pictures into a single repository. Nothing will substitute for the benefits of talking with a qualified estate attorney who is licensed in your state and who specializes in the work. They keep up with the ever-changing laws and have relationships with professional tax preparers, should your estate require taxation by either the federal or state government.

There's nothing like the word "legacy" to make you really think. What do you want to be remembered for? Who do you want to be remembered by? I think of my father almost every day, though he was never rich. There were values he shared with me that I will hold onto forever. There was also a sense of humor.

My father planted a seed of ambition within me to accomplish goals—not just for myself, but also for my family and community. I hope someone close to you has done the same. And I hope this book can impress upon you some of the techniques you can use to make those goals become reality.

A Final Word on Legacy

There is always a danger in thinking more about the future (or the past) than the present. The good news is that legacies are created almost exclusively by what we do day by day, regardless of who's looking. When I was studying for the CFP® exam, I held onto a quote inspired by the Holy Bible: "You will be rewarded in public for what you do in private." The inspiration comes from Matthew 6:4: "And your Father who sees what is done in secret will reward you." What kind of world would we live in if more of us believed that our efforts would unquestionably be rewarded? As citizens of the wealthiest nation in the world, what kind of legacies are we leaving behind for our families and our communities if we do not put forth our best efforts in everything we do as often as possible? I challenge you and the institutional leaders of our country to think about the actions you are taking today and the likely legacies they will leave when you are no longer with us. I make this challenge because I believe strongly that you matter—because it takes very few of us to change the world.

J.K. Rowling's 2008 commencement address to Harvard University graduates has gone viral. Towards the end of her speech, she seems to codify the thoughts I am trying to express here: "We don't need magic to transform our world. We carry all of the power we need inside ourselves already. We have the power to imagine better."

Agreed.

JOY OF OPPORTUNITY

Investing

"An investment in knowledge always pays the best interest."
~Benjamin Franklin

CHAPTER 30

BACKGROUND
& HISTORY

Capturing when and how investing began and what it means to you today was a daunting task. The game of setting aside wealth for a return or gain has been around for centuries. The ability for the common person to participate in that game grew slowly over time; today, almost anyone can get online and trade securities. Though trading securities isn't the only way to invest, it will be the focus of this section.

Mesopotamia to the Netherlands

Most researchers can trace the advent of investing all the way back to Mesopotamia, an area formerly known as Western Asia, but now known blithely as the Middle East. It's the land between the Euphrates and Tigris rivers, and cuts through parts of Syria, Turkey, Kuwait, Iraq, and even Saudi Arabia. (Considering its significance, it seems odd that "Wall Street" is in New York City.) Mostly land owners were allowed to invest, which dramatically isolated the number of people who could do any exchange of assets for returns. Any topic with a history that starts in Mesopotamia (or the advent of Stonehenge and the Egyptian Age) is a topic that basically has been around forever. Investing has been around since the beginning of recorded time.

Though it would be wonderful to explore the chronology of investing as authors Norton Reamer and Jesse Downing do in their acclaimed, *Investment: A History*, I will leave you to pick up that book on your own. I'll jump to what they call the "advent of public markets." There have been stock exchanges—markets where people could buy and sell stocks—since the 16th century. The Dutch East India Company was the first "multinational corporation" and publicly traded company. Thought it was a conglomerate of Dutch companies, it was involved in trading, shipping, and foreign direct investment. It paved the way for multinational corporations (and banks) of our era.

The Role of the Civil War

Understanding the role of the secondary investment markets begins with understanding the primary investment markets. Investment bankers raise capital (money) in what's called the "primary market" for large ventures; typically, corporations "go public" to offer stock (or bonds) in the secondary market. We typically buy them in the secondary market. When we buy stocks and bonds, we're essentially funding the expansive causes of corporations, states, or countries.

In 1861, the cause being funded was the **American Civil War**, and America's first investment banker was Jay Cooke. Jay Cooke & Company sold bonds for the Commonwealth of Pennsylvania and the Union by partnering with his friend, Treasury Secretary

Salmon Chase. Cook was a revolutionary salesman, hiring sub-advisors to market bonds throughout the country and advertising to individuals through newspapers. His teams sold *hundreds* of millions of dollars of bond notes to individuals (and earned handsome commissions). Though his life and his firm ended in failure post-conflict, he is credited with financing the Union during the critical early and final months of the Civil War. The existence of the "United States" of America proves that money makes a difference.

Names You Recognize

The mid-19th century to the early 20th century brought about the investment banking names many people recognize even today. This is in large part because many of their firms have endured many crises, survived and thrived. The year 1854 initiated a partnership in London between George Peabody and Junius S. Morgan. The firm name was eventually changed from Peabody, Morgan and Co. to J.S. Morgan and Co. By 1871, the firm was renamed again, this time in the name of Junius' son, J. Pierpont Morgan. The old-world (read: deep pocket) connections of J. P. Morgan had an outsized impact on the growth of the United States during the Gilded Age of the early 20th century. There would be no U.S. Steel or acknowledgement of Andrew Carnegie without the financing provided by what eventually became known as the House of Morgan on 23 Wall Street.[1]

Later in the 20th century, additional investment banks like Goldman Sachs, Lehman Brothers, Merrill Lynch & Co., Bear Sterns, and Salomon Brothers (Citigroup) were established. These

---

1   "Company History," J.P. Morgan, https://www.jpmorgan.com/global/company-history, 2019.

institutions provided financing for everything from war bonds to U.S. Steel Corporation to Microsoft Corporation to Amazon, Inc. They are not only "market makers," they are "economy makers." Investment banking, the source of primary markets that create the secondary markets we invest in, are a large part of what has made the United States, the United States.

The Laws of Investment Advice

Where does the history of investment advice come from? And how is it different from the emotional selling that Jay Cooke did during the **Civil War**, or the trickery that Jordan Belfort (the man portrayed by Leonardo DiCaprio in *The Wolf of Wall Street*) performed? For that answer, we can go back about a decade, to the Great Recession of 2008, and further back to the Great Depression of 1929. In each case, our United States Congress tasked the Securities and Exchange Commission (SEC) to fix what was wrong with the financial markets—the financial industry. In each instance, the intent of the SEC was for the public's best interests. The **Investment Advisers Act of 1940** was meant to cure society of the ills of hucksters and charlatans who fooled the public into buying products (stocks) when they had no idea what, in fact, they were buying. Initially, the 1940 act was meant to compel people who gave advice and charged for it—the true mark of a professional—to register with the SEC so they could be monitored. Later, this act led to a "fiduciary duty of care," meaning that investment advisers would be held legally responsible for their advice.

Since 1940, it should have been clear who were the aptly titled "advisors" (people hired to give advice for a fee) and who were the salespeople (people paid a commission for their ability to sell financial products). But as the decades have passed, those distinctions have blurred into near-nonexistence.

The **Dodd-Frank Wall Street Reform and Consumer Protection Act of 2010** had many good intentions when reacting to the near loss of liquidity by global markets. Tucked into the 2,000-page law was the ask that the SEC conduct a study of regulatory standards. On April 6, 2016, the U.S. Department of Labor (DOL) issued its infamous **DOL Fiduciary Rule**, "expanding the investment advice fiduciary definition." This rule now meant that every broker, insurance agent, financial advisor, or financial planner—no matter what they called themselves or what rules they thought they were under—would now have to operate in the best interests of their clients when it came to retirement dollars, or face legal liability. In March of 2018, the 5th Circuit Court of Appeals struck down the fiduciary rule. And with that, the financial world of confusion around who is selling products and who is selling advice, remains.

May Day

In the early 1970s, the public started to slow their investments in the stock market; it just cost too much. But on May 1, 1975, that all began to change. On that day, the Securities and Exchange Commission (SEC) ruled against fixed-rate commissions on trading stocks. This might seem counterintuitive, but brokers wanted to fix prices so they could all effectively charge large fees just to trade stocks. This is part of the reason that investing is still associated with rich people: Only rich people could afford to spend $50, $100, or more each time they performed a transaction in the markets. Now, we can trade stocks and bonds for as little as $4.95, and some of the so-called "discount brokers"—Fidelity, TD Ameritrade, E-trade, etc.—offer $0 trades of their funds. Effectively, it can be as little as FREE to participate in the markets. Without the friction of high costs, what separates the investing public from the non-investing public? Not much.

This isn't to say that you can't pay trading fees that are as high as $39.95 or more. The SEC gave brokers the option to charge whatever they wanted. Those that decided to reduce their transaction fees attracted a lot of business; other brokers simply went out of business. Charles Schwab and Co., TD Ameritrade, and Vanguard are three of the firms that tie their history to "May Day" and have obviously succeeded. Once the internet became available to the public in the mid-1990s, the growth of these firms exploded, further bringing down the costs to trade and invest over the long term. Some traditional brokers were able to continue business as usual by folding into banks and insurance companies. And those organizations still charge way too much.

John Bogle, founder of Vanguard, was one of the most well-known advocates of low fee investing. I think I happened to notice the ads for "no-load funds" because I worked in banking in the early-mid 1990s, but it took me a while to figure out what those commercials were talking about. I was just a bank teller— what did I care?

Loads were fees. By the 1990s, people were used to paying up to 8.5% up front just to buy a mutual fund. This meant that if you invested $100,000 on day one in a "load" mutual fund, by day two, you would effectively have $92,500 left over. With market fluctuation and other transactions, I imagine most investors didn't even know that the funds they were buying cost them that much. I know this because even now, there are investors that pay for "loaded" mutual funds sold at banks and many brokerage firms, and still don't know that they don't have to.

Back in the 1990s, technology and monopolies limited access to institutional funds that did not charge a fee up front or when you took your money out. Those funds were typically restricted to people who were investing at least $50,000, $100,000, or more. Today, we just don't have those limits. With $5 or $10, you and I have access to the stocks (fractions of stocks, if necessary), mutual funds, or exchange traded funds of our choice. Today, the only people that pay "loads" or high transaction fees are the people who don't know better. Now, you know.

The internet has made buying or selling securities cheap, easy, and frictionless. The majority of the investment universe is available to be bought and sold directly by the public. This has removed the barriers of cost and minimums to entering the investment markets. You can look up almost any individual investment or group of investments and make a purchase on online investment platforms like TD Ameritrade, Vanguard, or E-Trade. There is no longer a buffer between you and the securities markets that fund the world. This is quite different from the days of Mesopotamia, when investing was only available to a select few. And that is the opportunity and the challenge.

CHAPTER 31

INVESTING

There is no topic in financial planning as popular as investing. Whether I tell someone I am a financial planner, adviser, or wealth manager, their thoughts immediately turn to buying stocks and bonds. Understandably, there's probably no sexier topic in finance than the power of investing and its lottery-like ability to grow your income. Yes, I said lottery-like. Life insurance is lottery-like too, but someone you know has to die first (so that's no fun). Investing is different! No one has to die for you to succeed, but even though everyone loves investing, no one wants to lose. And some do.

This chapter is about taking the money you have saved and making it work harder than it would in a typical savings account. We will learn when it is important to invest in primarily the stock market and when it is appropriate to sit on the sidelines. We will define terms like "asset allocation" and "diversification," along with phrases like "the market" and "the index." We will also discuss the fees that are a part of investing, and what the smartest people do to ensure they don't lose in the long run. Finally, we will round out the chapter with the concept of investment philosophy, discussing a few of the differences between passive investing and active investing.

This is one of the most important sections in this book, because learning how to leverage the power of making money upon itself will help you achieve growth beyond yourself. The wealthiest investors do not worry about sending their kids to college or their retirement. They worry about what they can do to achieve the dreams they set out for themselves, their families, and their communities.

PERSONAL EXPERIENCE

I can tell you from experience that I found the joy of investing at an early age. Unfortunately, I just didn't continue. Because I worked full-time at a bank in college, I was exposed to a lot of the financial world from the bottom up. In the 1990s, the bank was where you went to deposit your paycheck, cash your paycheck, open an account, and even check your balance. There was certainly no online banking, because there was no "online." Back then, I dabbled, and despite not having a huge savings account, I wanted to learn about this stock market thing. So, I bought a stock, or ownership interest, in Intuit Corporation. As an accounting major, buying my first share of stock in the company that owned Turbo Tax made sense to me. I also invested $50 per month in either T. Rowe Price or Janus Funds and kept that going for a while. I got lucky with the Intuit stock, as it increased over the six or seven months I owned it. That year, I sold the stock and bought Christmas presents with my gains. As for the $50 per month I contributed to the mutual fund company, I know that I eventually cashed out the account; looking back, I wish I had kept contributing and left that account alone. The compounding over these last twenty plus years would have increased my net worth significantly.

Over the years, investing then selling after some accumulation success has been my pattern. I remember in 2005 having some extra money and deciding between buying some Garmin stock (the company that, at the time, dominated GPS systems) and Apple. Apple had just launched iPhone and the iPod a few years before. I invested in Garmin, and when I sold about a year later, had an 80% gain, which was good. Over that same period, had I invested in Apple, I would have had a 300% gain. And of course, had I invested in Apple and held that stock until 2018, the growth would have likely been over the 1000% range! The lesson it took me a while to learn was that if you believe in a company that you choose to invest in, hang onto it for a while. Even if you're investing in pools of companies with mutual funds or exchange traded funds, hang onto them for a while. Investing is not a short-term game. The only reason to invest is to beat inflation, and inflation is a long-term concern. When we invest your money in education, the stock market, or the housing market, we shouldn't expect to see the returns for a few years. Managing your expectations by taking a long-term view will help you beat inflation and ensure your money has time to make money.

PROFESSIONAL EXPERIENCE

More than any other topic in financial planning, friends, family, clients, and prospective clients want to know my "investment philosophy." They don't always ask the question in the same way, but they get the same answer regardless of what they ask: "Hey Jason, what do you think of the markets?" "Do you have any good stock tips for me?" "How would you invest my money?" "What advice would you give me for investing my retirement account at work?" All of these questions are slightly different, but the answer is simply: "I believe in the growth of the world economy and I believe the U.S. stock markets and exchanges are efficient and fair."

What that statement means is I primarily practice **passive** investment management. The following is an excerpt from my company's standard investment policy statement:

Passive investing involves building portfolios that are comprised of various distinct asset classes. The asset classes are weighted in a manner to achieve a desired relationship between correlation, risk, and return. Funds that passively capture the returns of the desired asset classes are placed in the portfolio. The funds that are used to build passive portfolios are typically exchange traded funds.

Passive investment management is characterized by low portfolio expenses (i.e., the funds inside the portfolio have low internal costs), minimal trading costs (due to infrequent trading activity), and relative tax efficiency (because the funds inside the portfolio are tax efficient and turnover inside the portfolio is minimal).

Our investment philosophy can be summarized as our best interpretation to date of Nobel Laureate Eugene Fama's view of efficient market theory. He believed value stocks outperformed growth stocks (and by definition, value ETFs will compare similarly with growth ETFs). This, among other concepts—for which he earned a Nobel Prize—has historically, though not necessarily predictably, allowed for higher returns with lower risk.

We also invest to proportionally represent the global market for securities by weighting our allocations representatively between international and domestic securities.

I try to match the market performance of various classes of stock. I do not try to "beat the market." There are professional "traders" and professional "investors." Professional traders can be highly credentialed and knowledgeable, but they are trading securities for short-term gains, trying to minimize short-term losses. Professional *investors* provide a service to clients based on academic research that they are always wrapping their minds around to grow their money intentionally, alongside a long-term plan. This is the service I provide for my clients. This is why one of the most important questions I ask clients before investing their money is, "When do you need access to this money?" Another way I might ask the same question is, "What do you need this money for?" By getting a sense of their timing, I learn which risks I can eliminate on their behalf.

Risk

At its core, investing is leverage: yours and the people or institution you are investing in. Of course, the smart investors know that whenever you invest your money, you are investing in people. You are taking a bet (a risk) that your money will do better in the hands of someone else. For example, if you choose to buy a share of Microsoft stock, you are making a bet on the CEO of Microsoft and his management team. If you choose to invest in debt like a municipal bond for Detroit, you are making a bet on the mayor of Detroit and perhaps the governor of Michigan. Behind every investment, there is a steward. When you choose an investment—or more indirectly, when you choose a financial advisor to invest on your behalf—you choose a steward of your money.

No matter what you do with the money you don't spend, you will incur a risk. The only questions are what kind of risk are you willing to take with your hard-earned money, and for what trade-off? The higher the likelihood you could lose your money, the higher potential return. Risk and return go together. For example, if you put $10,000 in a FDIC insured bank account, your money is fairly safe because it's backed by the U.S. government. In fact, since its founding on January 1, 1934, no bank customer has lost money due to a bank failure. Since FDIC insurance per depositor is currently $250,000, I guess we can say that your $10,000 would be more than "fairly safe." That being the case, you wouldn't have any **liquidity risk** (the risk that you couldn't access your money), but you would have **inflation risk** (the risk that the price of goods will rise at a higher percentage than the interest you are being paid by the bank). For example, if your bank is paying 1% in interest but inflation is close to 2%, in the short-term, that 1% point doesn't matter, but in the long run, your money will lose purchasing power (compounded at 1% per year). When you invest in markets—whether the stock market, bond market, or housing markets, for example—your money is susceptible to **market risk**: the risk that the market might go into a downward trend. In the short-term, this is a much riskier option than banks, because any market could drop at any given moment for any given amount. In the long term, however, history has shown that our U.S. stock market, on average, has trended up at a higher rate than inflation.

So, in summary, investing in the securities markets (long-term) helps to mitigate market risk and inflation risk, and setting money aside for the short term helps to mitigate liquidity risk.

CHAPTER 32

INVESTMENT PHILOSOPHY

With literally thousands of options, you can invest according to your tolerance for risk and how long you have to invest. How you sort through the thousands of options will depend, in large part, on your investment philosophy. Two of the more popular investment strategies are nicknamed "**active**" and "**passive**." They are based in part on whether your goal is to perform better than the overall stock market (active) or whether matching the market's performance is enough (passive). The passive approach is a bet on the overall economy. The technique here is investing broadly, in a way that represents the overall market. You'll hear people talk about investing in an index like the S&P 500 or Dow Jones Industrial Average. By way of example, the S&P 500 Index is a measure of value that represents the 500 largest companies in the world. The way to invest in the S&P 500 Index is with an S&P 500 index fund, which is essentially a collection of securities that mimic the S&P 500. You typically invest in index funds for a long, long time, regardless of the ups and downs, with confidence that in the long term, you will beat inflation. With this strategy, you make a bet on the overall market economy rather than an individual or small collection of companies.

The **active** strategy requires more analysis, knowledge, and experience. This strategy requires that you make educated guesses on which securities will outperform the overall market indexes. Because stock markets are "markets," by definition, for every buyer, there is a seller. Like every market, the prices of stocks and bonds are based on the laws of supply and demand. If you believe you can "beat the market," then you believe those prices are wrong. **Fundamental analysis** is one method for evaluating the company behind the stock or bond. This analysis might require you look at the financial statements of the company, the leadership, and where this company is positioned in its industry. Hundreds of analysts on Wall Street are paid to do this kind of work every day, and the prices of stocks are represented by that work in the stock market. If you believe you know something they don't, then the active strategy says make a move to buy or sell a security. **Technical analysis**, the other popular method for evaluating securities, asks you to analyze what's happening in the overall economy that might be affecting a particular company's stock. With this method, you would measure stock charts that represent stock price trends and averages. You ignore the individual company and focus squarely on stock prices.

Within the active trading philosophy, there is a debate over whether fundamental or technical analysis is better for evaluating stocks; for passive investors, that argument is a moot point. Over time, most stock traders don't beat the overall market approach with the active philosophy, so many famous investors, including the likes of Warren Buffett, suggest investing using the passive approach.[1]

---

1   Martin, Emmie, "Warren Buffett just won a $1 million bet—and highlighted one of the best ways to grow wealth," January 3, 2018, https://www.cnbc.com/2018/01/03/why-warren-buffett-says-index-funds-are-the-best-investment.html, 2019.

The **passive** approach provides for low portfolio expenses, minimal trading costs, and tax efficiency (because turnover of the funds inside the portfolio is low). Even with this philosophy, there are still choices between growth and value investing, domestic and international, large and small, and many other factors. Strong arguments can be made for all kinds of nuanced strategies. What's important is that you or your financial adviser choose a strategy and stick with it. If that happens, investing has a chance to help you progress towards your goals. Inconsistency, on the other hand, will eventually eat away at whatever gains you accumulate. The markets are just too unpredictable to outguess.

What you invest in largely depends on where you invest: through a retirement account at work, through a broker, or on your own.

Investing in Securities

Traditionally, when people think of investing, they think of stocks and bonds. **Stocks** are part of the equity (or ownership) markets, and **bonds** are part of the debt markets. Of course, you could also invest in real estate, commodities, futures, or even yourself! But by and large, the public approaches me as a financial planner about the investment news, which is typically focused on stocks and bonds. If I limited the investing options to just securities, what where would that leave us?

First, note that buying any iteration of "stocks or bonds" is a discussion about the secondary markets. The primary market is the world of investing in companies before they are **publicly held,** meaning before they have gone through the scrutiny of the SEC and partnered with investment banks to issue stocks and bonds for the first time. After the stocks and bonds are issued to the public through an initial public offering (IPO), that's when the majority of us have a chance to buy.

As a side-note, if you could buy the stock at its IPO price (the first price it was issued at on the day of sale), you would get a heck of a deal. This is because you would be able to buy before everyone else. Assuming the company is a good one and the stock goes up, you would have purchased the lowest general public price. Of course, it could also go down in the future, but that's investing.

Because of this risk, since 1982, the SEC has only allowed **accredited investors** to participate in pre-IPO sales. An accredited investor is defined as someone with a net worth of $1 million either individually or with a spouse, or an individual who has made $200,000 in the past two years (or $300,000 with a spouse). Some of you reading this may think, "That's me!" Even though you qualify, gaining access to pre-IPOs is tough; it's a crowded space due to the benefits I explained earlier. For the purposes of this book, rather than focusing on the primary market, I will focus more explicitly on the more widely available secondary market.

The Secondary Market

According to the World Federation of Exchanges Database (part of the World Bank website), there are just under 45,000 publicly listed companies across the globe. That's a large number, but note that there were just over 8,000 publicly traded companies in the United States in December of 1996; today, there are fewer than 5,000.[2] The United States has just about 11% of the number of public companies, but just over 40% of the world's equity market

2   Halbert, Gary D., "Number Of U.S. Public Companies Falls By Almost 50%," Value Walk, July 31, 2018, https://www.valuewalk.com/2018/07/number-of-us-public-companies-fall-50/, 2019

share. According to Bloomberg Market Cap Indices, Japan is the second largest, with just under 8%.

If you were concerned about investing in one of those 45,000 companies individually, you can reduce your choices by about 80% by choosing to invest in mutual funds (there are only about 10,000). **Mutual funds** are an open investment fund that pools your money with other investors so you don't have to choose individual stocks or bonds. Portfolio managers sell mutual funds à la carte and you can buy them through brokerage firms online (like TD Ameritrade, Vanguard, or Schwab). A mutual fund is an investment vehicle that gives individual investors access to hundreds of stocks or bonds in one little package.

If you aren't too interested in wading through 10,000 mutual funds, you could choose from the even smaller pool of funds: the 5,000 or so **exchange traded funds**. Exchange traded funds are similar to mutual funds, but they can be traded more like a stock and your choices are more likely to represent a certain sector/industry as well as **index**. An index is a measure of the overall market through representation of a group of securities. If you've ever heard of the **Dow Jones Industrial Average**, that's an index of thirty large, publicly traded companies that attempts to measure the overall market. If those thirty companies happen to be "up" one day, then the Dow is up, and vice versa. Similarly, the S&P 500 is a measure of 500 large companies. With mutual funds or exchange traded funds, you can invest in an index like the DOW or S&P that represents the entire equity market, or you can invest in an index that represents the bond market, small companies, large companies, international companies, and on and on. As I mentioned, there are 10,000 mutual funds and about 5,000 exchange traded funds. Thanks especially to the internet, we all have inexpensive access to all of them.

You can now invest in securities markets with smaller

amounts of money than used to be possible. This only helps, of course, if you know what you are doing.

Warren Buffet, one of the best investors in the history of investing, only invests in what he understands. He never invested much in the dot-com companies of the 1990s, because he just couldn't understand how those companies were going to make any real money. At first, he looked like a fool—the stock prices of the first internet-based companies rose greatly throughout the mid-1990s—but investing is a long-term game. By March of 2000, many of the internet stock values came crashing down, and all of a sudden, people like Buffet looked pretty smart.

What Buffet highlighted is if you don't understand what you are investing in, you are gambling (or speculating) without a basis in fact. Speculating is not investing; it is hoping that you're right based on biases you may not recognize.

When you gamble, you're just playing the odds, and in the long run, the "house" usually wins. There's a reason my industry has been able to afford so much real estate in Manhattan.

CHAPTER 32 TAKEAWAYS

Investing in the securities markets does not have to be random. Credible investors have an investment philosophy that is a guiding principle for their decisions (or non-decisions). Active strategies require either fundamental or technical analysis to make decisions based on a belief that you recognize something that is not recognized by the rest of the market. Passive management subscribes to the efficient market theory that the market at large is fairly pricing securities, and your investments are a bet on the global market.

There are literally thousands of options to choose from just in the securities markets: 45,000 individual securities, 10,000 mutual funds, and 5,000 exchange traded funds. Mutual funds and exchange traded funds help to decrease the complexity by investing in the broader market through pools of investments.

Actionable Strategies:

- Make a decision about your investment philosophy: active, passive, or a mix
- Make a decision about what you will invest in: individual securities, mutual funds, ETFs
- Compare the benefits of investing in indexes versus other strategies

CHAPTER 33

WHEN & WHERE TO INVEST

Before thinking about investing your money, stop to ask yourself a few questions: Do I have insurance policies to cover emergencies I can't afford? Do I have enough savings for other emergencies (i.e., the ones I should be able to afford)? If you have the right amount of savings and insurance, then you just might be prepared for the risks and rewards of markets.

When investing, take into account *when* you might need the money available. The sooner you need access to the money (i.e., cashed out), the higher your risk of losing money. The stock market going up or down is based on many factors, including global and national economic conditions, analysts' opinions, and the leadership behind the company or the government where you invest. If you have more than ten years before you will need to cash out the money, then statistically, based on past performance of the markets (which is legally no guarantee of future results), you have a better chance of recovering from a drop in the stock market. So, statistically, market risk is lower with a longer time horizon. Planning to take the money out of investments before ten years increases the risk that you will lose money. That kind of risk I'll call "personal timing" risk. Personal timing risk is the risk that you're getting ahead of yourself.

Again, the simplest and most important question I ask clients when they ask me to invest their money is "When will you need it?" That helps to determine their **risk capacity,** i.e., their ability to take on risk considering other factors in their financial plans. There is a lot of time and money put towards **risk tolerance**: an investor's ability to see the value of their money fluctuating, but stick to their plan. I believe that once you understand how markets work over a period of time, the bigger factor is risk capacity. This should give every investor the ability to take a deep breath. Your investing prowess does not have to depend on your stock market feelings. Instead, it can be based on factors you can determine based on your life goals and timing. The stock market will be there when you are absolutely ready.

Investing at Work

Since the 1980s, the most common way to invest is through your employer's retirement account. When you invest through work, you are limited by what your employer has decided will be good investment options. Your employer was sold a package by a retirement plan advisor, who designed a retirement plan that suits you and your co-workers. It was based on the number of employees and the fees your employer was willing to pay the retirement plan advisor (and the fees your employer chose to pass on to you and your co-workers). This is how you got your investment options at work. Usually this means you will use a retirement account to invest in groups of companies through mutual funds or exchange traded funds. There have been lawsuits brought by employees against their employers for having limited investment choices through their work retirement accounts.

The fees are typically low, though that depends on how your employer negotiated the structure of the retirement account. The best way to ensure you're not paying fees you should not is to read the **Summary Plan Description (SPD)** of your retirement account at work. Identify what the fees are for the overall account (usually under $100 per year) and whether there's a management fee (typically 1 to 1.5% per year). The management fee is similar to the advisory fee you might pay to your personal financial adviser. If you are paying this fee for your 401(k) or 403(b) work retirement account, at least use the service. Ask your employer for the brokerage's contact person who set up the account, to receive at least their version of advice.

You will typically have either **mutual fund** or **exchange traded fund** options rather than individual stocks or bonds in an employer-based retirement account. As an investor, you get the benefit of not having to buy or evaluate individual stocks or bonds to get access to them. A portfolio manager, employed by the mutual fund company, does the selecting in the background. Your investment gets blended along with others in a pool of funds, which, in turn, are invested in stocks, bonds, or mimic an index much like a mutual fund.

For the packaging and the portfolio manager, the investor (this is you, the employee) pays a fee called an **expense ratio**. This expense, or cost to you, is paid every year, so you want to know what it is; they vary from 0.01% to just under 2% per year. This is the difference between investing $1,000 and paying $1 in fees per year or just under $20. That's a 2,000% difference in fees, which you can imagine, over the years, will make a big difference in the growth of your retirement account.

Exchange traded funds (ETFs) work much the same way as

mutual funds in an employer account. One of the major differences is that ETFs are traded on a stock exchange, so their value fluctuates throughout the day like a stock and unlike a mutual fund, which has its value calculated at the end of the day. Most ETFs contain cheaper expense ratios than their mutual fund counterparts. If your employer has ETFs for you to invest in, celebrate. If they don't, ask, "Why not?"

Investing Outside of Work

It used to be that you had to go through a broker to invest in the markets outside of work. Using a broker meant that you had to meet certain dollar amount minimum before you could invest, and willing to pay a certain level of fees for their expertise. A large amount of a broker's expertise was based on the limited access and exposure the public had to investment instruments available through debt and equity markets. The public used to also pay high fees for "execution" of transactions, or buying and selling. This, of course, was all before the aforementioned "May Day."

When investing outside of your employer's options, you have so many choices. Not only is there the universe of securities to choose from, there is a universe of brokerage options to choose from to buy and sell those securities. You can go directly to discount brokers like Vanguard, TD Ameritrade, Schwab, E-Trade, or Fidelity. They have constantly improving solutions that will move your money from your bank, brokerage account, or old 401(k), and allow you to invest on your own or with the help of their phone bank folks. You can also work with one of the newer firms, like Betterment or Wealthfront, who will minimize your human interaction while providing the cutting edge of technology to manage your money. You could also work with an investment adviser.

Investment Advisers

You can eliminate many of the decisions by working with a financial planner or investment adviser who has access to a brokerage account. You will still have the responsibility of evaluating the kind of investment adviser you are working with. Here are just a few questions you should ask:

- Do you work as a fiduciary all of the time?
- What is your investment philosophy?
- How are you paid and how can I calculate my total fees?

You can do a quick background check on supposed investment advisers on *Brokercheck.finra.org* or *AdviserInfo.Sec.gov* to at least see if the person you are evaluating is licensed and whether anyone has filed a complaint. You can also confirm credentials like the CPA license or the CFP® professional marks on *CPAVerify.org* and *CFP.net*. Regardless, you will find there are many licensed professionals, unlicensed professionals, professionals who pretend to have an investment philosophy, and professionals who don't have an investment philosophy at all, and they have one thing in common: they would *love* to manage your money. Whether you choose to learn how to invest on your own or hire someone, you will need to do some ongoing research.

CHAPTER 33 TAKEAWAYS

Timing is everything in the world of investing. There is little need to invest in the long-term opportunities of the stock market unless you are saving money over and above your immediate (one-year needs). With ten years or more before you need to spend the money you plan to invest, you will have a high statistical chance of earning a return versus a loss. Note that using time as your greatest determinant for investing pays greater attention to your risk capacity versus the feelings of your risk tolerance.

Investing through an employer-based plan limits your investment options. The smaller universe of mutual funds and exchange traded funds allows you to focus on fees rather than the choice of 45,000 different securities. Working with investment advisers outside of work is an option whether you have an employer-based plan or not. Evaluating an investment adviser's credentials and background can be as exhausting as learning to invest for yourself. Choose accordingly.

Actionable Strategies:

- Create your financial plan, emergency fund, and insurance plan before investing
- Commit to investing for ten years before exposing your money to securities markets
- Review the fees in your employer-based retirement plans
- Choose to learn gradually about investing as you evaluate investment advisers

JOY OF OPPORTUNITY

Summary

Investing is mostly about opportunity, leverage, and risks that you can afford when you have created the proper risk capacity. There's a proper order of things, and you ought not invest until you have the ability to save and set aside three to six months' worth of your non-discretionary expenses. It's not easy to save that kind of money when you have credit card debt, so paying that down along with any other high interest debt should happen first. It's hard to pay down debt if you spend more than you make or, put another way, unless you spend much less than you make. Investing is so easy to do today because it can be so inexpensive, but that creates the moral hazard of people dabbling in the stock market before they are ready financially.

Once you are "ready," then deciding upon an investment philosophy is important (and writing it down will help). An investment philosophy is not meant to change, and it will help to manage your instinctive behavior of "protecting yourself" by selling out of positions when the values are low or buying in when the values are high. Understand that even when you do participate in the markets, you will have to decide whether you would like to incur the transaction costs of purchasing individual securities or purchase funds that will incur ongoing costs called "expense ratios." Most people benefit from investing in swaths of the entire market, which can be done more readily by investing in funds. There are discount fund families like Vanguard, Fidelity, and Schwab that will allow you to invest for yourself for fees as low as $0 per year. Yes, $0.

Though investing in the securities markets is much easier than it used to be, this may not be the best place to make your money work for you. You can invest in the housing market, your own business, or your education. Whichever you choose, be as clear about the risks as you are about the opportunities.

My industry makes the selfish mistake of pretending the only way you can invest is in the financial markets. Reading this book is an investment in yourself, and I hope that you continue investing in your education before you participate in the wild markets of finance. You may invest in a home, you may invest a business, and you may even invest in the securities markets. But the investment you make in yourself and your community will mean a lot, perhaps the most, in the long history of the world.

A Final Word on Opportunity

One of the greatest gifts my father gave to me was moving to California before I was born. As a natural-born U.S. citizen, the entire world of opportunities is available to me, including becoming president or vice president of these United States! But even being a naturalized citizen or a permanent resident of this country means you have been gifted a lucky break in life. What you and I do with that lucky break is the question. As part of the wealthiest nation on the planet, there is plenty of opportunity for us to create financial wealth here, of course. Capitalism ensures some of the people are going to get rich. How about the rest of the people? How about the next generation of your family? Will the opportunities always be available, or will the rising costs of healthcare, housing, and formal education crowd out more and more of us? I hope not.

The American Dream is the ideal that no matter who you are, you can win (whatever "winning" means to you). As President Kennedy said in the inaugural speech I've referenced before, "I don't believe any of us would exchange places, with any other people or any other generation." We have new challenges (including some old challenges that have arisen again), but we also have new opportunities. We can create income and wealth in ways that our grandparents could never dream about. And with that wealth, we can work to fight disease, give opportunities to the oppressed, and yes, heal the planet. I like my chances in a world with these opportunities, and I believe you do, too.

JOY OF TIME

Retiring

"Lose no time; be always employed in some-thing useful; cut off all unnecessary actions."
~Benjamin Franklin

CHAPTER 34

BACKGROUND
& HISTORY

Retirement Income vs. Retirement Savings

Too often, the topic of retirement winds up strictly in the weeds of saving and purely financial decisions. This is what happens when the tail wags the dog, and especially when there's a financial incentive for the tail waggers. The biggest scam people in my industry played upon the public was the idea that you needed to save up millions of dollars before you could enjoy the freedom of retirement. Yes, that is one way, but a more predictable way to attain control of the second part of life is by creating an ongoing income stream.

The modern idea of an ongoing income stream provided by the government to citizens as they age dates back to 1881 in Germany. Those ideas turned into what we could call legislation, with the passing of the **Old Age and Disability Insurance Law of 1889**. The law created a pension for workers who miraculously lived to age seventy (life expectancy was closer to forty-five back then). It was considered distinctly progressive at the time, because the national government was expected to be at least one of the underwriters. In a historical irony, German Chancellor Otto von Bismarck, aka the "Iron Chancellor," would be the singular individual to bring about the "welfare state" to the modern world.[1]

The 1889 law was preceded by the **Accident Insurance Law of 1884** and the **Sickness Insurance Law of 1883**. During the 19th century, many workers in the United States (firefighters, railroad workers, teachers, police, the military) were part of public pension systems, but there was not yet a true national welfare program. Corporate pensions began in 1875 with American Express, followed by many legendary companies like General Electric, U.S. Steel, Standard Oil, Goodyear, and others. The **Revenue Act of 1921** came on the heels of **World War I**, and was this country's first tax cut legislation. It not only repealed a wartime corporate tax, it also eliminated taxes on pension plan contributions for employees. This undoubtedly increased the popularity of pension programs, albeit with long vesting periods (upwards of twenty years).

Social Security

The Social Security Act of 1935 was signed into law by President Franklin Roosevelt to limit poverty brought on (in part) by the Great Depression of the early 1930s. The original law was designed to compensate workers, but two years later, in 1937, benefits were extended to the spouse and minor children. Over the years, additional benefits were added to Social Security, including a disability program in 1954 and the landmark Medicare health benefits in 1965. In 2017, 58.5 million people received Medicare benefits,

---

1   Ebeling, Richard, "Marching to Bismarck's Drummer: The Origins of the Modern Welfare State," Fee, December 1, 2007, https://fee.org/articles/marching-to-bismarcks-drummer-the-origins-of-the-modern-welfare-state/, 2019.

according to the Centers for Medicare and Medicaid Services. The Old-Age, Survivors, and Disability Insurance (OASDI) is the comprehensive name for benefits associated with Social Security, Medicare, and disability programs. The program is paid for by the **Federal Insurance Contributions Act** (FICA) that serves as the payroll tax on all of our paychecks.

Employee Retirement Income Security Act (ERISA)

The **ERISA** law of 1974 was signed by President Gerald Ford, but its development came about early in President John F. Kennedy's Committee on Corporate Pensions in 1961. By 1961, pensions had become so popular that a commission was necessary to explore the ramifications of their growth on the economy. Those concerns were validated by the closing of automaker Studebaker Corporation in 1963. Plainly, they just didn't have enough money to pay out the pensions they had promised. ERISA was eventually enacted to bring transparency and regulation to a tax haven for corporate trustees, who before then had very few rules to follow. The law also chartered the Pension Benefit Guaranty Corporation (PBGC), meant to act much like the Federal Deposit Insurance Corporation (FDIC) for bank members. It has a mandate to both to assist with uninterrupted pension payments while also keeping insurance premiums as low as possible for member firms.[2]

Inaccurate actuarial assumptions and overestimated market returns have put both public and private pension benefit payouts at risk. Some might say the ERISA Act was too late, and by the **Revenue Act of 1978**, the pensions obituary had already been written.

2   "History of EBSA and ERISA," Employee Benefits Security Administration, https://www.dol.gov/agencies/ebsa/about-ebsa/about-us/history-of-ebsa-and-erisa, 2019.

401(k), 403(b), TSP

The mid-point of the 20th century had employers jockeying with the Internal Revenue Service (IRS) to create new cash or other deferred compensation arrangements (CODA). Edwin T. Johnson and his employee Ted Benna are credited with being the godfather and father of one of those options: the current 401(k). Though a seemingly innocuous provision of the tax code, through their benefits consulting firm and a little lobbying, the 401(k) provision was signed into law by President Jimmy Carter in 1978.[3]

The Revenue Act of 1978 officially provided a tax break for employees who deferred their compensation. By 1981 (one year after the law went into effect), the IRS had issued the regulations that allowed employees to use salary deductions for retirement plan contributions. Immediately, employers started replacing their old pension plans with 401(k)s. Within two years—just two years—half of ALL large firms were preparing to offer or were already offering a 401(k) plan. These included firms like Honeywell, Johnson & Johnson, and PepsiCo.[4] Five years later, the Federal Employees Retirement System Act of 1986 (FERS) brought Thrift Savings Plans (TSPs) to the government (which was effectively a 401(k) plan for federal government workers).[5]

3   Arnold, Lawrence and Margaret Collins, "Edwin Johnson, 'Godfather' of 401(k) Retirement Plan, Dies at 82," Bloomberg, August 30, 2012, https://www.bloomberg.com/news/articles/2012-08-30/edwin-johnson-godfather-of-401-k-retirement-plan-dies-at-82, 2019.

4   Adams, Nevin, "The Birth of a Notion," PSCA: Plan Sponsor Council of America, November 6, 2018, https://www.psca.org/blog_nevin_2018_1, 2019.

5   Isaacs, Katelin P., "Federal Employees' Retirement System: The Role of the Thrift Savings Plan," Congressional Research Service, March 10, 2015, https://fas.org/sgp/crs/misc/RL30387.pdf, 2019.

Gig Economy

Recent studies published by McKinsey and a handful of academics were reported by the *Harvard Business Review*. The report of sixty-five workers revealed that they spent most of their time designing a "physical, social and psychological space for their work."[6] Not unlike retirees, these gig workers were (and are) constantly seeking the elusive comforts of place, routine, purpose, and people. In a way, this "new" workstyle is like any form of entrepreneurship. The "gig economy" is a new term for an old form of making money: working odd jobs. The internet has facilitated the reach of service providers and the visibility. It used to be that if you had a skill but little money, your challenge was letting enough people know about it to keep your billable hours up. The revolution of the gig economy is really about the (sometimes free, usually variable cost) platforms that make freelance workers visible without any fixed costs. It's the same old world, but the platform economy is one of the unique opportunities we have to combat the new challenges we face.

---

6   Ashford, Susan J., et al., "Thriving in the Gig Economy," Harvard Business Review, March/April 2018, https://hbr.org/2018/03/thriving-in-the-gig-economy, 2019.

CHAPTER 35

JOY OF TIME

Ellis Boyd Redding. Your files say you've served forty years of a life sentence. Do you feel you've been rehabilitated?

Rehabilitated? Well now, let me see. You know, I don't have any idea what that means.

Well, it means you're ready to rejoin society...

I know what you think it means, sonny. To me, it's just a made-up word. A politician's word, so young fellas like yourself can wear a suit and a tie and have a job. What do you really want to know? Am I sorry for what I did?

Are you?

There's not a day goes by I don't feel regret. Not because I'm in here, because you think I should. I look back on the way I was then: a young, stupid kid who committed that

terrible crime. I want to talk to him. I want to try to talk
some sense to him; tell him the way things are. But I can't.
That kid's long gone; this old man is all that's left. I gotta
live with that. Rehabilitated? It's just a bullshit word. So,
you go on and stamp your form, sonny, and stop wasting
my time. Because to tell you the truth, I don't give a shit.

That scene from *The Shawshank Redemption* reminds me of how useless the word "retirement" is to many people. Do an online search for "retirement statistics," and you will find a slew of articles on how terrible the retirement outlook is for large amounts of people. The sharp decrease in pension plans, the high cost of housing and college, the accumulated effect of low interest rates since the 2008 financial crisis, and the low growth in salaries since the 1970s have all put pressure on the ability to prepare for retirement. But so too has the decrease in the quality of our food, which has taken and a toll on our overall nutrition. President Kennedy's admonition to explore the "wonders of science" are keeping us alive, despite chronic heart disease and diabetes. We may live longer, but how well will we live?

For those who have been fortunate enough to prepare well for wealth and health, the season of retirement is an opportunity to finally control your time. In your sixties and seventies, you may not get up as quickly as you used to, you may have less hair, and the hair you do have has turned gray. No one mistakes you for someone in their twenties or even thirties anymore; you could be a fitness model, but to people under thirty, you are still unquestionably "old." That's just part of growing up and being lucky enough to have experienced multiple decades of this game called life. I remember watching Andy Rooney during his final years on *60 Minutes*. His segment on the show at the end was always seemingly about something he wanted to complain about. On this particular episode, however, it was personal. Someone had written him a letter claiming he was too old to be on television anymore. After a few caustic remarks, he closed with, "I didn't get old on purpose, it just happened. If you're lucky, it could happen to you." Something about that quote has stayed with me.

If you prepare well, the season of time will slowly transform your perspective. You don't doubt yourself or your decisions like you used to; you know what you like and what you don't; you know what love is and what is isn't. You've lived long enough to have experienced pain, and can appreciate the simplicity of a good day, a great drink, and someone to share both. And that is enough. If you have children, they have their own lives, but they might visit you and you might visit them, and you can spoil grandchildren on occasion. You can travel, because you are able and have enough money to see a little more of the world with a little life experience to understand it. You can volunteer, because you don't need the money, you need the purpose. You can consult to share your wisdom with people you would like to mentor. You can truly live the way you had intended, had you won the lottery thirty years prior.

This chapter is about changing the perspective of your current lifestyle to prepare for a positive reality in your sixties and seventies. Could your traditional retirement phase, the phase when you are winding down, begin in your eighties instead of your sixties? During your sixties, you may want to work, volunteer, vacation, or have intermittent cycles of all three. You can't know that for sure in your thirties, forties, or even fifties, but you can give yourself the options. The "gig" economy allows for you to become your own employer, so why can't you plan for ongoing income later in life? And if you plan to be "up and at them" later in life, your health is going to need to be a partner in that effort. Your heart, your joints, your teeth, and your skin could last into your hundreds.

The **Joy of Time** is the opportunity to predict the future (catastrophes and emergencies aside). You can become successful today and enjoy the season of life when you look and feel pretty "seasoned." You can give yourself a new story with an ending that matches the picture in your mind of what an ideal life could look like. If you don't have the life you want today, at least lay the foundation to have that life tomorrow.

PERSONAL EXPERIENCE

My father died at sixty-five; in fact, just days after he turned sixty-five. I had applied for Medicare paperwork on his behalf; unfortunately, by the time I had received that paperwork in the mail, he had already passed away. So, my father died too soon, but even if your parents are approaching or made it to their given life expectancy of about eighty, it's a model that we cannot follow. Have you noticed how much younger most of us look compared to our parents at a relatively similar age? It seems like nature's way of telling us to prepare for a longer future. I promised myself that I'd workout on a consistent basis when I graduated college and that was a promise I kept. Recently I have taken a hard look at nutrition; what's recommended versus what's *actually* good for me. To make the best of my time on this earth, so far, I've learned to cut my sugar intake and increase my vegetables and protein. Not a eureka moment, but it's made a difference.

I believe deeply in income versus accumulated wealth. About six years ago, sitting at my desk, I made a decision to maintain my interest in nearly all things and remain a jack of all trades, but I committed to becoming a master of one. That "one" was financial planning. The funny thing about becoming a master is that true mastery means committing to a never-ending process of improvement. This isn't too unlike the Japanese word for continuous improvement: Kaizen. "Kai" means change and "Zen" means good. Making good changes is what I aspire to do every year. Becoming a better version of myself is a constant aspiration, one that my children forced upon me during the few times I wanted to "grow" slower.

Children, of course, force you to consider your mortality. Long before my children were born, I kept fitness goals, but now those goals have greater meaning. I have noticed the difference in my thirty-year-old back versus my forty-year-old back; that younger back would have been helpful, had my kids come a little sooner into my life. I want to be a grandfather like my father-in-law, who can still play with children, or at the very least, interact with them without a cane. So, I focus less on my bench press in the gym and more on my ability to heave my own bodyweight. Think pullups, pushups, dips, and sit-ups. Of course, I do a lot with free and machine weights, but that's mainly because the bodyweight stuff is harder! Eventually, I will make regular trips to a yoga studio and learn a few more ways to lift myself off the floor. Maybe my back pain will even go away.

Writing this book was the latest iteration of me getting better. It's helped me to consolidate my thoughts, coordinate my messaging (through the magic of editing), and deliver a product that everyone can afford. And next, I will dabble into other technologies, like podcasting and webinar creation, to push myself further forward.

Honing the skills of writing and speaking will far outlast my abilities to use a financial calculator to compute the future value of a client's IRA. These skills are my opportunity to remain active and relevant in my later years, whether or not the investment of the day is tulips or bitcoins.

I don't dare imagine what my life will look like twenty years from now. Looking back over the last ten years—even predating progeny—my life has seemed to evolve every eighteen months. I do believe I am on a course of some sort: building a business, honing a message, and giving to causes that seem important (organizations and family). The practice of those traits should create that joy of time. I hope.

PROFESSIONAL EXPERIENCE

For years, retirement planning has been the key selling point of financial planning. Ever since that **Revenue Act of 1978**, the financial industry has been able to scare people into getting their financial houses in order, to plan for that day when their jobs went away. Today, financial planning can stand on its own, with retirement planning and investment management as only parts of a grand purpose. Most of my clients are Gen Xers, with kids and a lot more on their minds than playing golf or cruising the Atlantic Ocean. We have seven categories to work through, and I like to separate retirement planning from the obvious reliance on investment conversations. I talk to clients about where they want to live in retirement, what they would like to spend time doing, and what state their health is in. After all, it's a lot cheaper to be healthy in your seventies and eighties than the alternative.

Numbers are not divorced from this conversation. If their money isn't projected to outlive them, there are tradeoffs we discuss. This is where having spent time on earning, spending, saving, and goal-setting make a difference. Becoming familiar with every area of my client's financial life allows me to help them make sense of the tradeoffs. We prioritize concerns and values. I answer questions, but I let the client make the tradeoffs. Sometimes tradeoffs aren't necessary, because "retiring at age sixty-five" doesn't mean what it used to mean (for one, full Social Security benefits don't kick in until age sixty-seven for anyone born after 1960). Many of my clients admit they want to work a little. With their knowledge and experience, we find that working "a little" could mean $100,000 per year or more as a consultant, dictating the days, the hours, and the vacations.

When we get to the stage of retirement conversations, we're not just talking about money, we're talking about life. It's this portion of life where my aspiration for them is to imagine what living into older age will look like for them. How do they really want to spend their time? Our twenties, thirties, and forties are just training wheels for the fifties, sixties, seventies, and eighties. After figuring out what's possible for financial life, we are free to plan out long-held dreams.

Calculating Your Retirement Needs

You may be decades away from retirement or just a few years. What you will need financially during this new period of life will depend on how much you intend to spend, how much you intend to earn, how much you have already saved, and how much you choose to save going forward.

There are simple formulas for **spending** that estimate 75% or 80% of what you spend currently. That takes into account all of your current living expenses and assumes they will be relatively the same, just less. None of the clients I work with have it that easy. Travel tends to be a category that increases in retirement, but whether that's domestic or international travel of course depends on the client (and where any grandkids may live). If you don't travel $10,000 per year now, but plan to in retirement, you can take 80% of your current living expenses and add $10,000. Similarly, many clients tend to become more generous financially to their favorite charities, grandkids, or even their kids. This could be thousands of dollars per year, which will make a difference in your projections. I also happen to have clients who have adult children that need a $5,000 or $10,000 gift/loan. Transitioning to a fixed income or budget is not just an adjustment for you, but also your friends and family. Depending on the financial situation, you may have to learn to say "No."

The ability to **earn** money in old age has never been easier. Yes, there may be ageism (there always has been), but if you are at all entrepreneurial, you can leverage all of the knowledge and wisdom you've picked up in a career well-lived and share it for a fee. Some people write books on their expertise, some conduct seminars or webinars, and others just become consultants. Leveraging your expertise as a "wisdom worker" is a fantastic idea as long as you (and your loved ones) are healthy. With the gig economy, the choice is always yours. Should you have a pension, this will become part of your earnings in retirement, as does the estimated Social Security benefit (until you hear otherwise).

Your long-term **savings** gets the most focus from the financial industry. What you have set aside or choose to set aside for decades will become a big part of your decisions as you age. With unlimited earning potential, savings are only needed when you can't work. Saving is not the only way you can retire, but building the proverbial nest egg will give you more options.

Your total estimated annual spending less your total estimated annual earnings will tell you exactly how much extra you will need to take from savings (or can add to savings) per year. Calculating your retirement needs is not much different than calculating your current budget: if you don't plan to earn as much income as you plan to spend, you're probably planning to spend too much. The stress about retirement is built on the premise that one way or another you will not be earning an income. Change the premise, change your life: reincarnate.

Two Checks

In the United States, the retirement age of sixty-five became popular because up until Ronald Reagan's presidency, just about everyone received full Social Security benefits at age sixty-five. This made it a lot easier to figure out "when" retirement was going to happen. The Frequently Asked Questions page of the Social Security website shares the short story of how the federal government chose sixty-five as the retirement age in 1935: state pension systems, including the Federal Railroad Administration, used age sixty-five. There's a subtle mention that the actuarial tables also proved that paying out the benefits would work best at that age, which is to say, they knew enough people would die fast enough to make the program work. According to World Bank data, in the United States at that time, life expectancy was seventy for men and seventy-eight for women. The thought of waiting any longer than sixty-five to retire was essentially preposterous! And, of course, it also helped that most women and minorities were excluded from receiving benefits because of the types of jobs they usually worked in those days.

As of this writing, most everyone who is not already taking Social Security benefits can receive their full benefits at age sixty-seven. The neat thing about Social Security benefits is that it's income. And pensions were also income. It wasn't until the advent of the 401(k) plan that the average worker started thinking of retirement as something to save up for. Retirement benefits, for most people, were something to earn through loyal work over a long period of time, at the end of which you would receive two checks:

- A pension benefit check from your employer
- A Social Security benefit check from your federal government

Notice that neither of these checks used to be called "entitlements," but rather, "benefits."

When I worked for an insurance-based brokerage company that sold income annuities, we positioned them as paychecks for the rest of your life (just like the old pensions). We called them "play checks." You would spend that money in retirement and, thanks to the strength of the insurance company (and the OASDI program), you could expect to see another check the very next month without fail. Since then, I've learned that there are options to income annuities that could perform with similar functionality, but with different risks. But all of those ideas still involve saving up a lump sum of money. All except the idea of creating persistent income from your ongoing efforts.

Wisdom Work

"Wisdom," in the area of building a financial foundation, is working for an education, then working for people, then having people work for you, then having money work for you—for the rest of your life. Getting educated, getting work and getting leverage (people), and then getting money for the trouble is a virtuous cycle you can put in place as you become a "wisdom worker."

When my father was a young man, he moved from Trinidad and Tobago to Canada, where he met my mother. In the 1960s, moving to Canada from the Caribbean was kind of an in-between stage of becoming a young adult. When my parents were pregnant with their first born (my older sister), they decided that it was time to move to the United States; it was time to grow up.

On a track scholarship, my dad was invited to a university in California—where he quickly lost his track scholarship. Five years later, I was born in Orange County, so all wasn't lost! My dad eventually enrolled in Claremont University, where he took classes with famed management guru/consultant Peter Drucker. (Eventually, I learned that was pretty cool.) Drucker coined the phrase "knowledge worker" to highlight an emphasis on non-routine, problem-solving work that requires complex thinking. He predicted that this was the work of the future in his 1959 book, *The Landmarks of Tomorrow*.

Look around—Drucker was right. Most of us work in the safe confines of carpeted walls (cubes) or drywall (offices). While it is true that Drucker said, "The technology impacts which the experts predict almost never occur," in his book *Management* in 1973, it would be wrong to assume that he did not understand the ramifications of advancement and automation. In many of his books, he wrote about the effects of technology on the number of jobs and the political and socioeconomic effects of technology. Peter Drucker died in 2005, but I think he would have understood the plusses and minuses of artificial intelligence, and he would talk about what humans would need to do and learn to stay employed (or continue generating an income).

Whereas everyone is certain who coined the phrase "knowledge worker," no one is quite certain where the term "wisdom worker" came from—but it is an important concept. Wisdom is knowledge with experience applied. It is the power of discernment; the ability to create meaning from information. My dad used to say I could be as smart as I wanted, but I could never have more wisdom than him. That may have been true while he was still alive—experience matters, and our experience, properly applied, will keep us gainfully employed. We can use wisdom built upon the foundation of years in our current careers to outsmart the machines.

Consulting

A simplified concept of wealth accumulation was a trick my industry played on hardworking people about a generation ago, when the 401(k) was invented. The idea that saving 3% of your money for thirty years (even with a match) would be enough to live off of for thirty more years may have been true arithmetically, but for everyone? And what if you lived for forty or fifty years longer in "retirement?" Or worse, what if you neglect to save for a decade or two? What then?

Just because we don't have pensions anymore doesn't mean we have to give up on retiring into a life where we control our time or the opportunity to focus on the needs of our communities. Life is consistently expensive, and since advances in science are going to keep us around a while, we are going to need income to support our lifestyle and our causes for as long as we live. The "gig economy" can play a role during our golden years.

Income is the key to retirement. When I work with clients who talk about retiring early, I ask them what that means. It typically means not having to work behind a desk, under the direction of a boss and within the imperfect management of a large organization. Living and working in the Washington, D.C. area means competing intellectually, almost every working moment.

We are all consultants and we are all effectively self-employed. Unlike singing and dancing or running and dunking, we can be consultants well into our eighties, and with technology, forever. In addition to whatever you are learning through osmosis in your profession, there are certain skills you need to develop over the next ten, twenty, or thirty years to become a wisdom worker and keep yourself ahead of the machines. Those skills include empathy, relationship building, public speaking, prolific writing, and multi-model content creation. In a world where cash is still king, but information is infinite and "data is the new oil," content curation is the future. The ability to articulate and deliver your wisdom is the future. The ability to leverage the latest technologies is the future. The ability to compete with artificial intelligence with the combination of human intelligence and technology is the future. (That's right, the future is *RoboCop*.)

Technology already competes with knowledge workers. As a financial planner, I am well aware of the technology available for investing, buying insurance, and soon, financial planning. Turbo-Tax took the place of a lot of tax preparers. LegalZoom—rightly or wrongly—is replacing the legal services of local attorneys. Firms like Expedia (which owns Trivago, Hotels.com, Orbitz, etc.) have taken most of the jobs from travel agents. I determined early on that the way I stay relevant is to keep acquiring intelligence: academic, business, and emotional intelligence. We can still out-wise, out-ethos, and out-personalize technology. Those are the skills we can develop for now *and* the long term.

As you get older, you will become more tired of having a boss, but you may not mind working. But how does a sixty-year-old compete with a twenty-two-year-old for work? With experience, of course! As you build your career, you'll have decades to earn an expertise through education and experience. It is this experience that will invite you to the world of wisdom workers. The future belongs to the wisdom worker who can take their knowledge (expertise) and wisdom (experience) to another level of value. Work on your speaking, writing, and networking skills, and in the future, use them to earn an income well into your eighties.

CHAPTER 35 TAKEAWAYS

Preparing for retirement is a lot like preparing for life: you do the best you can do with the information that you have. You calculate how much money you'll need in retirement based on similar best practices you use today: budgeting, saving, and earning an income. With the opportunity of the internet and cloud computing, there are fewer reasons to be afraid of the future. The advent of "wisdom workers" means that if you are intentional about your expertise and comfortable distributing that knowledge, you will always have an opportunity to create income. The longer you can create income, the farther whatever amount of savings you have will go.

Actionable Strategies:

- Sign up for access to your Social Security benefits on SSA.gov
- Calculate your retirement budget by projecting your income and your expenses
- Identify the expertise you are building (or have built) over the years you can leverage
- Build your skills in empathy, public speaking, writing, and content creation

CHAPTER 36

GOOD HEALTH

Are you coming down into the pit? Wesley's got his strength back; I'm starting him on the machine tonight.

Tyrone, you know how much I love watching you work. But I've got my company's 500th anniversary to plan, my wedding to arrange, my wife to murder, and Guilder to frame for it. I'm swamped!

Get some rest. If you haven't got your health, you haven't got anything.

The Princess Bride was an instant classic when it came out in 1987. (As an aside, "instant classic" is how I hope people remember me one day when I'm no longer around.) The line, "If you haven't got your health, you haven't got anything," rings true to anyone who has experienced anything from stomach pain to a bad headache, all the way to debilitating cancer. "Health is wealth," my dad used to say. And he was absolutely right.

Healthcare needs can dramatically affect post-retirement life plans. Some of the most prevalent diseases in America, like pneumonia and arthritis, are hard to predict and protect against. Others that attack the cardiovascular (heart disease) and endocrine system (diabetes) are affected by lifestyle, but also inherited genetics. So, you can't avoid every disease, ailment, or medical accident in life, because chances are, genetics and luck are not on always on your side. But you can try. Benjamin Franklin is quoted to have said that, "An ounce of prevention is better than a pound of cure."

Watching the prescription medicine commercials in between segments of the nightly news or *60 Minutes* should scare anyone into believing that. The "cures" we have for common ailments to serious diseases are likely to have side-effects that will force additional "cures" and additional side-effects. No thank you. We all know that our health is positively affected by proper diet and exercise. But what's a proper diet, and how much exercise? And bottom line: when are we going to look like Tom Brady and Giselle?

A major study published in *JAMA (The Journal of the American Medical Association): Internal Medicine* has linked sugar to dying of heart disease. We could all easily assume that consuming a lot of sugar would lead to Type 2 diabetes. And we could have figured out that eating too much sugar would pull us further away from looking like athletes and models. But what surprised me about this fifteen-year study is that they didn't exactly figure out how it affected the heart; just that it did. Harvard's Health Blog did an assessment of the study and indicated that previous studies have shown that drinking sugar raises blood pressure and may stimulate the liver to "dump more harmful fats into the bloodstream."[1] Okay, so obviously neither of those are going to be good for the heart.

---

1   Corliss, Julie, "Eating too much added sugar increases the risk of dying with heart disease," Harvard Health Publishing, February 6, 2014, https://www.health.harvard.edu/blog/eating-too-much-added-sugar-increases-the-risk-of-dying-with-heart-disease-201402067021, 2019.

Not too long ago, I ran a little experiment on myself. After literally years and a few very intense months of sitting while studying for the CFP® exam, I decided to throw myself at another challenge: creating six-pack abs. When I shared this plan with one of my friends, she quickly replied that the only six-pack I was going to get would be bought at the store. (Ah, that's what friends are for!) I had only given myself about six weeks to accomplish this task, and I thought it would be fun. It wasn't exactly fun and (spoiler alert) I didn't get more than the outline of a two-pack. Unintentionally, though, I lost seventeen pounds and about four inches around my waist.

What did I do? Besides rededicating myself to a workout that had gotten stale, I drastically reduced my sugar intake. I had heard about both the Atkins and "keto" diets, but even with the easy access to information online, I didn't look either up. I just looked at the labels on the food that I ate and I looked at the food on my plate. With my wife's help, I moderated my portions, eliminated anything that felt "heavy," like pasta, and even substituted mustard for ketchup. I stopped drinking all sugar. I didn't know it at the time, but that *JAMA* study noted that sugar-sweetened beverages are the largest source of sugar in the American diet. Goodbye, processed orange juice!

Simple Healthcare

Too often, actual health strategies get buried in the conversation around healthcare. Many of us become experts in discussing medical care, but discussing how to stay healthy or get healthy almost seems too personal. Like financial management, health management is an evergreen discipline. Falling short of perfection means we are doing something wrong, that there's something wrong with *us*, because why else wouldn't we work to master something so important? Probably because we are human.

Like neuromarketing, there are scientists who work very hard to help us make choices that we would otherwise not when it comes to food. In David Kessler's book, *The End of Overeating: Taking Control of the Insatiable American Appetite*, the former Food and Drug Administration (FDA) commissioner speaks about the use of our brain chemistry, which reacts to "hyper-palatable" foods that are typically just high in sugar, salt, and fat. (And you thought you just liked the taste of ice-cream.) Understand that the reward system built into your mind is "controlling" your urge to eat (you're not necessarily still hungry).

Most personal trainers I talk with say 75% of good health is based on diet. I think they're underestimating the effect of nutrition. Getting up and going with exercise will likely help your "get up and go" (check with your doctor), but what we put in our mouths tends to most determine our weight and energy. Vigorous exercise may not be an option for you (right now), but taking control of nutrition is a simple technique for managing your healthcare that we can do at any age. Monitor your portions of carbohydrates, proteins, and vegetables. Discuss with your doctor how anything you eat will affect your digestive system.

Preventative Care

The Center for Disease Control (CDC) has a list of screenings (tests) that can help you identify diseases, sometimes earlier than you start seeing symptoms. Taking advantage of these screenings (especially when you have the medical insurance to cover the costs) is a great opportunity to extend your quality of life. A few examples (listed on their website):

- Blood pressure checks (every 1 to 2 years)
- Cholesterol checks (every 5 years)
- Colorectal cancer check (adults ages 50 – 75)
- Get Important vaccines (as necessary)

Keeping up with all of these "checks" can seem like a hassle. The easiest way to plan for good health is to get consistent guidance from a medical doctor through a regular physical. Annual physicals are often touted, but if you miss a year, don't let that prevent you from scheduling your next one.

Medicare

Are you turning sixty-five years-old soon? Medicare is waiting for you! Enacted in 1968 as an addition to the **Social Security Act of 1935**, Medicare is considered one of the few remaining "safety nets" for United States citizens. Like Social Security, Medicare was meant to solve one problem (healthcare for older Americans), but eventually grew to serve people under age sixty-five with disabilities (1972), hospice services (1982), and prescription drugs (2003) via the **Medicare Prescription Drug Improvement and Modernization Act of 2003**. This latest change added prescription drug coverage as a benefit, and is known as "Medicare Part D."

Here are the parts of Medicare we hear so much about:

- Part A: Hospital Insurance (typically free)
- Part B: Medical Insurance (typically deducted from your Social Security benefits)
- Part C: Medicare Advantage (prices vary because it's considered private insurance)

- Part D: Prescription Coverage (prices vary because it's considered private insurance)

The trickiest part of Medicare begins with whether or not you need to sign up or whether you are automatically enrolled. If you're already receiving Social Security benefits or Railroad Retirement Benefits (RRB), then you will be automatically signed up for Medicare Part A and B (unless you live in Puerto Rico, which requires you to sign up for Part B). And if you are sixty-five and working, the size of your firm and your healthcare coverage will determine whether or not you need to sign up or not.

Medicare was designed to take care of both hospital (Part A) and doctor (Part B) coverage, but you pay a flat fee for Part B, which is deducted from your Social Security benefits depending on your income. The higher the income, the higher the fee. As of 2019, total monthly premiums for Part B start at $135.50 and can rise to $460.50 for the highest incomes. Part A (hospital coverage) has no premium, but there are "co-insurance" costs that patients pay when hospitalized, depending on the length of hospital stay. As of 2019, a hospital deductible will cost $1,364 for the first sixty days of admittance. On the sixty-first through ninetieth day, hospital co-insurance will cost $341 *per day*, and $682 per day after that. Part A premiums may be free, but the cost to use it is definitely not!

Medicare Advantage is a lot like buying private insurance to use in lieu of Medicare Part A, Part B, and sometimes Part D. Whether it's more cost effective for you to sign up for Medicare Advantage depends on many personal factors, like whether you need a lot of prescriptions, it's cheaper than paying for a Medigap plan (see next section), you're still employed, how much you are paid, etc. Like most things in this book, you can't make a decision from reading this one source, but you can use this information as a foundation for finding out more. For example, Medicare.gov is a terrific resource.

Medigap

Because Medicare doesn't cover everything (does any health-care policy?), a market for Medicare Supplement Insurance (aka Medigap) was created. Unlike Medicare Advantage, Medigap is extra insurance you buy to complement your Medicare insurance coverage (rather than replace it). It is used to cover those Part A and Part B coverage "gaps," like co-pays, co-insurance, and deductibles. Insurance companies who offer Medigap insurance are required by law to conform to standards that seek to protect consumers from fraud and abuse. The **Medigap Fraud and Abuse Prevention Act of 1990** sought to increase:

- The maximum civil penalty which may be imposed on agents who use fraudulent and deceptive practices to sell Medicare supplemental insurance policies
- The percentage of premiums which must be returned to policyholders as benefits

It is illegal for anyone to sell you a Medigap plan if you already have a Medicare Advantage (Part C) plan, in part because of the duplication of benefits.

Purchasing Medigap coverage during the open enrollment period will give you your best chance to pay the lowest possible premium. Although there is still medical underwriting (meaning the insurance company will look at your health records), you can't be denied for preexisting conditions during open enrollment (the six-month period beginning the first day of the month of your sixty-fifth birthday). Although Medigap is described as "filling in the gaps" that Medicare doesn't cover, you will still need to find a solution for vision care, dental care, and long-term care.

Pharmacogenomics

Identifying how individuals respond to medicines or any kind of treatment is the future of healthcare. For example, tracking the activity of liver enzymes in the body can help predict how a person breaks down or eliminates medicines. This can lead to better, more customized prescriptions, rather than the one-size-fits-most approach we have to medicinal care today. According to the National Institutes of Health (NIH), pharmacogenomics is "the study of how genes affect a person's response to drugs." The future of medicine—"precision medicine"—is in the hands of people who are using the human genome to map exactly what drugs are most effective in your exact body (not one like yours). Franziska Moeckel, formerly with INOVA Hospital's Personalized Health department, has won many awards for her work helping to create MediMap®, a trademarked testing program that can use a saliva or blood test to show your doctor your body's ability to break down medicine. The NIH website says the intention of pharmacogenomics is to tailor treatment for some of the most chronic and debilitating diseases like heart disease, Alzheimer's disease, and cancer.

If medical science handles those big ones, we owe it to ourselves to manage our nutrition, exercise, dental, and skincare. We might be around a while! If we can take care of some of the low hanging fruit of healthcare, like exercise, sleep, and proper nutrition, over the course of the next twenty to thirty years, barring accident, we can plan for active lifestyles even at the ages of sixty, seventy, and beyond.

Perceptions will soon change about what you are capable of in the long term. You can be the catalyst for that change by first believing it is possible you can maintain your physical and mental acuity well into your seventies. Don't lean into the jokes around being forgetful and "getting senile." Decide not to call yourself "old" just because you are earning some gray hair. Some people say age is "just a number." I disagree. Age is a number, a lifestyle, and a mindset. There will be nothing you can do to prove that say, sixty-seven years old isn't old to a twenty-five-year-old, but you can ensure that their definition of old has varying degrees: active, able, and stopped. Never stop. Science is giving us a new life in older ages. What will you do?

Mesolimbic Pathway

To be a good fiduciary financial planner, I need to be a kind of low-budget neuroscientist. I mean *really* low-budget, like pop-psychology low. Because a fiduciary financial planner has to first plan for contingencies or emergencies, many of us find ourselves discussing how to protect against all of the things that could go wrong. We're wet blankets when it comes to investing in the stock market too—we talk about things like passive investing, and assert that no one can beat the market. What fun is that? Maybe this is part of the reason that so many financial planners, wealth managers, financial advisers, and others prefer just to work with really wealthy people. It's efficient for the business—more money, more complex work, higher fees—but it also gives us an opportunity to walk clients towards the brain's reward centers, allowing them to dream and imagine what they could do with all of the wealth they somehow amassed. This part of the brain is called the "mesolimbic pathway," and at this point of your life, spending your time utilizing that part of your brain is the goal.

Giving Time or Talent

As you age into the second part of your life, you may find that increasing your time and talent contributions becomes more possible and more impactful. This is what *Joy of Financial Planning* is supposed to be about, at its core: using the skills of planning to succeed so you can give before you die. On the non-financial side, there are dozens of organizations located all around us who could probably use your time and/or expertise.

I don't cook often, but I had the most fun chopping onions for the D.C. Central Kitchen in Washington, D.C. A brief plug for them: D.C. Central Kitchen is a community kitchen that develops and operates social ventures targeting the cycle of hunger and poverty. I laughed and cried (a lot) because of the friends, the onions, and the friends laughing at me crying over the onions. And because of my efforts that day, their mission was moved forward.

I volunteer for my church, my alma mater, and my networking group, in leadership positions that have little to do with my skills as a financial planner. Never mind that I also take the opportunity to serve family and friends on an ad hoc, pro bono basis using my expertise.

Part of your long-term personal financial strategy is transforming your formal and informal education, along with your work experience, into expertise that someone is always willing to pay for. To get paid for that expertise, you will also need to learn how to deliver the content of your mind into various platforms.

Today, those platforms include blogs, podcasts, and social media. I don't know what delivery platforms will look like in twenty years, but I have to imagine that public speaking and business writing will still hold value. So, while you are honing these skills for your own professional development, allow the organizations you support to use you for what you are becoming.

Location, Location, Location

Where you live has a lot to do with how you will live during the final third of your life. Planning ahead gives you something to prepare for years in advance. Do you want to live near family? Do you want to live where you spent your wealth-building years? Would you rather live where you grew up? Of course, deciding where to live during your final years will have everything to do with where you are "domiciled" when it comes to federal and state estate taxes. Most people won't have to worry much about federal estate taxes, but for state estate taxes, it's best to keep up with *Forbes* magazine's *"Where Not to Die"* list. In the 2019 article, for example, it lists New York state as generous, with an exemption of estate taxes for up to $5.74 million. But if that estate value creeps up to $6.027 million (or just $287,000 more), it would be hit with a $514,040 tax! That's known as the "tax cliff," where a proportionally small increase in value can tip an estate into owing a lot of tax.

For planning purposes, an area with a lower cost of living could help with how you spend your time in retirement. You may not have to work if, for example, you are moving from San Francisco, California or Washington, D.C. to a town like Raleigh, North Carolina or Morehead, Kentucky.

CHAPTER 36 TAKEAWAYS

More than any other factor, your physical and mental health can make your life after full-time work enjoyable or terrible. Working with your doctor to uncover the best nutritional practices for your body will save you money later. It is so much cheaper to be healthy during the later stages of our lives.

Medicare is the default safety net for healthcare as we age, but it will take time to make the right decisions for you and your family. Fully ingest Medicare.gov before making decisions about coverage, but make a decision before age sixty-five.

Thanks to the study of pharmacogenomics, we will likely live longer and better than previous generations. If we can control our nutrition, amount of exercise, and skincare, science will do the rest.

There are parts of our brains that respond positively to giving; it's part of our nature (if not our nurture). Preparing for a time in our lives when we can spend our time giving, volunteering, and sharing some of our time and talent with causes we believe in can be exciting. Decide where you want to live by deciding how you want to live during this special time in life's cycle. And between now and then, let's get ready!

Actionable Strategies:

- Take a look in the mirror, be honest, decide to make improvements
- Talk with your doctor about a safe exercise regimen that will work for your fitness level
- Talk with your doctor about reducing sugar and other ideas for improving your nutrition
- Research MediMap® and find out when you can get the saliva test

- Be wary of the Medicare deadlines, do your research, and make a decision by age sixty-five
- Review the current cost/benefit differences between Medicare Advantage and Medigap
- Create a separate savings fund for healthcare costs in your later years
- Identify the causes with which you want to share your time and talent

JOY OF TIME

Summary

Now is the time to make promises to yourself about what the next phase of your life will look like. As hard as it is to predict the future of the world, it's common sense to assume that if you keep doing the same things, you will get similar results. Looking to the future with fear is a waste of time. Retirement is no more an event to anticipate than turning thirty, forty, or fifty. Like those moments, how you feel the first day may end up surprising you, or it may be a non-event. Regardless, what you do after makes the difference. Here's what you can do before:

- Acclimate yourself now to your future health insurance options
- Don't get caught up on "retirement," it's just a made-up word
- Save a little money when you can—eventually, it adds up
- See your current job as an opportunity to build your expertise
- Work on your writing and public speaking skills

- Become familiar with digital ways to share what you know (podcasts, social media, etc.)
- Find opportunities to increase your nutrition knowledge and reduce your sugar intake
- Incorporate time for exercise in your busy schedule
- Start working on causes you believe in now

Taking advantage of time during your older years begins with the way you treat yourself and your life today. Where I used to work, they would talk about retirement like it was planning for a vacation you don't come back from. Well, not all of us will save a huge lump of money that will allow us to golf all day, but most people reading this book have an expertise, borne from a passion, that they can sell well into their eighties. Keeping your health and your income wealth will ensure you out never run of money.

You will eventually retire from full-time career work. How, when, and where you retire are entirely different subjects. Will you get tired of the grind? Will you be "pushed" out? Will you "die in your boots," found face down on your keyboard in your office? I hope not. I hope you have a choice in how, when, and where you retire. I hope you have the ability to give your time, talents, and treasure to causes you believe in. I hope you maintain your health. I hope you can be an example of the elusive American Dream that so many around the world—and around the block—are looking to achieve. Let's try to figure how to do that; let's try to predict the future.

A Final Word on Time

One of the more thought-provoking statements I've heard was from a funeral director named Pete Hause. He and I attend the same church, and he has the best sense of humor and best taste in clothes (in "church" clothes, anyway). He said to me, "You know, we spend a lot more time dead than we do alive." I am certain that line was followed with a laugh and another one-liner, but it has stuck with me. I have no explanation for time; I see life as a clock that ticks, no matter what. Until it doesn't. If you are so lucky to have a long life, especially one blessed with good health and mobility, I hope you can look back every year with a sense of achievement and progress, whatever your endeavor.

Almost everyone is "busy," which is usually an indication of how frustrated they are with their use of time. I know I don't want to miss anything important, and being busy forces you to do that. We all have self-interests and family interests, and on our best days, community interests and global interests. I see a world where we are able to spend time involved in them all. And I see you looking back on your progress with a smile.

CONCLUSION

Turning Vegetables into Candy

One Saturday, my little family and I switched the channel to the CW because of its edutainment programming. It was 10 A.M., and the program *Chicken Soup for the Soul's Animal Tales* was just beginning. It was sponsored by *Chicken Soup for the Soul* dog food, to which my wife Jennifer and I had two questions:

1. When did *Chicken Soup for the Soul* start sponsoring TV shows?
2. *The Chicken Soup for the Soul* people make dog food?

I looked them up online; as it turns out, the *Chicken Soup* folks also sell cat food! If this doesn't prove that you can do anything you set your mind to, I don't know what will (from books for humans to food for pets).

My goal in writing this book was to turn vegetables into candy. We all *know* that financial planning is important, just like we know all about flossing and cutting the carbs. Some of us are great at all of those things, and others of us will get around to it when we can. I understand the latter group. My career began in banking, continued into accounting, then I ran for office on a finance platform—and I still didn't commit to any of the stuff in this book until my wife and I had our first kid.

Joy of Financial Planning

There are hundreds of books on personal finance. Many of those books are factual; some are not. Many of those authors are well-meaning; some are not. I could have written a book for consumers that parroted the way we practitioners are taught. Had I done that, the outline for financial planning would have broken down this way:

- Establishing and defining the client-planner relationship
- Gathering client data including goals
- Analyzing and evaluating the client's current financial status
- Developing and presenting recommendations and/or alternatives
- Implementing the recommendations
- Monitoring the recommendations

If I wrote the book that way, well, it wouldn't take that long to write…because I know that I wouldn't be able to finish it, ever. In fact, I tried to write a book that was much more clinical in nature, but I couldn't finish it, so I had to start over. If this were 1980 and I had a typewriter instead of a computer, there would have been a pile of paper in a trash can. Every hour, my wife would have heard me tear out a sheet of paper from the roller pin, crumple it up, and toss it in the can. But since I had a computer, (thankfully) she couldn't tell if I was typing or just deleting.

That said, this book would be lacking if I didn't share a little about how the financial planning process came to be and the organization that stands behind the process.

The CFP Board is the non-profit organization that serves the public by regulating CERTIFIED FINANCIAL PLANNER™, or CFP® professional certification. They are the ones that identified the six steps in the financial planning process above.

The six steps serve as a guide for all financial planners who become certified as a standard of excellence when working with a client. Eventually, the CFP Board hopes the public will come to recognize these steps and the associated process as something they should expect from all advisers.[1]

Becoming Your Own Financial Planner

As a CFP® professional working with clients on both the big and the small picture of financial life, I know you will be well served by joining my family of clients. I also know that you don't have to work with a financial planner to walk through the financial planning process on a regular basis. This is another reason why I wrote this book: to give people a foundation for sourcing their own financial planning services or just doing it themselves. With the internet, you have access to most of the tools needed for your comprehensive financial plan. My only suggestion, if you work on this yourself, is to at least check with the kinds of professionals mentioned in this book to verify your understanding and your decisions.

Establishing the client relationship is akin to getting to know yourself and perhaps the people your money affects, like

---

1 "Financial Planning," CFP Board, https://www.cfp.net/for-cfp-professionals/
professional-standards-enforcement/current-standards-of-professional-conduct/
compliance-resources/frequently-asked-questions/financial-planning, 2019.

your spouse and children. Understanding where you are coming from when it comes to money before you get started with planning for the future is important. For example, recognizing that you or your spouse were raised without ever having to think about money will help you understand why it might be hard to begin a conversation about the subject.

Gathering client data for you just might mean logging into your accounts to find the balances, especially if you haven't combined checking, saving, or 401(k) accounts yet. It can also mean finding your insurance policies for property, liability, health, and life. Once you have all of the information, there's a lot you can do to ensure you are being intentional about your financial choices.

Analyzing or walking through all of that data is something you begin on your own. When you run into something you don't understand (like, "Why is my uninsured motorist coverage $1,000,000? Why do I pay a $15 bank fee? Why is all of my 401(k) invested in bond funds?"), you can just call the associated professional to help you figure it out.

Presenting your financial life is really about sharing what you learned about your finances with those they impact the most: your family. It's one thing to know how much you make, how much insurance coverage you have, how your retirement account is invested; it's quite another to say it all out loud. As a financial planner, I get to do this with my clients, and it's a significant moment. Every time you share your financial status with, for example, a spouse, it will be significant as well.

Implementing recommendations will come from some of the common sense you apply to the information you identified from looking at everything and the conversations you had with your significant other and yourself about concerns, goals, and hopes for the future. Taking action is where all of the improvements live; without making a plan to implement some of the new ideas you learned, you will not dramatically affect your financial life.

Monitoring how things are going is the heart of financial planning. Financial plans are out of date the moment they are put together. This can be one reason why you've hesitated to even try to complete one in the past. Why bother if it can't be current, right? If you acknowledge this fact up front, understanding that each plan is just a snapshot of your financial life, then completing one and redoing them every six months will seem more natural. Financial planning is an ongoing process with elements that will change as you age, as life throws new challenges your way, and as new opportunities come to your attention. This is part of the joy of financial planning: the opportunity to re-imagine how your life will be lived and how to make your money make it happen.

Transformation

In this book, I write about a lot of things, but in summary, this is a book about transformation.

Transforming pessimism to optimism. This generation of adults has every right to feel pessimistic about the future. The older generations did not do the hard political work that would fund Social Security and Medicare, calibrate capitalism to split profits with shareholders and workers, or embrace a myriad of other social causes that could have paved the way for all of us. That's too bad, but we can overcome those challenges. I am giving you a foundation for understanding how money works, which, we might all agree, is how the world works. Learn these tools, and then take up the mantle to fix the problems.

Transforming confusion to clarity. The regular consumer cannot keep up with the ever-changing financial industry without a foundation for understanding the history and a little time to keep up with the evolution. Money is confusing and emotional. We need clarity that begins with understanding the origins of the seven categories I shared in this book. Everything that followed in the chapters after each section may go out of date, but history is set in stone. Use that history and whatever else you can take from this book to clarify money and your family's future.

Transforming apathy into leadership. I ran for office once before. I had hoped that a run for office as a young adult would make a difference, like the old 1939 movie, *Mr. Smith Goes to Washington*, starring Jimmy Stewart. I lost, so in one respect, it did not. In another, I was fortunate to bump into the personal finance industry for perhaps the fifth time in my career. This time, I said yes, and I am emboldened by the work I do for my clients. It makes me think that there is a way for us to make a difference. That we aren't necessarily beholden to the station in life where we are. That economic mobility is real, and all it takes is for one generation of your family to try harder than all of the previous ones. One generation that creates a family governance system, for example, will set the bar high for every future generation of your surname.

Transforming potential into success. We are a generation of adults full of opportunity. In one way or another, I've been told that I have so much potential my whole life. All of those people were right, but that doesn't make me unique. Gen Xers grew up in another one of those American industry transitions—from the corporate age (think of the movie *Office Space*) to the true information age. We saw it all happen. We were the first kids to have computers in our homes. We added the internet and cell phones to our efficiency because we were born into the inefficiency of microfiche, the Dewey Decimal System, and rotary phones. Millennial adults are near-native techies. And tech is what is driving the disruption in the economy. Tech will be our downfall or our economic savior. Believe that if you get your financial life in order, you will be able to tackle all of the problems that we face both socially and economically as a country.

Transforming passion into action. Each of us has a cause that we care about. I don't mean a hobby; I mean a cause. Maybe you want to feed the hungry, free the oppressed, fight global warming, educate the poor, or improve the rights of women around the world. Whatever it is, it's hard to make a difference, to turn that passion into real action, when you're broke. Rallies are nice to attend, but real action comes in the form of real time and money invested in making the biggest break possible in the wall of fear, power, and apathy you are likely fighting. Join the fight for real. Work really hard to become really successful so you can really make a difference.

The Dash

I believe in the ideals of the American Dream, that everyone has an opportunity to succeed (whatever that means to you). I believe it doesn't matter how you start or how you finish. I believe it matters what you do in between.

THE DASH
by Linda Ellis[2]

I read of a man who stood to speak at a funeral of a friend.

*He referred to the dates on the tombstone
from the beginning...to the end.*

*He noted that first came the date of birth and
spoke of the following date with tears,*

*but he said what mattered most of all was
the dash between those years.*

For that dash represents all the time they spent alive on earth

*and now only those who loved them know
what that little line is worth.*

For it matters not, how much we own, the cars...

the house...the cash. What matters is how we live

and love and how we spend our dash.

So, think about this long and hard;

are there things you'd like to change?

*For you never know how much time is
left that still can be rearranged.*

To be less quick to anger and show appreciation

more and love the people in our lives

2   Ellis, Linda, "The Dash," https://thedashpoem.com/, 2019.

like we've never loved before.

If we treat each other with respect and more often wear a smile...

remembering that this special dash might only last a little while.

*So, when your eulogy is being read, with
your life's actions to rehash,*

*would you be proud of the things they say
about how you lived your dash?*

END

APPENDIX

Great Speeches

President John F. Kennedy
Inaugural Address, January 20, 1961

Vice President Johnson, Mr. Speaker, Mr. Chief Justice, President Eisenhower, Vice President Nixon, President Truman, Reverend Clergy, fellow citizens:

We observe today not a victory of party but a celebration of freedom—symbolizing an end as well as a beginning—signifying renewal as well as change. For I have sworn before you and Almighty God the same solemn oath our forebears prescribed nearly a century and three-quarters ago.

The world is very different now. For man holds in his mortal hands the power to abolish all forms of human poverty and all forms of human life. And yet the same revolutionary beliefs for which our forebears fought are still at issue around the globe—the belief that the rights of man come not from the generosity of the state but from the hand of God.

We dare not forget today that we are the heirs of that first revolution. Let the word go forth from this time and place, to friend and foe alike, that the torch has been passed to a new generation of Americans—born in this century, tempered by war, disciplined by a hard and bitter peace, proud of our ancient heritage—and unwilling to witness or permit the slow undoing of those human rights to which this nation has always been committed, and to which we are committed today at home and around the world.

Let every nation know, whether it wishes us well or ill, that we shall pay any price, bear any burden, meet any hardship, support any friend, oppose any foe to assure the survival and the success of liberty.

This much we pledge—and more.

To those old allies whose cultural and spiritual origins we share, we pledge the loyalty of faithful friends. United there is little we cannot do in a host of cooperative ventures. Divided there is little we can do—for we dare not meet a powerful challenge at odds and split asunder.

To those new states whom we welcome to the ranks of the free, we pledge our word that one form of colonial control shall not have passed away merely to be replaced by a far more iron tyranny. We shall not always expect to find them supporting our view. But we shall always hope to find them strongly supporting their own freedom—and to remember that, in the past, those who foolishly sought power by riding the back of the tiger ended up inside.

To those people in the huts and villages of half the globe struggling to break the bonds of mass misery, we pledge our best efforts to help them help themselves, for whatever period is required—not because the Communists may be doing it, not because we seek their votes, but because it is right. If a free society cannot help the many who are poor, it cannot save the few who are rich.

To our sister republics south of our border, we offer a special pledge—to convert our good words into good deeds—in a new alliance for progress—to assist free men and free governments in casting off the chains of poverty. But this peaceful revolution of hope cannot become the prey of hostile powers. Let all our neighbors know that we shall join with them to oppose aggression or subversion anywhere in the Americas. And let every other power know that this Hemisphere intends to remain the master of its own house.

To that world assembly of sovereign states, the United Nations, our last best hope in an age where the instruments of war have far outpaced the instruments of peace, we renew our pledge of support—to prevent it from becoming merely a forum for invective—to strengthen its shield of the new and the weak—and to enlarge the area in which its writ may run.

Finally, to those nations who would make themselves our adversary, we offer not a pledge but a request: that both sides begin anew the quest for peace, before the dark powers of destruction unleashed by science engulf all humanity in planned or accidental self-destruction.

We dare not tempt them with weakness. For only when our arms are sufficient beyond doubt can we be certain beyond doubt that they will never be employed.

But neither can two great and powerful groups of nations take comfort from our present course—both sides overburdened by the cost of modern weapons, both rightly alarmed by the steady spread of the deadly atom, yet both racing to alter that uncertain balance of terror that stays the hand of mankind's final war.

So, let us begin anew—remembering on both sides that civility is not a sign of weakness, and sincerity is always subject to proof. Let us never negotiate out of fear. But let us never fear to negotiate.

Let both sides explore what problems unite us instead of belaboring those problems which divide us.

Let both sides, for the first time, formulate serious and precise proposals for the inspection and control of arms—and bring the absolute power to destroy other nations under the absolute control of all nations.

Let both sides seek to invoke the wonders of science instead of its terrors. Together let us explore the stars, conquer the deserts, eradicate disease, tap the ocean depths and encourage the arts and commerce.

Let both sides unite to heed in all corners of the earth the command of Isaiah—to "undo the heavy burdens...(and) let the oppressed go free."

And if a beachhead of cooperation may push back the jungle of suspicion, let both sides join in creating a new endeavor, not a new balance of power, but a new world of law, where the strong are just and the weak secure and the peace preserved.

All this will not be finished in the first one hundred days. Nor will it be finished in the first one thousand days, nor in the life of this Administration, nor even perhaps in our lifetime on this planet. But let us begin.

In your hands, my fellow citizens, more than mine, will rest the final success or failure of our course. Since this country was founded, each generation of Americans has been summoned to give testimony to its national loyalty. The graves of young Americans who answered the call to service surround the globe.

Now the trumpet summons us again—not as a call to bear arms, though arms we need—not as a call to battle, though embattled we are—but a call to bear the burden of a long twilight struggle, year in and year out, "rejoicing in hope, patient in tribulation"—a struggle against the common enemies of man: tyranny, poverty, disease and war itself.

Can we forge against these enemies a grand and global alliance, North and South, East and West, that can assure a more fruitful life for all mankind? Will you join in that historic effort? In the long history of the world, only a few generations have been granted the role of defending freedom in its hour of maximum danger. I do not shrink from this responsibility—I welcome it. I do not believe that any of us would exchange places with any other people or any other generation. The energy, the faith, the devotion which we bring to this endeavor will light our country and all who serve it—and the glow from that fire can truly light the world.

And so, my fellow Americans: ask not what your country can do for you—ask what you can do for your country.

My fellow citizens of the world: ask not what America will do for you, but what together we can do for the freedom of man.

Finally, whether you are citizens of America or citizens of the world, ask of us here the same high standards of strength and sacrifice which we ask of you. With a good conscience our only sure reward, with history the final judge of our deeds, let us go forth to lead the land we love, asking His blessing and His help, but knowing that here on earth God's work must truly be our own.

President Ronald W. Reagan
Farewell Address, January 11, 1989

My fellow Americans, this is the 34th time I'll speak to you from the Oval Office, and the last. We've been together eight years now, and soon it'll be time for me to go. But before I do, I wanted to share some thoughts, some of which I have been saving for a long time.

It's been the honor of my life to be your President. So many of you have written the past few weeks to say thanks, but I could say as much to you. Nancy and I are grateful for the opportunity you gave us to serve.

One of the things about the Presidency is that you're always somewhat apart. You spend a lot of time going by too fast in a car someone else is driving, and seeing the people through tinted glass—the parents holding up a child, and the wave you saw too late and couldn't return. And so many times I wanted to stop, and reach out from behind the glass, and connect. Well, maybe I can do a little of that tonight.

People ask how I feel about leaving, and the fact is parting is "such sweet sorrow." The sweet part is California, and the ranch, and freedom. The sorrow? The goodbyes, of course, and leaving this beautiful place.

You know, down the hall and up the stairs from this office is the part of the White House where the President and his family live. There are a few favorite windows I have up there that I like to stand and look out of early in the morning. The view is over the grounds here to the Washington Monument, and then the Mall, and the Jefferson Memorial. But on mornings when the humidity is low, you can see past the Jefferson to the river, the Potomac, and the Virginia shore. Someone said that's the view Lincoln had when he saw the smoke rising from the battle of Bull

Run. Well, I see more prosaic things: the grass on the banks, the morning traffic as people make their way to work, now and then a sailboat on the river.

I've been thinking a bit at that window. I've been reflecting on what the past eight years have meant, and mean. And the image that comes to mind like a refrain is a nautical one—a small story about a big ship, and a refugee, and a sailor.

It was back in the early Eighties, at the height of the boat people, and the sailor was hard at work on the carrier *Midway*, which was patrolling the South China Sea. The sailor, like most American servicemen, was young, smart and fiercely observant. The crew spied on the horizon a leaky little boat—and crammed inside were refugees from Indochina hoping to get to America. The *Midway* sent a small launch to bring them to the ship, and safety. As the refugees made their way through the choppy seas, one spied the sailor on deck, and stood up and called out to him. He yelled, "Hello, American sailor—Hello, Freedom Man."

A small moment with a big meaning, a moment the sailor, who wrote it in a letter, couldn't get out of his mind. And, when I saw it, neither could I.

Because that's what it has to—it was to be an American in the 1980's; We stood, again, for freedom. I know we always have but in the past few years the world—again, and in a way, we ourselves—rediscovered it.

It's been quite a journey this decade, and we held together through some stormy seas. And at the end, together, we are reaching our destination.

The fact is, from Grenada to the Washington and Moscow summits, from the recession of '81 to '82 to the expansion that began in late '82 and continues to this day, we've made a difference.

The way I see it, there were two great triumphs, two things that I'm proudest of. One is the economic recovery, in which the people of America created—and filled—19 million new jobs. The other is the recovery of our morale: America is respected again in the world, and looked to for leadership.

Something that happened to me a few years ago reflects some of this. It was back in 1981, and I was attending my first big economic summit, which was held that year in Canada. The meeting place rotates among the member countries. The opening meeting was a formal dinner for the heads of government of the seven industrialized nations. Well, I sat there like the new kid in school and listened, and it was all Francois this and Helmut that. They dropped titles and spoke to one another on a first-name basis. Well, at one point I sort of leaned in and said, "My name's Ron."

Well, in that same year, we began the actions we felt would ignite an economic comeback: cut taxes and regulation, started to cut spending. Soon the recovery began.

Two years later, another economic summit, with pretty much the same cast. At the big opening meeting, we all got together, and all of a sudden just for a moment I saw that everyone was just sitting there looking at me. And then one of them broke the silence. "Tell us about the American miracle," he said.

Well, back in 1980, when I was running for President, it was all so different. Some pundits said our programs would result in catastrophe. Our views on foreign affairs would cause war, our plans for the economy would cause inflation to soar and bring about economic collapse. I even remember one highly respected economist saying, back in 1982, that "The engines of economic growth have shut down here and they're likely to stay that way for years to come."

Well, he—and the other "opinion leaders"—were wrong. The fact is, what they called "radical" was really "right"; what they called "dangerous" was just "desperately needed."

And in all that time I won a nickname—"The Great

Communicator." But I never thought it was my style or the words I used that made a difference—it was the content. I wasn't a great communicator, but I communicated great things, and they didn't spring full bloom from my brow, they came from the heart of a great nation—from our experience, our wisdom, and our belief in the principles that have guided us for two centuries.

They called it the Reagan Revolution, and I'll accept that, but for me it always seemed more like the Great Rediscovery: a rediscovery of our values and our common sense.

Common sense told us that when you put a big tax on something, the people will produce less of it. So, we cut the people's tax rates, and the people produced more than ever before. The economy bloomed like a plant that had been cut back and could now grow quicker and stronger. Our economic program brought about the longest peacetime expansion in our history: real family income up, the poverty rate down, entrepreneurship booming and an explosion in research and new technology. We're exporting more now than ever because American industry became more competitive, and at the same time we summoned the national will to knock down protectionist walls abroad instead of erecting them at home.

Common sense also told us that to preserve the peace we'd have to become strong again after years of weakness and confusion. So, we rebuilt our defenses—and this New Year, we toasted the new peacefulness around the globe. Not only have the superpowers actually begun to reduce their stockpiles of nuclear weapons—and hope for even more progress is bright—but the regional conflicts that rack the globe are also beginning to cease. The Persian Gulf is no longer a war zone, the Soviets are leaving Afghanistan, the Vietnamese are preparing to pull out of Cambodia and an American-mediated accord will soon send 50,000 Cuban troops home from Angola.

The lesson of all this was, of course, that because we're a great nation, our challenges seem complex. It will always be this way. But as long as we remember our first principles and believe in ourselves, the future will always be ours.

And something else we learned: once you begin a great movement, there's no telling where it'll end. We meant to change a nation, and instead, we changed a world.

Countries across the globe are turning to free markets and free speech—and turning away from the ideologies of the past. For them, the Great Rediscovery of the 1980's has been that, lo and behold, the moral way of government is the practical way of government. Democracy, the profoundly good, is also the profoundly productive.

When you've got to the point where you can celebrate the anniversaries of your 39th birthday you can sit back sometimes, review your life and see it flowing before you. For me, there was a fork in the river, and it was right in the middle of my life.

I never meant to go into politics: it wasn't my intention when I was young. But I was raised to believe you had to pay your way for the blessings bestowed on you. I was happy with my career in the entertainment world, but I ultimately went into politics because I wanted to protect something precious.

Ours was the first revolution in the history of mankind that truly reversed the course of government, and with three little words: "We the People."

"We the People" tell the Government what to do, it doesn't tell us. "We the people" are the driver—the Government is the car. And we decide where it should go, and by what route, and how fast. Almost all the world's constitutions are documents in which governments tell the people what their privileges are. Our Constitution is a document in which "We the People" tell the Government what it is allowed to do. "We the people" are free.

This belief has been the underlying basis for everything I tried to do these past eight years.

But back in the 1960's when I began, it seemed to me that we'd begun reversing the order of things—that through more and more rules and regulations and confiscatory taxes, the Government was taking more of our freedom. I went into politics in part to put up my hand and say, "Stop!" I was a citizen-politician, and it seemed the right thing for a citizen to do.

I think we have stopped a lot of what needed stopping. And I hope we have once again reminded people that man is not free unless government is limited. There's a clear cause and effect here that is as neat and predictable as a law of physics: as government expands, liberty contracts.

Nothing is less free than pure Communism, and yet we have, the past few years, forged a satisfying new closeness with the Soviet Union. I've been asked if this isn't a gamble, and my answer is no, because we're basing our actions not on words but deeds.

The detente of the 1970's was based not on actions but promises. They'd promise to treat their own people and the people of the world better, but the gulag was still the gulag, and the state was still expansionist, and they still waged proxy wars in Africa, Asia and Latin America.

Well, this time, so far, it's different: President Gorbachev has brought about some internal democratic reforms and begun the withdrawal from Afghanistan. He has also freed prisoners whose names I've given him every time we've met.

But life has a way of reminding you of big things through small incidents. Once, during the heady days of the Moscow Summit, Nancy and I decided to break off from the entourage one afternoon to visit the shops on Arbat Street—that's a little street just off Moscow's main shopping area.

Even though our visit was a surprise, every Russian there

immediately recognized us, and called out our names and reached for our hands. We were just about swept away by the warmth—you could almost feel the possibilities in all that joy. But within seconds, a K.G.B. detail pushed their way toward us and began pushing and shoving the people in the crowd. It was an interesting moment. It reminded me that while the man on the street in the Soviet Union yearns for peace, the Government is Communist—and those who run it are Communists—and that means we and they view such issues as freedom and human rights very differently.

We must keep up our guard—but we must also continue to work together to lessen and eliminate tension and mistrust.

My view is that President Gorbachev is different from previous Soviet leaders. I think he knows some of the things wrong with his society and is trying to fix them. We wish him well. And we'll continue to work to make sure that the Soviet Union that eventually emerges from this process is a less threatening one.

What it all boils down to is this: I want the new closeness to continue. And it will as long as we make it clear that we will continue to act in a certain way as long as they continue to act in a helpful manner. If and when they don't—at first pull your punches. If they persist, pull the plug.

It's still trust—but verify.

It's still play—but cut the cards.

It's still watch closely—and don't be afraid to see what you see.

I've been asked if I have any regrets. Well, I do.

The deficit is one. I've been talking a great deal about that lately, but tonight isn't for arguments, and I'm going to hold my tongue.

But an observation: I've had my share of victories in the Congress, but what few people noticed is that I never won anything you didn't win for me. They never saw my troops; they never saw Reagan's Regiments, the American people. You won every battle with every call you made and letter you wrote demanding action.

Well, action is still needed. If we're to finish the job, of Reagan's Regiments, we'll have to become the Bush Brigades. Soon he'll be the chief, and he'll need you every bit as much as I did.

Finally, there is a great tradition of warnings in Presidential farewells, and I've got one that's been on my mind for some time.

But oddly enough it starts with one of the things I'm proudest of in the past eight years; the resurgence of national pride that I called "the new patriotism." This national feeling is good, but it won't count for much, and it won't last unless it's grounded in thoughtfulness and knowledge.

An informed patriotism is what we want. And are we doing a good enough job teaching our children what America is and what she represents in the long history of the world?

Those of us who are over 35 or so years of age grew up in a different America. We were taught, very directly, what it means to be an American, and we absorbed almost in the air a love of country and an appreciation of its institutions. If you didn't get these things from your family you got them from the neighborhood, from the father down the street who fought in Korea or the family who lost someone at Anzio. Or you could get a sense of patriotism from school. And if all else failed, you could get a sense of patriotism from the popular culture. The movies celebrated democratic values and implicitly reinforced the idea that America was special. TV was like that, too, through the mid-Sixties.

But now we're about to enter the Nineties, and some things have changed. Younger parents aren't sure that an unambivalent appreciation of America is the right thing to teach modern children. And as for those who create the popular culture, well-grounded patriotism is no longer the style.

Our spirit is back, but we haven't reinstitutionalized it. We've got to do a better job of getting across that America is freedom—freedom of speech, freedom of religion, freedom of enterprise—and freedom is special and rare. It's fragile; it needs protection.

We've got to teach history based not on what's in fashion but what's important: Why the pilgrims came here, who Jimmy Doolittle was, and what those 30 seconds over Tokyo meant. You know, four years ago, on the 40th anniversary of D-Day. I read a letter from a young woman writing to her late father, who'd fought on Omaha Beach. Her name was Lisa Zanatta Henn, and she said, we will always remember, we will never forget what the boys of Normandy did. Well, let's help her keep her word.

If we forget what we did, we won't know who we are. I am warning of an eradication of that—of the American memory that could result, ultimately, in an erosion of the American spirit.

Let's start with some basics—more attention to American history and a greater emphasis of civic ritual. And let me offer lesson No. 1 about America: All great change in America begins at the dinner table. So, tomorrow night in the kitchen I hope the talking begins. And children, if your parents haven't been teaching you what it means to be an American—let 'em know and nail 'em on it. That would be a very American thing to do.

And that's about all I have to say tonight. Except for one thing.

The past few days when I've been at that window upstairs, I've thought a bit of the shining "city upon a hill." The phrase comes from John Winthrop, who wrote it to describe the America he imagined. What he imagined was important, because he was an early Pilgrim—an early "Freedom Man." He journeyed here on what today we'd call a little wooden boat, and, like the other pilgrims, he was looking for a home that would be free.

I've spoken of the shining city all my political life, but I don't know if I ever quite communicated what I saw when I said it. But in my mind, it was a tall proud city built on rocks stronger than oceans, windswept, God blessed, and teeming with people of all kinds living in harmony and peace—a city with free ports that hummed with commerce and creativity, and if there had to be city walls, the walls had doors, and the doors were open to anyone with the will and the heart to get here.

That's how I saw it, and see it still.

And how stands the city on this winter night? More prosperous, more secure and happier than it was eight years ago. But more than that: after 200 years, two centuries, she still stands strong and true on the granite ridge, and her glow has held steady no matter what storm.

And she's still a beacon, still a magnet for all who must have freedom, for all the Pilgrims from all the lost places who are hurtling through the darkness, toward home.

We've done our part. And as I "walk off into the city streets," a final word to the men and women of the Reagan Revolution—the men and women across America who for eight years did the work that brought America back:

My friends, we did it. We weren't just marking time, we made a difference. We made the city stronger—we made the city freer—and we left her in good hands.

All in all, not bad. Not bad at all.

And so, goodbye.

God bless you. And God bless the United States of America.